v. 1

AGRICULTURAL POLICY IN DISARRAY

VOLUME I

Edited by
**Vincent H. Smith, Joseph W. Glauber,
and Barry K. Goodwin**

AMERICAN ENTERPRISE INSTITUTE

ISBN: 978-0-8447-5016-3 (hardback)
ISBN: 978-0-8447-5017-0 (paperback)
ISBN: 978-0-8447-5018-7 (ebook)

American Enterprise Institute
1789 Massachusetts Avenue, NW
Washington, DC 20036
www.aei.org

*This volume is dedicated
to the memory of D. Gale Johnson,
whose seminal work on agricultural policy
has inspired the authors throughout their careers.*

Contents

Foreword

Americans admire our nation's farmers. Few industries require such discipline and hard work, and fewer still so clearly change millions of lives for the better each day. Unfortunately, our agricultural policies do not live up to such a high standard and poorly serve both farmers and the American public.

Agricultural Policy in Disarray is a collection of work that seeks to improve this. This two-volume compendium of 19 studies continues a storied AEI tradition: Dating back to the work of D. Gale Johnson and Hendrik Houthakker in the 1960s and 1970s, the Institute's scholars have examined the economic flaws and consequences of US agricultural policy for decades.

This work is a culmination of a three-year program of research, and it includes a wide range of studies, authored by prominent agricultural economists and written for a nontechnical audience. These evidence-based reports capture the complex, chaotic, and often internally inconsistent structure of US federal agricultural policy.

Today's policies have their roots in the 1930s New Deal legislation originally enacted to provide support for a struggling agricultural sector. But these policies have long outgrown their original purpose. By and large, US agricultural policies now merely transfer dollars from taxpayers to owners of financially sound farm businesses.

As the studies in this work document, agricultural interest groups have regularly found bipartisan support for their preferred policies in Congress, while other interested parties—such as agribusinesses and shipping companies—have used votes and campaign contributions to obtain favorable treatment. And although these policies serve desired ends for a select number of interests, they come at the expense of taxpayers, consumers, and especially families and children in poverty. Thus, the deepest flaw in agricultural policy today is not merely that it creates economic inefficiencies, whether involving the country's resource base, market mechanisms, long-run productivity growth, or US international trade relations; it is that the cronyism still present in our system reduces our ability to direct resources and opportunities to those who need them the most.

Agricultural Policy in Disarray is a self-recommending contribution to an underappreciated area of public policy. Without sacrificing substance, it breaks down the labyrinthine world of agricultural policy in accessible language, offering readers a clear understanding of both how and why scarce government resources are so frequently mismanaged. Anyone who gives this volume the attention it deserves will gain two valuable insights. The first is that most agricultural programs shrink the size of the economic pie while redistributing a larger share of that pie to special interests. The second is why these flaws in policy matter—because they ultimately limit opportunities for Americans who would benefit most from a smarter use of government resources.

If policymakers take the lessons of this volume seriously, they will find themselves equipped with actionable ideas for reforms that will reduce the damage being done by current policy. But more than that, these studies demonstrate how we can secure a dynamic and productive future for the agricultural sector, all while positioning our economy to lift up those on the margins. And it is ultimately this aspirational element that makes *Agricultural Policy in Disarray* so crucial to the policy conversation. Happy reading.

Arthur C. Brooks
President, American Enterprise Institute

Introduction

About 45 years ago, in 1973, D. Gale Johnson published a seminal study of agricultural policy. For his title, Johnson settled on *World Agriculture in Disarray* to reflect the chaotic incentives and economic inefficiencies created by the agricultural policies of many countries, including Australia, Canada, the European Union, Japan, New Zealand, and the United States.

Beginning in the mid-1980s with a set of radical reforms to New Zealand's and Australia's agricultural policies, many member countries of the Organisation for Economic Co-operation and Development initiated reforms to their agricultural policies. Those reforms involved reducing levels of support (measured percentages of the value of production) and changing how farm revenues are enhanced. The shift has been away from support tied to production and input use and toward either fixed payments or payments tied to the provision of environmental amenities. Not surprisingly, in those countries, farmers have generally become more entrepreneurial and efficient, and agricultural productivity has improved more quickly than in other countries whose programs have sustained inefficient farms and reduced incentives for innovation.

So what about the United States? While the United States appeared to be moving away from subsidies that distorted agricultural markets in the early and mid-1990s, since then the House and Senate Agriculture Committees that largely determine the structure of US farm programs have indulged in a 180-degree turn, boosting support to provide protection against falling market prices and revenues. In many ways, recent US policy initiatives, including several programs introduced in the 2014 Farm Bill, have only made matters worse. Most of those programs will likely remain unchanged, and possibly even be expanded, in any future US agricultural policy legislation.

These sacred cows include the two most expensive programs in terms of federal outlays on subsidy payments. One is a major new (in 2014) direct subsidy program that offers farm businesses a choice between two alternative methods by which they can obtain tax dollars. The other is the much

1

older federal crop insurance program that benefits both farm businesses and, perhaps especially, crop insurance companies.

As a result, despite some major changes over the past four decades, in many respects US agricultural policy continues to vividly reflect the disarray about which Johnson wrote so elegantly almost half a century ago—hence the title of this two-volume examination of US agricultural policy, *Agricultural Policy in Disarray*, which includes 19 studies of a wide range of US agricultural policies authored by many of the world's leading agricultural economists.

The purpose of this work is to examine the complex and, in many ways, conflicted structure of contemporary US agricultural policy through a series of studies that are designed to be accessible to students, policymakers, and the general public. Each study examines a set of current programs that affect a particular subsector of the US agricultural economy (e.g., cotton, dairy, and sugar), a broader program area (e.g., conservation programs, the federal crop insurance program, and competition policy), or a major issue (e.g., domestic poverty alleviation) and evaluates the impacts of potential options for policy change.

Unfortunately, these studies are likely to be relevant for a long time, as the current chaotic amalgam of US agricultural programs appears unlikely to be altered in the near future. As this introduction is being written, the US House and Senate have passed separate versions of a new 2018 or 2019 Farm Bill. In the context of agricultural policy, the two draft bills are similar and essentially represent a "stay the course" approach. Both bills simply extend the current provisions of most agricultural subsidy programs while making some changes to, but maintaining overall funding for, conservation programs. Neither bill does anything substantive for public agricultural research funding. Therefore, in real terms, support is likely to continue to decline for one of the few initiatives that clearly generates widespread benefits for the economy as a whole.

Many of the studies reflect similar realities with respect to agricultural policy in the United States. First, policies are largely designed to benefit and are effectively determined by relatively small interest groups. Many of these organizations consist of farm businesses (e.g., the National Cotton Council and the American Soybean Association), producer organizations (e.g., the American Farm Bureau Federation and the National Farmers Union), and industries that service the agricultural sector, such as crop insurance companies and input supply organizations.

Second, other players in the agricultural policy process do include environmental and other more broadly focused interest groups (e.g., the World Wildlife Fund and the Sierra Club), but often the polices those groups seek involve payoffs to the agricultural sector (e.g., through paid land retirement programs and subsidies for changes to working-lands programs).

Third, little attention, if any, is paid to consumers or the poor in forming and implementing farm subsidy programs, despite assertions to the contrary from vested farm interest groups. Consumers, including the poor, are more likely to pay for farm programs either through higher taxes or higher prices for agricultural commodities because of tariffs and other forms of supply control. In fact, much of the recent debate on farm policy has focused on tightening work requirements for recipients of nutritional support and reductions in spending on such programs.

Fourth, US agricultural policies rarely take account of the international trade and trade relations implications associated with how they operate, notwithstanding that the US is a net exporter of agricultural commodities. Finally, in almost all cases, subsidy programs are intentionally structured to funnel federal funds to large farm businesses that in most cases would be financially successful without any help from the US taxpayer or consumer.

Volume I of this study focuses on policies and regulations intended to benefit farm businesses through direct subsidy payments (e.g., the federal crop insurance program), price controls (e.g., dairy marketing orders), and output restrictions through limits on domestic production or imports (e.g., the sugar program). It also examines the consequences of such policies on US trade relations. Volume II includes analyses of the effects of US domestic policies and international food aid programs on poverty and hunger (e.g., food stamp programs versus agricultural subsidies), the impacts of US conservation, environmental and renewable fuels programs and regulations, public agricultural research funding, the regulation of genetically modified (GM) technologies, and regulations affecting market operations, including agricultural commodity future markets and contracts.

As Vincent Smith et al. demonstrate in their detailed overview of contemporary US agricultural policy (Chapter 1, Volume I), in general, programs authorized by the 2014 Farm Bill channel substantial amounts of federal funds to households whose incomes and wealth are well above those of the average US household. Many of those programs also create incentives for farm businesses to operate in ways that waste economic resources, and the owners and managers of those businesses respond accordingly.

The issue of which farm businesses benefit from agricultural subsidy programs is considered in more detail by Anton Bekkerman, Eric Belasco, and Vincent Smith in Chapter 2 of Volume I. Using US Department of Agriculture (USDA) data, they examine the distribution of payments through the Agricultural Risk Coverage (ARC) and Price Loss Coverage (PLC) programs, which average over $6 billion a year, and crop insurance subsidy payments, which average just under $6 billion a year. Their analysis shows that farms in the top 10 percent of the crop sales distribution received approximately 68 percent of all crop insurance premium subsidies in 2014, and farms in the top 20 percent received more than 82 percent of ARC and PLC payments in 2015. Further, the astonishingly concentrated nature of those subsidy payments on the largest farm businesses was reflected by the fact that, in 2015, farms in the bottom 80 percent of crop sales received approximately the same total amount of ARC, PLC, and crop insurance subsidy payments as farms in the top 2 percent.

Vincent Smith, Joseph Glauber, and Barry Goodwin discuss the complex nature of the US federal crop insurance program in Chapter 3 of Volume I. They argue that, in effect, the US federal crop insurance program is a poster child for policies that waste economic resources, are poorly targeted, and involve substantial subsidies to an ancillary industry (the crop insurance industry) that, in response, becomes an effective and well-resourced lobby for the continuation and expansion of the program. From small beginnings, since 1981, the program has become a major source of subsidies for farmers, currently with more than 300 million acres and 130 crops enrolled in the program. In addition to being expensive—the program costs taxpayers over $8 billion a year, of which (one way or another) $2.5 billion is paid to crop insurance companies—as discussed by Bekkerman, Belasco, and Smith (Chapter 2, Volume I), federal crop insurance subsidies are targeted mainly to large farm businesses. Premium subsidies average about 60 percent, ensuring that a typical farm business receives more than $2 in indemnity payments for every $1 it pays in premiums. The program also encourages farmers to waste resources and has the potential to engage the US in World

Trade Organization (WTO) disputes with other countries over the trade impacts of US agricultural policy.

Two programs, ARC and PLC, were established by Congress in the 2014 Farm Bill. On a commodity-by-commodity basis, for a set of 17 "program commodities," many of which have received farm subsidies for seven or more decades, a farm business can select one of these two programs as a source of direct subsidy payments. In Chapter 4 of Volume I, Barry Goodwin explores the structure and economic implications of these PLC and ARC subsidy programs, which as discussed above involve income transfers averaging more than $6 billion annually. One important issue is whether subsidy payments made under these two programs are linked to current production decisions and therefore substantively affect resource-allocation decisions and distort markets. Payments under both programs are linked to historical production decisions within the period covered by the 2014 Farm Bill (2014–18) and therefore may appear to be decoupled from current production choices. However, as Goodwin notes, allowing farm businesses periodically to update their historical basis for payments, as in the 2008 and 2014 Farm Bills, reties such payments to current production choices. Such "recoupling" of support seems likely to occur in the future and raises substantial concerns regarding trade agreement obligations

The US crop insurance and ARC and PLC programs are not the only elements of US agricultural policy that have spillover effects on global markets, with consequences for the country's international relations with other countries. Joseph Glauber and Daniel Sumner (Chapter 5, Volume I) examine the interactions between US agricultural programs and international trade in agricultural and food products, demonstrating that trade has always been important for US agriculture. However, over the past 50 years, US consumers and producers of agricultural commodities have become increasingly linked to global markets. Since the 1980s, several changes to US programs, many due to trade agreements and the WTO's influence, have lowered tariffs and increased trade, fostering income growth for farm businesses and lowering prices for consumers. Nevertheless, distortionary policies that are problematic for the US in its trade relations remain, and the impacts of some have expanded which has adverse implications for global commodity prices and US trade relations. These include high tariffs for some commodities (e.g., sugar); substantial increases in price and income subsidies for other major commodities such as corn, soybeans, wheat, rice, peanuts, and milk; and the expansion of the federal crop insurance program.

Chapters 6–9 of Volume I focus on four sets of commodity-specific policies for sugar (Chapter 6), milk (Chapter 7), cotton (Chapter 8), and peanuts (Chapter 9). John Beghin and Amani Elobeid (Chapter 6) review the structure, welfare, trade, and world price implications of the US sugar program. The sugar program is a protectionist policy based on supply controls that increases the domestic price of sugar above the corresponding world price. It restricts imports of raw and refined sugar, depresses world sugar prices, and substantially changes the mix of sweeteners used in processed food. Domestic markets are distorted, sugar users are effectively taxed, and sugar producers are subsidized by the program. The welfare transfer to sugar growers and processors is quite large in the aggregate, hovering around $1.2 billion. Losses to households are diffused, about $11 per person per year, but are large for the population as a whole, in the range of $2.4–$4 billion. Gains to producers are concentrated in a few hands, especially in the cane sugar industry. Labor effects from lost activity in food processing are estimated to be between 17,000 and 20,000 jobs annually.

Daniel Sumner examines US dairy policy (Chapter 7, Volume I). Productivity gains in the US dairy industry, which now involves substantial exports of US dairy products, have shifted policies away from border protection, price supports, export subsidies, and government regulations. The 2014 Farm Bill terminated several outmoded programs but left some long-standing programs in place (e.g., marketing orders) and created new government programs. Those programs continue to be expensive for US consumers and taxpayers and create incentives for dairy farms to waste economic resources. They include dozens of high tariffs for specific dairy products and complex Federal Milk Marketing Orders that are costly to administer, and they generate resource misallocations within and beyond the dairy sector. A new income subsidy program was also introduced in 2014. The program is called the Margin Protection Program, which is notionally designed as a "risk-management insurance program."

Joseph Glauber examines cotton subsidies (Chapter 8, Volume I). They have been a major source of controversy in international trade relations and historically have been viewed as highly distortionary. However, as Glauber notes, among the reforms enacted in the 2014 Farm Bill, few were more significant than the changes made to the suite of federal subsidy programs for cotton. Direct and countercyclical payments were eliminated and replaced by a heavily subsidized supplemental insurance program, the Stacked Income Protection Plan (STAX), a program designed and promoted by the US cotton industry. The changes were made to resolve a long-standing trade dispute brought by Brazil to the WTO against US cotton price and income support programs. Subsequently, the US cotton industry became disenchanted with its own self-selected STAX program and pushed for access to the new ARC and PLC income and price support programs, which it eventually obtained for seed cotton. The seed cotton proposal was presented as a budget neutral initiative, but given the volatility of cotton prices, the potential for large subsidy payments exists. Moreover, the program clearly violates the US agreement with Brazil over cotton subsidies, will likely create market distortions, and could have detrimental effects on world prices. The new initiative is a classic example of a policy solely intended to benefit a relatively small but wealthy and politically influential interest group at a potentially substantial cost to US trade relations and other sectors of the economy.

Barry Goodwin and Vincent Smith examine the peanut program (Chapter 9, Volume I). They argue that the program is another compelling example of how relatively small, well-funded interest groups often successfully obtain funds from federal legislators. The peanut industry consists of about 6,000 generally affluent and financially secure farm businesses located in a small number of states. The peanut lobby's exceptional effectiveness in obtaining taxpayer funds is illustrated by the fact that between 2014 and 2016 peanut producers received, on average, over $340 an acre annually in taxpayer subsidies. Those payments amounted to almost half the total revenues farm businesses received from all sources of funds, almost matching their revenues from the sale of peanuts in the marketplace. Further, farm businesses raising peanuts enjoy exceptionally generous treatment in terms of limits on the subsidy payments they can receive. No other group of farm businesses, producing commodities such as rice, corn, and wheat, comes close to receiving such levels of government subsidies for a specific crop, and the program represents "an extreme among extremes" in the context of agricultural policy.

Farm interest groups have historically claimed that a major objective, if not the major purpose, of agricultural subsidy programs is to reduce rural poverty, especially poverty among farmers, and to mitigate urban poverty by lowering the prices paid by urban consumers for food. In the first study presented in Volume II (Chapter 1), Joseph Glauber, Daniel Sumner, and Parke Wilde review the current evidence about such impacts. They conclude that farm subsidy programs have little impact on food consumption, food security, or nutrition in the United States, despite any claims to the contrary. Further, as also discussed in Chapters 1 and 2 of Volume 1, the people whose household incomes are most improved by agricultural policies are the owners of large farm businesses, not struggling small-scale farmers or other rural families with low incomes who are at risk of poverty and hunger.

Farm bills include several nutrition assistance programs that do provide resources for low-income families. By a considerable margin, the Supplementary Nutrition Assistance Program (SNAP), examined by Diane Whitmore Schanzenbach (Chapter 2, Volume II), is the largest of these programs for both the number of people participating in the program and federal spending. Since 1960, SNAP has relied on the market system to increase access to nutrition by supplementing the resources that low-income families have to purchase food through regular channels of trade. The program is a cornerstone of the social safety net—estimated to have kept 8.4 million people, including 3.8 million children, out of poverty in 2014—and responds quickly to increased needs in times of economic downturns. Schanzenbach concludes that block granting the program would fundamentally undermine its ability to perform these benefits. However, access to SNAP is strictly time limited for able-bodied, unemployed adults without dependents during normal economic times and could be strengthened by doing more to assist participants with finding employment and rewarding work. Further, smart federal investments in monitoring could improve the program's integrity by reducing fraud and error. The SNAP program is frequently caught in the middle of debates between supporters and fiscal conservatives. The current debate over the 2018 Farm Bill is no different, with considerable rhetoric directed at restricting benefits through tighter work requirements, while many of the same legislators also argue that wealthy farmers in their constituencies need large subsidy payments.

Since 1954, the structure of US international food aid policy has largely been determined by farm bill legislation. Erin Lentz, Stephanie Mercier, and Christopher Barrett examine the current suite of food aid programs (Chapter 3, Volume II). They emphasize that US food aid programs have played a crucial role in saving and improving the lives of hundreds of millions of people around the world over the past 60 years. However, relative to other countries' food assistance programs, which have been extensively reformed over the past 30 years, the costs of US food aid are excessive, delivery of assistance is slow, and the programs have not kept pace with global emergency needs. They argue that three main opportunities exist to improve program efficiency and impact: (1) relaxing cargo preference requirements on shipments of US food aid, (2) expanding access to cash-based instruments rather than commodities, and (3) relaxing procurement requirements that compel food aid to be purchased in the US. Those changes are strongly opposed by the private companies that own US-flagged ships that benefit financially from cargo preference and the mandate to source food aid from the United States. Thus, even key elements of the current US international humanitarian food aid program represent a costly example of the role of rent-seeking by a small interest group at the expense of economic efficiency and, in this case, real lives.

Productivity growth is tied to, and in important ways driven by, public and private investments in research and development (R&D). Further, the productivity of private R&D investment is affected by public R&D investments, which continue to yield high rates of return for the economy as a whole. However, as Phillip Pardey and Vincent Smith show (Chapter 4, Volume II), beginning in the 1980s the rate of growth in US public R&D investments slowed down in real terms, and since the mid-2000s public R&D spending has been shrinking. The United States now spends less on both public and private R&D than China does, and, significantly, as the rate of growth in US public R&D investments has declined, so too has the US agricultural sector's productive growth rate. Pardey and Smith suggest that one important reason for the slowdown in the growth and eventual decline of public R&D investments has been the willingness of agricultural interest groups to sacrifice spending on R&D to maintain or increase spending on direct subsidies to farmers.

Technology regulation can also substantially affect productivity growth by impeding or encouraging innovation. Gary Brester and Joseph Atwood (Chapter 5, Volume II) explore whether GM crops have been responsible for increased crop yields. Comparing US yields to EU yields (where GM crops are banned) provides evidence that GM technologies have increased crop yields in the United States. They conclude, however, that such yield and productivity increases are not a fait accompli. Rather, they result from the development of new technologies. Banning investments in and the use of yield-enhancing technologies has potentially serious consequences; food crop production will be lower than would otherwise be the case, and more water, land, and other inputs will be needed to increase global food production.

In the United States, some programs and regulations intended to sustain or reduce the degradation of natural resources are determined by the provisions of the conservation title in the farm bill and managed by the USDA. Other policies and regulations are established by non–farm bill legislation and fall under the purview of the US Environmental Protection Agency (EPA). These include the recent EPA Waters of the United States (WOTUS) rule and the Renewable Fuel Standard (RFS) that mandate the use of minimum annual levels of biofuels by the nation's transportation system.

Erik Lichtenberg (Chapter 6, Volume II) considers the conservation provisions of the farm bill. He points out that, from the beginning, conservation provisions in the farm bill have been linked with farm income support. Further, beginning in the mid-1980s, spending on conservation programs in the farm bill increased and has subsequently remained relatively stable, so conservation now accounts for about 30 percent of direct farm program payments. Farm bill conservation programs are justified as ways of preventing farmland degradation and mitigating environmental externalities, notably, damage to water quality, wildlife habitat, and air quality. Clear economic efficiency grounds exist for policies that address environmental externalities from agriculture, and the empirical evidence indicates that conservation programs have resulted in reductions in the environmental damage associated with farming and forestry. In addition, the USDA has made some progress in reorienting conservation programs toward environmental goals rather than mainly income enhancements for farm businesses. Thus, prioritizing conservation spending, as in the most recent farm bills, has had some positive outcomes. However, the conservation budget has not been allocated in ways that most efficiently improve environmental outcomes. Shifts in the allocation of federal funds among and within the different conservation programs could increase the efficiency of conservation spending in the sense of getting the most environmental-quality protection from the federal conservation budget.

In Chapter 7 of Volume II, Nathan Hendricks examines the issues associated with the WOTUS rule promulgated by the EPA under the provisions of the 2015 Clean Waters of the United States Act. The rule, which addresses water pollution, extends the jurisdiction of the 2015 act to all waters linked to navigable waters. He points out that many farm businesses do not know whether, as a result, they are subject to those provisions, and, if they are, then even simply obtaining permits for their operations is a costly endeavor. Further, nonpoint source pollution (emissions from sources that cannot readily be identified) is a major source of pollution in navigable waters, and the WOTUS rule does nothing to mitigate such emissions. Thus, Hendricks argues, a completely different market-based approach to reduce pollution and reach the optimal cost and benefit trade-off should be considered. As theorized by Ronald Coase in 1960, property rights should be assigned to either farm businesses (right to pollute) or environmentalists (right to clean water). They would then make contracts in which a party would accept not to exercise its rights fully in exchange for compensation. Hendricks argues that initial allocations of property rights could be established by state governments. Those governments would then be responsible for ensuring that parties comply with their contracts and use their resources to support the development of the organizations that would represent the interests of the different groups of individuals.

Aaron Smith (Chapter 8, Volume II) examines the viability and efficiency of the current RFS managed by the EPA. The RFS requires that biofuels such as ethanol and biodiesel be blended into the national transportation fuel supply. Nevertheless, the RFS is at a crossroads. Under the RFS, cellulosic biofuels would supposedly generate most greenhouse gas emissions reductions, and, as authorized by Congress, the RFS mandate requires immediate and substantial increases in their production. However, technologies have not been developed to make cellulosic biofuels cost-effective, and most biofuels continue to be produced from corn or soybeans. Moreover, the RFS now requires more biofuel than the fuel industry can easily absorb. Congress and the EPA, which administers the program, face important decisions about the future path of the RFS. Aaron Smith draws three lessons from the RFS that are relevant to government policymaking in this and other areas. First, in developing policies based on speculative assessments about future technologies, policymakers should account for uncertainty when making and implementing new programs. Second, they should not give regulators in government agencies too much discretion because it enables political forces and legal challenges to undermine policy. Third, policymakers should not mandate the use of things that do not exist.

Scott Irwin (Chapter 9, Volume II) examines regulatory and other issues associated with recent technological innovations and other changes that affect the way commodity futures markets function. A global uproar about speculation in commodity futures markets ensued after the spike in food commodity prices during 2007–08, which coincided with emerging large-scale participation by a new type of speculator in commodity futures markets: financial index investors. Some market participants, regulators, and civic organizations argued that the inflow into new commodity index investments was the principal driver of the spike in agricultural and energy prices. The subsequent policy debate focused on more restrictive speculation position limits in commodity futures markets. The issue was largely resolved when most of the evidence indicated that commodity index trading was at most a minor player in recent price spikes. As the commodity prices spiked, coincidentally a serious episode of convergence failures in grain futures and cash markets occurred. When contract rules were altered to raise artificially low storage rates, most problems disappeared, although more recent moderate non-convergence events suggest that the issue needs continued monitoring and that further increases in storage rates may be necessary. In addition, the transition from a telephone and open outcry trading platform to a computer and electronic order matching platform represents a major structural change in how futures markets operate. The issues associated with this shift are currently not well understood and are likely to be the subject of considerable research and regulatory attention in coming years.

Periodically, farm interest and other groups raise concerns about potential anticompetitive behaviors associated with contracting between farm businesses and downstream processors or upstream agribusiness input suppliers. Tomislav Vukina and Xiaoyong Zheng examine these issues in Chapter 10 of Volume II, focusing mainly on contracting in the livestock sector. They point out that two main types of contracts are widely used in the US agricultural sector: marketing contracts and production contracts, which are sometimes jointly described as alternative marketing arrangements (AMAs). They conclude that AMAs benefit not only farmers and packers by eliminating marketing timing and capacity underutilization risks but also consumers because such contracts provide consumers with better-quality products. The authors conclude that AMAs should not be banned by regulators but that regulators should protect spot markets, improve mandatory price reports, and leave tournament settlements of broiler contracts intact, all of which would enable markets to function more effectively. Policymakers should also support the 2012 Grain Inspection, Packers and Stockyards Administration rule regarding additional capital investment requirement and provisions regarding breaches of contract and suspension of delivery of animals, again to ensure the more efficient operation of markets.

In summary, the 19 studies included in this two-volume examination of US agricultural policy provide insights about a wide range of issues. Those issues range from the economic welfare effects and environmental consequences of direct and indirect agricultural subsidy programs such as crop insurance and the sugar program to the efficiency and effectiveness or ineffectiveness of environmental and conservation policies such as the Conservation Reserve Program and the RFS managed by the EPA. The relevance and consequences of international agricultural trade and trade policies are investigated, as are important issues about the impacts of agricultural subsidies on poverty and hunger in the United States (of which there are few, if any) and the efficiency of US international emergency food aid programs. The causes and consequences of the changing trajectory of public R&D funding are investigated, as are the potential impacts of different technology regulation regimes. And policy issues associated with the management of futures markets and the regulation of contracting are explored.

Finally, each of the studies, while using state-of-the-art knowledge, is designed to be accessible to the nonspecialist—students, policymakers, public interest groups, and the general public—and of interest to economists and graduate students seeking insights about contemporary US agricultural policies.

Section I

Agricultural Policy in Disarray

1

Agricultural Policy in Disarray: An Overview

VINCENT H. SMITH, JOSEPH W. GLAUBER, BARRY K. GOODWIN, AND DANIEL A. SUMNER

Policymakers have pursued many objectives in successive farm bills and ancillary legislation over the past 80 years, and as a result, US agricultural policy has evolved into a complex swath of programs and regulations. The 2014 Agricultural Act—the 2014 Farm Bill—has 11 titles, more than 350 pages of changes to existing programs and new initiatives, and a multitude of rules and regulations. Given its breadth and complexity, the farm bill contains multiple programs that simply do not serve a useful public purpose. Many are ineffective and wasteful and often work at cross-purposes with other farm bill programs.

Much of the legislation in the current farm bill provides transfers of funds from taxpayers and consumers to farm and agribusiness interests with little or no broader public purpose. More than 50 percent of the approximately $7 billion spent annually on the new direct farm subsidy programs introduced in the 2014 Farm Bill also flows to the largest 10 percent of all farm businesses. Mandates for American sourcing and shipping of food aid funnel almost a third of the total US emergency food aid budget to domestic and foreign corporations that own US-flagged vessels instead of to millions of the poorest people in the world suffering from famine.[1] In addition, conservation programs target payments to specific kinds of agricultural operations with little regard for environmental benefits.[2]

The farm bill and related legislation also authorize numerous programs directed toward conflicting objectives. For example, the federal crop insurance program that accounts for about a third of all farm subsidies encourages farmers to plant crops on highly erodible soils, while the Conservation Reserve Program (CRP) pays farmers to take such land out of production.

The farm policy component of the farm bill is in no sense a poverty program. A recent analysis by Daniel Sumner, Joseph Glauber, and Parke Wilde showed clearly that current US farm subsidy programs provide no measurable economic benefits for the rural poor, either in higher incomes for low-income households reliant on farm revenues (those farms generally receive nothing) or improved employment opportunities for hired workers.[3] Nor do farm subsidy programs lower overall food purchasing costs for consumers.[4] Some policies raise food prices quite substantially; others lower them to some extent. In the farm bill, policies that raise food prices include the US sugar program and federal marketing orders for milk. Beyond the farm bill, import barriers[5] and the Renewable Fuel Standard increase the prices of corn and oilseed crops such as soybeans and also crops in linked markets such as wheat.[6]

Programs such as agricultural commodity price supports may originally have been intended to reduce rural poverty. That was the case for the 1933 Agricultural Act, which was one of the key pieces of New Deal legislation that introduced programs to increase farm incomes and farm gate prices.[7] For example, legislators established price supports and land retirement programs in the 1930s when farm household incomes were well below those of nonfarm incomes.[8] While many commenters have questioned the efficacy of New Deal farm programs, those programs did raise short-run prices and incomes for some farmers and ranchers.[9] In contrast, Mark Drabenstott concluded that farm payments did not provide a strong boost to the rural economy in those counties that most depend on them.[10]

The data show clearly that current and recent agricultural policies not only largely transfer funds to farm owners and operators through programs now often labeled as farm income "safety-net" programs or through import barriers but also send substantial government revenues to households whose incomes are several times the national average. These policies include the federal crop insurance program, which has cost taxpayers more than $8 billion a year or more over the past eight years. (In 2012 the cost to the federal government was about $18 billion.)

They also include two income transfer programs—Price Loss Coverage (PLC) and Agricultural Risk Coverage (ARC)—that the 2014 Farm Bill created to replace three other programs: direct payments (originally established as a Production Flexibility Payments program in the 1996 Farm Bill), countercyclical payments (introduced in the 2002 Farm Bill), and the Average Crop Revenue Election (ACRE) program (introduced in the 2008 Farm Bill). The same income transfer impact applies to import barriers such as those for sugar and some fruits and vegetables, which shift funds from US food consumers to farm owners and operators.

When farm prices were relatively high, the Direct Payment Program (DPP), under which payments were not tied to prices, was popular with farmers whose land was eligible for such payments. However, public criticism of the DPP increased in the mid-2000s when the media reported that farmers were receiving about $5 billion a year despite farm prices reaching record levels. By the next farm bill debate, the program had become politically untenable, and in 2011 congressional leaders informed House and Senate Agriculture Committees that the DPP had to go.

In contrast, the Countercyclical Payment Program (CPP) provided farmers with only small payments as market prices had generally exceeded target price levels, leading agricultural interest groups to seek program changes that would generate more subsidy payments. The ACRE program, based on farm and county per-acre revenue guarantees, was complex[11] and held little interest for most farms.[12] The 2014 Farm Bill reinvented the CPP, renamed it the PLC program, and substantially increased the target prices that would trigger subsidies, taking advantage of a sanguine budget baseline that projected high commodity price levels over the next 10 years. Similarly, the ACRE program was reborn as a simplified revenue guarantee program also likely to generate relatively large subsidy payments.

As Bruce Babcock points out, the restructured PLC and ARC programs have turned out to be considerably more expensive than the programs they replaced.[13] This was predictable given that commodity prices were already falling from their record levels in 2013.[14]

The PLC and ARC programs, coupled with federal crop insurance, a relatively small disaster aid program for forage and livestock losses, a special revenue insurance program for cotton, and a margin protection program for milk, form what farm interests refer to as the safety net. Supporters of these programs argued that the programs would help ensure farmers receive adequate revenues when prices or yields were low (or feed prices for dairy cows were high). However, in tandem with crop insurance subsidies, the

ARC and PLC programs have transferred $11–$12 billion annually, in many cases when farm incomes have been relatively high.

Fundamentally, the primary goal of the PLC and ARC programs, along with federally subsidized crop insurance, is simply to ensure farms receive revenues that are higher than they can expect from the market. In other words, in what would otherwise be lower-price and lower-income years, government programs raise farm revenues to what Congress, in response to farm group lobbying, would like farms to receive, while in good years farms retain the higher returns from the marketplace. The impact of such programs in the past has been to increase farm incomes, land rents, and land prices.

The Dairy Margin Protection Program and a new cotton program called the Stacked Income Protection Plan (STAX), also introduced in the 2014 Farm Bill, were designed with high subsidy rates. But in the first two years they provided few benefits, and most farms chose not to sign up. Both programs disappointed their advocates because they did not generate substantial payments in 2015 or 2016 even though advocates were unsatisfied with dairy and cotton revenues in those years. However, given the structures of the two programs, between 2014 and 2018, cotton yields, harvest prices, and dairy margins were too high to trigger substantial income transfers. In response, in a February 2018 omnibus bill (the Bipartisan Budget Act of 2018) primarily intended to provide funds for hurricane relief in Houston and Florida, the dairy program was modified to become "more attractive" to dairy farmers by increasing farmer benefits and reducing any costs that might be involved in their participation in the new program. Moreover, as Glauber discusses in more detail in Chapter 8 in this volume, a new subsidy program for seed cotton was also introduced in the same legislation.

The current dairy and cotton industry complaints about the dairy margin and STAX programs are revealing, as was producer dissatisfaction with the CPP. In each case, farmers were unhappy because the programs were not generating substantial payments. While the current rhetoric among farm program advocates is that subsidy programs should provide farmers with help only when they need it, their definition of "need" also includes periods of relatively normal and exceptionally high prices and yields.

Programs in the conservation title of the farm bill also mainly benefit farm owners and operators with relatively large operations. Erik Lichtenberg showed that in the 2014 Farm Bill most of the functions of the previous suite of conservation programs were retained, and funding for the Conservation Stewardship Program (CSP)—a program with only marginal conservation benefits, but popular among midwestern hog, grain, and oilseed growers—was expanded.[15] Most of the $6 billion spent on conservation programs goes to the largest farm operations for two reasons. First, the subsidies tend to be based on land or capital improvements, and thus larger operations receive most of the subsidy. Second, application processes are complex and require considerable managerial inputs. Costs of applying for support are often larger than the potential cost-share payments for small farms.

The farm bill does include some US agricultural policy initiatives that are beneficial for society as a whole. For example, public investments in agricultural research, development and technology transfer, and education have consistently provided substantial returns to society,[16] and the rate of return on taxpayer investment in such R&D programs is well over 25 percent.[17] This indicates that current investments will likely be as rewarding as past investments.[18] These high rates of return show that the United States is vastly underinvesting in agricultural research and that much of this must be supported by government, or it will not be done at all.[19] The farm bill authorizes funding for such efforts.

Government action to improve market access for imports into the United States and exports are useful in stimulating agricultural markets. Such efforts are addressed in the farm bill. However, the farm bill also includes farm subsidies, import restrictions (e.g., the US sugar program), and foreign aid initiatives that create import impediments and have the net effect of reducing US exports.

In summary, most programs send the vast majority of the subsidies they provide to a relatively small number of large farms that produce the overwhelming bulk of all US farm output. Among the two million farm entities (using the official definition of a farm as any entity with potential annual sales of agricultural commodities of $1,000 or more), the largest 15 percent receive 85 percent of subsidy payments. Further, the largest 10 percent of farms receive more than 50 percent, and the largest 1 percent receive more than 20 percent of total subsidy payments. In addition, subsidy programs that do not make direct government payments to farmers, such as trade barriers that raise market prices, also benefit the largest farms that produce most of the output.

Moreover, as discussed below, farms receiving the bulk of the payments do not need the government's help to manage year-to-year revenue fluctuations. They are financially sound businesses that successfully manage the business risks they face on a daily and yearly basis. In addition, as detailed next, the recent period of 2014–17 has been relatively normal in farm revenue and net returns for most of US agriculture. Advocates for subsidies have recently claimed that US farms are facing a potentially disastrous period of historically low prices that, without high farm subsidies, will lead to a collapse that threatens the US food production and distribution system. Such claims are simply not credible.

State of the Farm Sector

Recent US Department of Agriculture (USDA) reports projecting sustained relatively low commodity prices and low net farm income levels have raised concerns that the US farm sector has entered or is at least standing on the precipice of the worst farm financial crisis since the 1980s. Net farm income for 2017 is projected at $63.8 billion, which, if realized, would be 3.7 percent above 2016 estimates and about 50 percent below the (nominal) record net farm income levels reached in 2013. Citing "the largest three-year drop since the Great Depression," the current chairman of the House Agriculture Committee asserted:

> America's farmers and ranchers are facing very difficult times right now. . . . Farmers and ranchers have endured a 45 percent drop in net farm income over the last three years, the largest three-year drop since the Great Depression. . . . Overall, ERS is forecasting a 50 percent drop in net farm income since 2013. It is hard for any of us to imagine our income being sliced in half. We are told that one in 10 farms are now highly or extremely leveraged. Nominal debt levels are at all-time highs, and real debt levels are approaching where they were prior to the 1980 farm financial crisis. . . . There is real potential for a crisis in rural America.[20]

Already some proponents are arguing that the downturn in the farm economy will necessitate additional funding for farmers.[21]

The actual financial health of the US farm sector is far more complex than the picture legislators and other advocates sketched for farm subsidies. For specific sectors such as cotton and dairy, the net cash incomes for farm businesses are likely to increase substantially.[22] The picture is also different for the half of US agriculture that receives little from most subsidy programs, including livestock, fruits, hay, tree nuts, and vegetables. So why the discrepancy in farm income measures, and what does it mean for the farm economy's health?

Net Cash Versus Net Farm Income. Net cash income is a cash flow measure that compares cash receipts, including government payments and farm-related income, to cash expenses in a calendar year. It is therefore a measure of the current-year funds available to farm operators to purchase new machinery or other investments, make debt payments, and increase for-profit and returns for operator-provided capital and labor. Farm output must be marketed (i.e., exchanged for payment) before it is counted as part of the household's cash flow. For example, some crops are produced and harvested but then held in on-farm storage and not counted in net cash income, and income is often received in calendar years after the expenses for that year's crop are incurred.

Net farm income is a measure of a farm operator's share of the net value added to the national economy in a calendar year, independent of whether income and expenses are in cash or noncash form. In contrast to net cash income, net farm income includes the value of on-farm consumption of farm-produced goods, changes in inventories, capital replacement, and implicit rent and expenses related to a farm operator's dwelling, all of which are generally not reflected in cash transactions during the current year. Once a crop is grown and harvested, it is included in the farm's net income calculation, even if it remains in on-farm storage.

Net cash income is usually less variable than net farm income, reflecting that farmers can manage timing crop and livestock sales and purchasing inputs to stabilize the variability in their net cash income. For example, farmers can hold crops from large harvests to sell in the forthcoming year, when output may be lower and prices higher. Thus, while net farm income

Figure 1. Net Cash Versus Net Farm Income (Adjusted for Inflation Effects to Billions of 2017 Dollars)

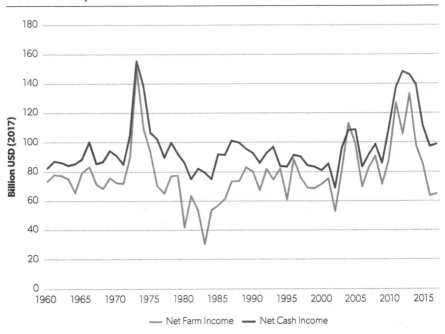

Source: US Department of Agriculture, Economic Research Service, "Data Files: U.S. and State-Level Farm Income and Wealth Statistics," https://www.ers.usda.gov/data-products/farm-income-and-wealth-statistics/data-files-us-and-state-level-farm-income-and-wealth-statistics/.

may be a more appropriate measure for national income accounts (measuring what is produced in the calendar year), net cash income is a better measure of current cash flow (the amount of money the farmer has on hand). Averaging either measure over several years tends to smooth out fluctuations associated with annual bunching or receipts or expenses.

Figure 1 shows US net cash income and US net farm income since 1960, adjusted for inflation. What is striking is how relatively flat both farm income measures have been over the period once the values have been adjusted for inflation, except in the early 1970s and then more recently following the price spikes of 2007–08, 2010–11, and 2012–13. Further, net cash income and net farm income have fallen back to their long-term averages after the recent price spikes in 2012–13.

Table 1. Average Net Cash Income for Farm Business by Farm Specialization

Farm Specialization	Forecast Net Cash Income for 2017 (Dollars per Farm)	Change from 2016 (Percentage)
Wheat	$54,300	−24.7%
Corn	$163,000	−12.8%
Soybeans	$130,100	−10.9%
Cotton	$337,800	43.8%
Specialty Crops	$298,300	−14.5%
Other Crops	$84,700	−8.4%
Cattle and Calves	$32,700	4.0%
Hogs	$216,400	25.7%
Poultry	$110,500	1.9%
Dairy	$197,900	34.9%
Other Livestock	$20,600	−3.4%

Note: Farm specialization is determined by a farm having more than 50 percent of its value of production from that commodity.
Source: US Department of Agriculture, Economic Research Service, "Net Cash Farm Income for U.S. Farm Businesses Forecast up in 2017," 2017, https://www.ers.usda.gov/topics/farm-economy/farm-sector-income-finances/farm-business-income/.

Adjusting for inflation and putting all years in 2017 dollars, the 2017 net cash income forecast of $98.6 billion is the second-lowest level since 2009 but 2 percent above the 1960–2016 average of $96.7 billion. Inflation-adjusted net farm income for 2017 is forecast to be $64.9 billion, about 17 percent below the 1960–2016 average of $76.8 billion, in part due to the expected drop in farm inventories and large capital consumption measures from machinery purchases during the high-income years of 2010–14. Both measures remain above the low levels of income experienced during the 1980s.

Net Cash Income for Farm Businesses Projected to Increase in 2017. Another measure of the health of the US farm sector is farm-business income. The USDA reports that farm businesses (farms with annual gross farm incomes over $350,000 or smaller operations in which farming is reported as the farm operator's principal occupation) account for less than half of US farms but about 90 percent of total value of production of the farm sectors.

Net cash income for those farms is projected to average $100,500, down 2 percent from 2016.

For most grain producers, net cash incomes are expected to continue to be down, with net cash income for wheat producers down almost 25 percent from 2016 levels (Table 1). Cotton producers might expect to see their net cash income increase about 44 percent over 2016 levels—a fourth year of increases after a large drop in 2014. Similarly, stronger dairy prices and increased production are likely to boost net cash income for dairy producers by 35 percent in 2017 compared to quite low levels in 2016. Net cash income for the cattle and calf sector are projected to increase 4 percent, while net cash income for hog producers is expected to increase 25 percent.

Farm Debt and Financial Exposure. Prices and incomes have declined from the atypical highs experienced between 2007 and 2013. At the same time, the dollar amount of farm debt has increased—and even modestly increased relative to the value of farm assets. However, in both nominal and inflation-adjusted terms, farm assets are projected to reach record highs in 2017 (Figure 2). Adjusting for inflation, as farm income has declined, land values have flattened (after more than doubling in many regions between 2007 and 2014), with projected values for 2017 only 3 percent above 2014 levels. Farm debt is projected to be at the highest level since 1982, adjusting for inflation.

Nevertheless, the forecast for the ratio of total farm debt to farm assets is 12.7 percent—slightly higher than the record-low levels in 2012 and 2013—which is still much lower than in the 1980s when debt-to-asset ratios rose to more than 20 percent (Figure 3). It is even a little lower than during 2000–06, the period preceding a substantial surge in corn, soybean, wheat, and other commodity prices that began in 2005.

Debt-servicing ratios describe the share of production used for debt payments. Higher debt-servicing ratios imply that a greater share of revenues from production is required for debt payments, indicating less liquidity. The USDA recently projected that the debt-servicing ratio will increase to 27 percent—the highest level since 2002—which is significantly below debt-servicing levels during the 1980s when loan principal payments plus interest expenses accounted for as much as 46 percent of the value of production.

Figure 2. Farm Debts and Assets: 1960–2018 (Adjusted for Inflation Effects to Billions of 2018 Dollars)

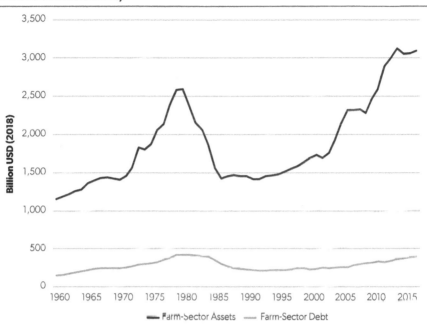

Source: US Department of Agriculture, Economic Research Service, "Data Files: U.S. and State-Level Farm Income and Wealth Statistics," https://www.ers.usda.gov/data-products/farm-income-and-wealth-statistics/data-files-us-and-state-level-farm-income-and-wealth-statistics/.

Farm Household Income. Another important measure of farm financial well-being is the household income of farm operators. Farm household income measures include income from on-farm and other sources. The USDA forecasts that median farm household income will reach $77,304 in 2017, up 1.2 percent from 2016 levels and, in nominal terms, second only to the records achieved in 2014.

In recent years, slightly more than half of all farm households are estimated to have lost money on their farming businesses in any given year, even while enjoying record prices. However, most of these households earn substantial incomes from other sources (off-farm employment, investments, etc.). As a result, the USDA forecasts that median off-farm income will increase in 2017 to $68,011. Moreover, many farm-business owners

Figure 3. Farm Financial Ratios: 1960–2018

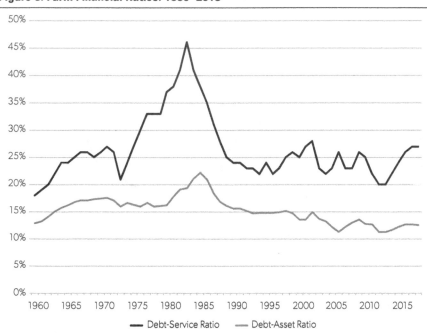

Source: US Department of Agriculture, Economic Research Service, "Data Files: U.S. and State-Level Farm Income and Wealth Statistics," https://www.ers.usda.gov/data-products/farm-income-and-wealth-statistics/data-files-us-and-state-level-farm-income-and-wealth-statistics/.

deliberately choose tax-related agricultural investment strategies to create current farm income losses that then offset their tax liabilities on other income while expanding the value of the farm assets they own.

As production and farm income have become more concentrated within a smaller proportion of farm households, off-farm income has become an increasingly important source of income for almost all households involved in farming (Figure 4). In 1960, about half the average farm household's income came from the farm, and the other half came from off-farm sources. In the mid-1990s, farm income accounted for only 10 percent of average total farm household incomes.

With the rise in farm income levels since 2005, income from farm operations has accounted for about 20 percent of average total farm household income. Therefore, for most of the two million households involved

Figure 4. Percentage of Total Household Income from Farm Enterprises Received by Households with Farm-Business Income: 1960–2017

Source: US Department of Agriculture, Economic Research Service, "Farm Household Income and Characteristics," https://www.ers.usda.gov/data-products/farm-household-income-and-characteristics/.

in farming, farm income is a relatively modest source of their economic well-being.

Income from nonfarm sources has also helped stabilize farm household income because it is less variable and relatively uncorrelated with farm income. Figure 5 shows year-to-year percentage changes in the portion of farm household income from farming compared to total farm household income since 1960. While the annual variation in the farm portion of household income was 40 percent over 1960–2015, the annual variation of total farm household income from all sources was only 12 percent.

Outlook for Farm Prices and the Budget Baseline

Federal expenditures on farm bill programs must fit in an overall budget that is closely tied to what is known as the baseline for those programs. An important political factor in the farm bill debate is the size of the projected 10-year budget baseline the Congressional Budget Office (CBO) prepares annually.

Figure 5. Percentage Annual Change in Household Income from Farming Enterprises Versus Total Household Income for Households with Farm Businesses: 1961–2014 (Incomes Adjusted for Inflation Effects to 2009 Dollars)

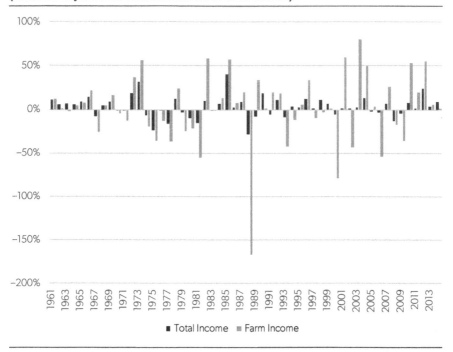

Source: US Department of Agriculture, Economic Research Service, "Farm Household Income and Characteristics," https://www.ers.usda.gov/data-products/farm-household-income-and-characteristics/.

The CBO baseline projects government spending, assuming that programs authorized under current law remain in place over the life of the baseline.

For agricultural commodity programs, the CBO forecasts supply, demand, and prices for the major crops receiving subsidies and calculates the estimated outlays under each of the major farm programs. Typically, the CBO releases a preliminary estimate of the baseline budget in January and then a final version in late winter or early spring. The costs of any proposed changes to farm programs are then calculated and compared to the baseline cost estimates. In this way, proposals are scored relative to the baseline. The 2018 Farm Bill will likely be scored using the baseline that the CBO prepared in April 2018.

The CBO's baseline assumptions about supply, demand, and prices for major program commodities are crucial because those assumptions

Figure 6. Projected Corn Prices Under the 2013 CBO Baseline Compared to Actual and Projected Corn Prices Under the 2017 CBO Baseline

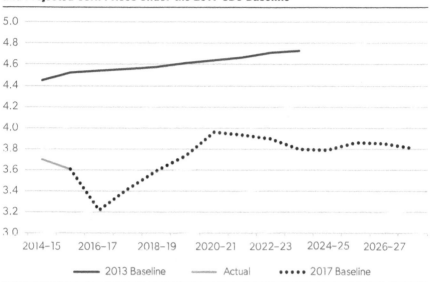

Source: Congressional Budget Office, "Baseline Projections for Selected Programs," 2017, https://www.cbo.gov/about/ products/ baseline-projections-selected-programs#20,

determine the CBO's estimates of the size of expected budgetary outlays. Many farm programs are countercyclical with respect to prices or revenues. Thus, low projected prices can mean large expected outlays under countercyclical programs, and vice versa. Moreover, price forecasts often vary significantly from one year to the next as current market conditions can largely affect expectations about future price levels. For example, compare projected corn prices under the 2013 CBO baseline to actual prices through 2016–17 and price projections under the June 2017 baseline. When the 2013 baseline was prepared, farm prices were at record highs, and the CBO projected that corn prices would remain well above $4.00 per bushel throughout the 10-year projection period (Figure 6). Instead, record global grains crops over 2014–16 resulted in large global inventories. In response, corn prices declined by about 40 percent.

The June 2017 CBO baseline projected a modest recovery for corn prices over the next five years, but prices are still expected to remain far below the projected levels reported in the CBO 2013 baseline. Because of

Table 2. Projected Outlays for Selected Agricultural Programs, FY2018–27

					Fiscal Year						Total 2018 –27
	2018	2019	2020	2021	2022	2023	2024	2025	2026	2027	
					Billion Dollars						
SNAP	67.7	67.4	67.4	67.2	67.2	67.2	67.5	68.1	68.9	70.6	679.2
Commodity Programs	8.5	6.4	4.8	6.7	5.4	5.5	5.8	6.3	6.3	5.9	61.8
Conservation	5.2	5.7	6.0	6.0	6.0	6.1	6.1	6.2	6.2	6.2	59.8
Crop Insurance	7.1	7.2	7.5	7.9	8.0	8.0	7.9	7.9	8.0	8.1	77.4
Total	88.5	86.7	85.7	87.8	86.6	86.8	87.3	88.6	89.5	90.8	878.2

Source: Congressional Budget Office, "Baseline Projections for Selected Programs," 2017, https://www.cbo.gov/about/products/baseline-projections-selected-programs#20.

lower-than-expected prices, actual commodity program spending for the ARC and PLC programs has been higher than originally projected under the 2013 baseline.[23]

Over the 2018–27 federal fiscal year (FY), current farm and nutrition programs are projected to cost the budget about $878.2 billion (Table 2). About 77 percent of the spending is for the Supplemental Nutrition Assistance Program (SNAP). Of the remainder, the federal crop insurance program is projected to cost about $7.7 billion annually. Annual outlays under the price and income support programs are projected to average about $5.9 billion, while annual spending on conservation programs, including the CRP, is estimated to average about $6.0 billion.

The CBO projects that outlays under the price and income support programs are expected to fall over the next 10 years, due in part to rising crop prices and because ARC program revenue guarantees are projected to decline. The reason for the forecasted decline is that the ARC guarantees are based on a five-year Olympic average price (computed discarding the highest and lowest prices) of the prices in the five previous marketing years, which cannot fall below the prices used to trigger payments in the PLC program. This wrinkle essentially guarantees that if prices for crops such as corn

Table 3. Actual 2014–18 Enrollment and the Projected Enrollment for 2019–27 in the PLC Program Assumed in CBO 2017 Baseline

	2014–18	2019–27
Corn	6.6%	82.1%
Soybeans	3.1%	48.7%
Wheat	42.5%	82.1%
Rice	100.0%	100.0%
Peanuts	100.0%	100.0%
Sorghum	66.4%	82.1%
Barley	74.8%	74.4%
Oats	32.0%	93.3%

Source: Congressional Budget Office, "CBO's June 2017 Baseline for Farm Programs," June 2017, https://www.cbo.gov/sites/default/files/recurringdata/51317-2017-06-usda.pdf.

fall to their long-run average levels, then farmers who enrolled in the ARC program would still receive substantial subsidies.

Under the 2014 Farm Bill, program crop producers had to choose to sign up for either the ARC or PLC program for the life of the farm bill (i.e., through the 2018 crop year). In 2014, almost all corn and soybean producers signed up for the ARC program, while nearly all rice and peanut producers signed up for PLC. Wheat producers split their land somewhat more evenly, depending on geographic region (Table 3). The current CBO baseline forecasts assume that many corn and soybean producers will switch from ARC to PLC in 2019 because of lower ARC guarantees.

Almost 40 percent of all PLC and ARC price and income support payments are projected to go to corn producers (or producers who have historically produced corn). Corn payments are projected to decline as ARC guarantees fall due to lower prices since 2013 but then average about $2.5 billion per year over the 10-year period. Wheat payments average about $1.3 billion a year, while annual payments for soybeans, peanuts, and rice each average about $500 million. Upland cotton was excluded from the ARC and PLC programs as part of a settlement with Brazil in a World Trade Organization (WTO) dispute over US cotton subsidies.

Conservation program spending is projected to increase modestly over the baseline period, from $5.6 billion projected in FY2018 to $6.2 billion in

FY2027 (Table 2). The three largest programs—the CRP, the Conservation Stewardship Program, and the Environmental Quality Incentives Program—account for about 93 percent of total spending.

Projected crop insurance outlays are tied to the level of crop prices. When expected crop prices fall, expected crop insurance premiums fall. As a result, expected outlays for premium subsidies and delivery costs (which are tied to premium levels through underwriting gains and administrative and operating costs) fall as well. Delivery costs are estimated to account for about one-third of total crop insurance expenses. As crop prices are expected to appreciate marginally throughout the baseline period, crop insurance outlays rise from $7.2 billion in FY2018 to $8.1 billion in FY2027.

Wide variations in commodity prices due to weather and other factors often cause CBO baseline forecasts to be poor predictors of actual market prices, a characteristic they have in common with other price forecasts. The strong market environment assumed in the 2014 CBO baseline was widely viewed as overly optimistic when it was announced and had given way to a much less sanguine outlook by March 2015. Price and income support programs tend to be countercyclical with respect to actual prices and revenues. As a result, budget forecasts swell when the outlook is for lower prices and shrink when the outlook for prices improves.

To obtain the most accurate estimate of budgetary costs, legislation should be scored using the most current baseline. However, there have been instances in which Congress has chosen to maintain an outdated baseline (for example, when the farm bill debate is unresolved and extended into a subsequent year) to take advantage of the fact that the market outlook has changed and projected payments are higher or lower.

For example, in 1996 Congress passed farm legislation that established direct payment rates based on projected budget outlays using the 1995 baseline rather than the 1996 baseline, which projected lower payments due to increased price prospects.[24] The 2014 Farm Bill was scored against the 2013 budget baseline that projected high prices over the 10-year period and as a result showed much lower subsidies and much larger savings than if the farm bill had been scored against the 2014 baseline.[25]

Rationalizations for Agricultural Subsidies: Assertions and Evidence

The statement by the current chair of the House Agriculture Committee and similar assertions by other supporters of farm subsidies reflect the contemporary pro-subsidy view surrounding farm subsidies. Their arguments consist of several questionable claims. They argue that (1) farms are facing financial crises, (2) farms are facing enormous business risks (because they do face production risks associated with weather and disease) that other types of businesses do not face, (3) farmers are in a poor position to manage variations in their farm incomes, and, implicitly, (4) farm households are at risk of facing poverty. As a direct consequence, the rhetoric asserts that without subsidies the US farm sector is on the verge of collapse and that the US food system is likely to fail.

None of those claims is supported by the empirical evidence. Following several years of record-high farm incomes, net farm household incomes have fallen back to levels relatively close to the long-run average. Figure 1 illustrates the long-run evolution of net cash farm income in the US in real (2009 dollar equivalent) terms.

Two facts are obvious. Farm income in 2017 is considerably lower than it was in the 2009–14 period. However, 2017 farm income is similar to the farm income that households engaged with agriculture received throughout the preceding 10 years (from 1999 to 2008). Thus, while it is true that farm operations have endured big drops in incomes over the past three years, real farm incomes remain above their long-term, inflation-adjusted average.

It is difficult for many of us to imagine our incomes falling by half from one year to the next. However, it is also equally difficult for us to imagine that our incomes may double overnight, as occurred for many farms in the late 2000s. Of course, most farms (1) expect the revenues they obtain from their farm businesses to be volatile and (2) do not get all or even most of their incomes from farming and intentionally have extensive arrangements to smooth out variations in their household's incomes from one year to the next. Thus, in the context of the longer-run trend in incomes from farming activities, an "unimaginable 50 percent drop" between 2013 and 2016 is perhaps more reasonably characterized as an entirely imaginable reversion to normal farm income times.

Figure 7. Ratio of Average US Farm Household Incomes to All US Household Incomes

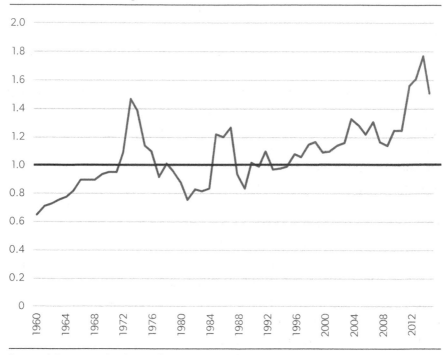

Source: US Department of Agriculture, Economic Research Service, "Farm Household Income and Characteristics," https://www.ers.usda.gov/data-products/farm-household-income-and-characteristics/.

In addition, recent claims by various House and Senate Agriculture Committee members about the current "difficult times" in agriculture, the precipitous drops in income, and increases in financial leverage and stress are also familiar. They resonate with lobbying efforts in relation to previous farm bill debates both in using largely cherry-picked data to justify the arguments and using the associated pleas flowing from agricultural interest groups and their representatives in Congress for higher levels of subsidies to address these issues. Finally, the net contribution of farm activities to the incomes of households engaged in farming is no more than 20 percent of those households' total annual incomes, and it only achieved that degree of significance during 2007–13, a period of near-record prices for many agricultural commodities.

A straightforward assessment of a few empirical facts about US agriculture helps clarify the relevance of these arguments. As discussed previously, farm incomes and gross revenues from market sales rose substantially during 2007–13 and have recently contracted to levels that were common before the significant increases. The extent to which these changes have crossed the thresholds that threaten the viability of farms is questionable. The farm sector, like many other portions of the aggregate economy, is subject to cycles and boom-and-bust events. From the perspective of a longer-run examination of the financial standing of farms, today's incomes remain equivalent to or above long-run averages.

Further, the claim that in the United States farmers need help because their families have low incomes relative to those of nonfarm families has little to recommend it. For example, only 2 percent of all farm households have incomes that fall below the federal poverty line, while, using that metric, more than 14 percent of all households are in poverty. The claim that on average farm families are poorer than other families may have been true 80 years ago, but it carries no water today.

When compared to nonfarm households, farm households have enjoyed household incomes significantly above those of nonfarm households for well over two decades. Figure 7 illustrates the ratio of farm household incomes to all household incomes. Farm households have realized average incomes that exceed the average US household incomes since the early 1990s. While this ratio did fall from 177 percent to 151 percent between 2014 and 2015, farm families on average still enjoy significantly higher household incomes.

The argument that farms are poorly placed to cope with financial risks is also misleading. An examination of the long-run trend in the ratio of debts to assets (the typical measure of financial leverage) does show modest sector-wide increases in leverage in the past couple of years. However, in the five preceding years (2009–14) average leverage ratios and other indicators of financial stress were at their lowest levels since the USDA began collecting such data in 1960.

As shown in Figure 3, the ratio of debts to assets peaked in 1985 at 22 percent and then steadily declined to about 11 percent over the next 30 years. The debt-to-asset ratio has risen to just over 14 percent, but the level remains low when compared to its long-run average and with leverage ratios in other sectors of the economy. For example, AT&T, a company widely viewed as being modestly leveraged, has a current debt-to-asset ratio of 26.4 percent.[26] Viewed in the context of any reasonable metric, financial

Table 4. Farm Household Financial Characteristics by Farm Type

Item	Residence Farms	Intermediate Farms	Commercial Farms	All
Number				
Number of Farms	1,215,011	631,942	185,346	2,032,300
Income, Median Dollars per Household				
Farm Income	−$2,100	$788	$146,466	−$765
Off-Farm Income	$82,987	$55,750	$40,250	$67,500
Earned Income	$62,500	$31,789	$22,500	$38,270
Unearned Income	$24,000	$25,013	$9,000	$25,013
Total Household Income	$82,925	$59,102	$197,980	$76,735
Balance Sheet, Median Dollars per Household				
Total Household Assets	$868,500	$933,625	$3,256,500	$966,000
Farm Assets	$335,200	$537,400	$2,680,455	$438,775
Nonfarm Assets	$449,129	$252,541	$362,750	$297,000
Total Household Debt	$50,438	$93,299	$435,399	$90,562
Farm Debt	$547	$1,472	$314,500	$938
Nonfarm Debt	$38,750	$37,917	$32,500	$37,917
Household Net Worth	$759,306	$799,345	$2,586,944	$827,307

Source: US Department of Agriculture, Economic Research Service, "Farm Household Income and Characteristics," https://www.ers.usda.gov/data-products/farm-household-income-and-characteristics/.

stress in US agriculture remains low, both in comparison to its own history and to other sectors of the economy.

Strident arguments for subsidies and other support measures almost always focus on measures such as net farm income and compellingly ignore that farm households are typically actively engaged in the nonfarm workforce and receive substantial and relatively stable incomes from their off-farm work. Chairman Michael Conaway's statement is clearly consistent with the standard "we need farm subsidies" approach that ignores the role of off-farm income. Since at least the early 1940s, farm households have been extensively involved in nonfarm employment.[27]

Today, as has been the case for more than 40 years, the majority of a typical farm household's family income comes from off-farm activities. This is true even for households that own and operate large commercial farms and is not just a phenomenon concentrated among farms operated by what many describe as hobby farmers.

Financial indicators are reported in Table 4 for three different classes of farms—residence (hobby), intermediate, and commercial. Among all two million farms in the United States, about 88 percent of total household income is derived from off-farm activities. Even among large commercial farms (farms with more than $350,000 in annual sales), more than 20 percent of farm household income comes from off-farm activities. Table 4 also documents that farm households tend to be quite wealthy, with the average household having about $1 million in assets.

In short, farms in the US agriculture sector are facing economic conditions consistent with the sector's long-run history. In the past three years, farm incomes have declined from recent record levels, but they remain above long-run averages. At the same time, while US farms have become more leveraged since 2013, leverage rates remain close to the all-time low. Rhetorical reflections on the well-being of US farm households typically neglect to consider the extensive involvement of household members in the nonfarm workforce.

Significant off-farm work is prevalent, even for large commercial farming operations. Economic conditions, as evidence by the actual data, do not point to the onset of a financial crisis in rural America that many advocates for farm subsidies claim is just around the corner. Rather, economic conditions remain favorable, and US households involved in farming continue to enjoy high incomes and significant wealth.

Another claim legislators with farm constituencies are making is that farm programs were cut during the last farm bill; that is, the 2014 Farm Bill reduced farm subsidy payments. Overall, while farm bill–related spending has been lower than anticipated, it is not because spending on farm subsidies has moderated but because spending on nutrition programs (especially SNAP) has declined.

In fact, total spending on major commodity subsidy programs authorized by Title I of the farm bill increased substantially after the 2014 legislation. And while spending on crop insurance subsidies moderated after 2014 largely because of lower commodity prices, the fundamental highly subsidized structure of the crop insurance program was untouched, and the program's scope expanded. Congress established ARC and PLC support at high levels that were always likely to trigger significant payments when prices retreated from their record-high levels in the years preceding passage of the 2014 Farm Bill. As a result, total subsidy payments to farms increased relative to the amounts they obtained under programs authorized by the previous legislation (the 2008 Farm Bill).

Recently, the House Agriculture Committee claimed that the committee's sacrifices in the 2014 Farm Bill, by implication especially with respect to farm subsidies, have saved taxpayers $100 billion over a 10-year time horizon. To the extent that such savings exist, they do not come from reductions in direct farm subsidy payments. In summary, neither assertions that the farm economy is entering a period of dire economic conditions nor claims that the farm programs introduced in 2014 resulted in less spending on farm subsidies square with the evidence.

The International Trade Implications of Current US Farm Subsidy Programs. One important concern about current US farm bill agricultural subsidy programs is their impacts on US trade relations with other countries. Since the 1930s, such subsidies have been criticized for their distortionary impacts in world markets.[28] During the 1950s and 1960s, for example, US price supports resulted in large inventories of grains and cotton. Those surpluses were often dumped on world markets through concessional food aid[29] or, as in the 1970s and 1980s, through direct export subsidies.[30]

While food aid recipients may have benefited through lower food prices and increased food availability, foreign producers were disadvantaged through lower prices, and subsequently, in many instances, commercial exports were displaced from the United States and other countries. High price supports also insulated producers from market signals, which distorted production decisions and further depressed prices in international markets.[31]

As, to some extent, US agricultural supports have shifted away from direct price support based on actual plantings to income support programs decoupled from production, their distortionary effects have become less obvious. For the most part, PLC and ARC subsidy payments for crops such as corn and soybeans are not tied to current planting decisions and are viewed by some as barely affecting domestic or global markets.

However, in the context of the WTO agreements, both the PLC and ARC subsidy program are viewed as "amber box," or production-distorting programs, because per-acre payments are driven by current market prices and, in the case of ARC, current yields for specific crops. In addition, scholars such as Barry Goodwin, Ashok Mishra, Nathan Hendricks, and Daniel Sumner have questioned whether payments are truly decoupled from production, even if the effects are less commodity specific than payments tied to the areas planted to specific crops.[32]

Further, some US subsidy program payments, including those made in the federal crop insurance program, are unambiguously tied to farm businesses' crop-specific production decisions. Moreover, other initiatives such as the US sugar program deliberately restrict imports to raise prices paid to US sugar beet and cane producers, lowering world prices by expanding US sugar production and diverting sugar production from other countries into global markets.[33] Marketing orders for milk, fruits, and vegetables designed to segment markets and raise average prices paid to US producers may also encourage domestic production with adverse implications for producers of those commodities in other countries (e.g., Mexican tomato growers, Chilean grape producers, and New Zealand dairy farmers).

Domestic support levels in the United States, as measured by the Aggregate Measurement of Support (AMS) estimates that the US is required to file for each year to the WTO, have remained below the levels specified as binding under the current WTO agreement since reporting began in 1995.[34] Some subsidy payments, known as de minimis supports, are excluded from the US AMS in accord with the terms of the current WTO agreements. However, if those payments were included, the total AMS would have exceeded limits in 1999–2001. The countercyclical nature of many US farm programs causes subsidy expenditures outlays and AMS levels to fluctuate year to year in response to fluctuations in commodity prices.

This issue has raised concerns that, because of subsidies associated with the new PLC and ARC programs, the US could breach its AMS bindings if prices for major commodities were to fall to low levels.[35] Farm bills since 2002 have included authority for the secretary of the USDA to cut agricultural spending if it became likely that subsidy spending would exceed WTO limits. However, as this situation has not yet arisen, it is unclear how the secretary would make such cuts.

The United States may well not exceed its domestic support WTO commitments under the terms of the current WTO agreement on aggregate measures of support. However, that does not mean that US agricultural subsidy programs remain immune to challenges under other parts of the WTO agreements. In the Brazil cotton case (the United States–Upland Cotton dispute), Brazil charged that a wide range of US cotton programs were distorting US cotton production and trade and causing serious prejudice to Brazil cotton producers through the subsidies' effects on world cotton prices.

In 2014, Brazil agreed to a settlement of the case with the United States in return for changes made to the cotton program as part of the 2014 Farm Bill. However, dissatisfaction with STAX, which replaced programs the WTO Dispute Resolution Panel in the Brazil cotton case found to be production distorting, prompted the US cotton industry to argue that cotton production should be eligible for the PLC and ARC programs. Congress agreed and within four years of passage of the 2014 Farm Bill reversed earlier reforms by making seed cotton eligible for ARC and PLC. Such a program could likely trigger another WTO case by Brazil.

Whether United States–Upland Cotton provides a ready legal template for challenges to other crop programs as some have argued remains to be seen.[36] However, it has shown that domestic support programs are subject to successful WTO challenges. Congress should therefore view the WTO US–Upland Cotton case as a serious cautionary note. Policy innovations such as PLC subsidies for seed cotton may not result in agricultural support levels that exceed aggregate US-WTO-AMS commitments. However, they may lead to successful WTO challenges by other countries that could involve punitive actions against US agricultural exports or hurt other sectors of the US economy.[37]

The Economic Efficiency Effects of US Farm Programs. As discussed previously, US farm programs essentially do nothing for the rural poor and instead, for the most part, redistribute federal funds to relatively and very wealthy households that own or operate farmland, scarcely an iconic public policy goal for anyone other than the recipients of the largesse. In addition, as briefly discussed in relation to trade issues, many of the programs create incentives for resource waste.

Ironically, for example, federal crop insurance program supporters often describe the initiative as a risk-management program. In fact, from a societal perspective, it is nothing of the sort. As discussed by Smith, Goodwin,

Glauber, and Brian Wright, farmers systematically take on more risk when they insure their crops with heavily subsidized crop insurance products because they do not bear the consequences of those risky actions.[38] The costs associated with adverse outcomes from taking more risk are transferred to taxpayers, while farmers reap any benefits when their risky gambles pay off.

For example, farmers use less fertilizer and crop-loss protection inputs[39] and plant crops on poorer-quality land.[40] They distort their crop mixes; shift to being single-enterprise operations, sometimes adopting monoculture practices; and in a myriad of other subtle ways adjust their resource uses and production practices. These shifts are profitable for the farms but costly for society as a whole.

Programs that restrict imports (i.e., the sugar program) or create opportunities for price discrimination (i.e., milk marketing orders) to exploit market power raise average returns and encourage inefficient expansion in producing the commodities to which they are applied. As discussed previously, they may also create trade relations problems because of impacts on global market prices that expand well beyond the farm sector's products.

In addition, programs such as PLC, ARC, and the long-standing US loan rate program (which still exists and occasionally can provide substantial support to producers, as in the case of cotton recently) distort production decisions and generate inefficient uses of resources in the agricultural sector. Moreover, they require substantial government funds (Table 5).

Raising tax dollars has real social costs, beyond the direct costs to the families that pay those taxes. Income taxes and other forms of payroll taxes shift incentives for work in ways that waste resources, and taxes involve collection costs. To the extent those taxes are used in wasteful ways (e.g., as gifts to wealthy farmers or to encourage wasteful resource practices), they involve additional costs for society.

Ideally, tax dollars would support activities that have positive net social returns. Worryingly, there is little or no data-based evidence that such is the case for most US farm subsidy programs. In fact, the evidence is overwhelmingly to the contrary, with one unambiguous exception. Public investments on agricultural research have consistently been shown to generate substantial returns to society over the past 90 years, and recent and current investments have equally high returns.[41]

Table 5. US Agricultural Program Payments: 2013–17

Year	2013 ($)	2014 ($)	2015 ($)	2016 ($)	2017 ($)
Total Government Direct Farm Program Payments	11,003,796	9,766,845	10,804,486	12,996,932	12,473,139
Fixed Direct Payments	4,288,531	18,733	–3,509	N/A	N/A
Cotton Transition Assistance Payments	N/A	459,927	24,018	N/A	N/A
Cotton Ginning Cost-Share Program	N/A	N/A	N/A	328,032	283
Average Crop Revenue Election Program	206,896	255,084	13,738	N/A	N/A
Price Loss Coverage	N/A	N/A	754,928	1,960,000	3,200,000
Agricultural Risk Coverage	N/A	N/A	4,376,892	5,940,000	5,380,000
Countercyclical Payments	–839	–527	–60	N/A	N/A
Loan Deficiency Payments	–331	61,894	154,844	171,000	108,000
Marketing Loan Gains	0	32,955	53,528	148,000	23,000
Certificate Exchange Gains	N/A	N/A	N/A	93,000	19,000
Milk Income Loss Payments	231,704	–129	–40	16	0
Dairy Margin Protection Program	N/A	N/A	686	–10,580	–15,000
Tobacco Transition Payment Program	647,974	646,399	2,574	N/A	9
Conservation	3,679,896	3,561,396	3,618,928	3,687,334	3,260,915
Biomass Crop Assistance Program	7,078	5,444	7,364	7,000	6,600
Supplemental and Ad Hoc Disaster Assistance	1,942,908	4,725,718	1,800,619	673,162	490,367

Source: US Department of Agriculture, Farm Service Agency, "CCC Net Budgetary Expenditures and Other Financial Data," April 10, 2013, https://www.fsa.usda.gov/Assets/USDA-FSA-Public/usdafiles/AboutFSA/Budget/pdf/pb14_table_09a09ba.pdf.

Yet, for all their public affirmations of the importance of agricultural research, over the past 30 years farm interest groups have been far more effective in protecting subsidy programs such as PLC and ARC that give their members regular checks in the mail. Over the same period, however, farm bill–funded federal spending on agricultural research has atrophied. Currently, for example, as Pardey and Smith discuss in Chapter 4 of Volume II, the farm bill gives the crop insurance industry (about $2.6 billion a year) twice as much as agricultural research (about $1.3 billion a year).[42]

Summary

Many of the farm-oriented programs the current farm bill authorizes mainly funnel federal funds to households whose incomes and wealth are well above those of the average US household. Those programs also generally create incentives for farm businesses to operate in ways that waste economic resources, and the owners and managers of those businesses respond accordingly.

The federal crop insurance program creates incentives for moral hazard behaviors that expand crop production on highly erodible land and generate some reallocation of existing cropland among crops. The sugar program encourages beet and cane operations to expand production, often with adverse environmental consequences. This also hurts world prices, creating challenges for the United States in its trade relations with other countries.

Marketing orders for milk, fruits, and some vegetables also distort production incentives, leading to misallocations of scarce land and water resources. Even subsidy programs that are notionally decoupled from farmers' planting decisions, such as the PLC and ARC programs that cost US taxpayers more than $8 billion in 2017, have adverse resource-misallocation effects. In contrast, federal support through the farm bill has atrophied for the one program that has generated substantial benefits for all US families—publicly funded agricultural research.

So what about the farm interest groups' arguments for continued subsidies? Farm subsidies continue to be justified on the basis that (1) the US agricultural sector is facing a financial crisis as Congress moves toward developing a new farm bill in 2018 and the future of US agricultural production and (2) US food security will be seriously threatened without continued and substantial federal support. There is nothing new in such assertions. Interest groups vested in the farm sector have made similar claims for the past 90 years. Effectively, since at least the late 1930s, such claims have been overblown and, over the past 40 or more years, simply without merit.

The evidence, as laid out in this overview, is that the US agriculture sector is neither experiencing a financial crisis nor about to enter an era of extreme financial stress. Current sector-wide net cash income is close to its long-run historical average. Farm debt-to-asset ratios, while slightly higher than at their record lowest values in 2012 and 2013, are still close to those record lows and well below any levels that would indicate a major financial crisis for the sector.

Households with incomes from farm operations in which a member of the household is actively engaged (that is, manages or provides labor) work in farming mostly on a part-time basis, even when the farms are defined by the USDA as commercial operations. Those households have average incomes well above the national average for all US households and are many times wealthier than nonfarm households. Further, in the sector as a whole, more than 80 percent of those households' incomes come from off-farm sources, and even for the few households (less than 10 percent of all farm households) for which farming is a substantial source of income, a substantial portion of the farm owners' incomes comes from other nonfarm sources.

A second major claim put forward by farm interest groups is that farming is a much riskier enterprise than any other form of business operations and, therefore, farm households face unacceptable volatility in their incomes. Farming as an economic activity does face production risks associated with weather, plant and animal disease, infestations of insects and predators, and so forth. However, whether farming as a business faces more severe financial risks than enterprises in other sectors of the economy is entirely another matter.

The evidence indicates that farming is in fact a much less risky financial business than most other types of business. For example, farm business failure rates, at less than 0.5 percent a year, are many times lower than in any other private sector of the US economy. In addition, farm household incomes are relatively stable, not least because on average income from farming contributes less than 20 percent to the total incomes of farm households. To put the matter succinctly, most farm households are not poor—they are generally well off or very well off in terms of annual incomes—and farm household incomes are not highly volatile. There is therefore no "financial need" or "risk management" case to be made for farm subsidies.

What, then, should Congress do in the 2018 Farm Bill? Ideally, Congress would terminate many farm subsidy programs such as the ARC, PLC, federal crop insurance, the sugar programs, and marketing orders that waste scarce economic resources, raise some consumer prices, and send taxpayer-funded checks to relatively wealthy and very wealthy individuals. These programs certainly do not provide measurable benefits to farmers in households with incomes below the federal poverty line or the rural poor who are not engaged in farming. Some of the $16 billion in federal funding currently tied up in the PLC, ARC, and crop insurance subsidy program should be reallocated to programs that do provide US households with genuine positive benefits, one clear example of which is agricultural research. The rest could be reallocated to other uses, including lower tax rates.

Absent a genuine major shift in agricultural policy, many changes in existing programs that would improve their economic efficiency, reduce their "redistribution to the well-off" effects, and lessen adverse effects on US trade relations with other countries deserve serious consideration. These programs' specific issues are discussed in Volumes I and II by leading agricultural economists that address a wide range of farm bill–related concerns, including direct farm subsidy programs, crop insurance, the sugar program, cotton subsidies, the dairy program, and conservation policies. In the end, the findings remain similar to those laid out by Professor D. Gale Johnson over 40 years ago: US agricultural policy is in disarray and needs to be substantially reformed.[43]

Notes

1. Christopher Barrett, Erin Lentz, and Stephanie Mercier, *International Food Aid and Food Assistance Programs and the Next Farm Bill*, American Enterprise Institute, October 19, 2017, http://www.aei.org/publication/international-food-aid-and-food-assistance-programs-and-the-next-farm-bill/.

2. Erik Lichtenberg, *The Farm Bill, Conservation, and the Environment*, American Enterprise Institute, November 13, 2017, http://www.aei.org/publication/the-farm-bill-conservation-and-the-environment/.

3. Daniel A. Sumner, Joseph W. Glauber, and Parke E. Wilde, *Poverty, Hunger, and US Agricultural Policy: Do Farm Programs Affect the Nutrition of Poor Americans?*, American Enterprise Institute, January 9, 2017, http://www.aei.org/publication/poverty-hunger-and-us-agricultural-policy-do-farm-programs-affect-the-nutrition-of-poor-americans/.

4. Sumner, Glauber, and Wilde, *Poverty, Hunger, and US Agricultural Policy: Do Farm Programs Affect the Nutrition of Poor Americans?* The farm bill includes the legislation that authorizes SNAP, previously known as the Food Stamp Program. SNAP substantially

increases the real incomes of eligible families. See Diane Whitmore Schanzenbach, *The Future of SNAP: Continuing to Balance Protection and Incentives*, American Enterprise Institute, November 6, 2017, http://www.aei.org/publication/the-future-of-snap-continuing-to-balance-protection-and-incentives/. Our focus here, however, is on programs targeted to farm and ranch businesses.

5. Joseph W. Glauber and Daniel A. Sumner, *US Farm Policy and Agricultural Trade: The Inconsistency Continues*, American Enterprise Institute, October 19, 2017, http://www.aei.org/publication/us-farm-policy-and-trade-the-inconsistency-continues/.

6. Christopher R. Knittel, *Corn Belt Moonshine: The Costs and Benefits of US Ethanol Subsidies*, American Enterprise Institute, July 12, 2011, http://www.aei.org/publication/corn-belt-moonshine-the-costs-and-benefits-of-us-ethanol-subsidies/; and Aaron Smith, *Biofuels, the Renewable Fuel Standard, and the Farm Bill*, American Enterprise Institute, December 6, 2017, http://www.aei.org/publication/biofuels-the-renewable-fuel-standard-and-the-farm-bill/.

7. For a detailed history of US agriculture in the 20th century, see Bruce Gardner, *American Agriculture in the Twentieth Century* (Cambridge, MA: Harvard University Press, 2002); and Ezekiel C. Pasour and Randall Rucker, "Plow Shares and Pork Barrels: The Political Economy of Agriculture," Independent Institute, 2005.

8. E. C. Pasour and Randall R. Rucker, *Plowshares and Pork Barrels: The Political Economy of Agriculture* (Oakland, CA: Independent Institute, 2005).

9. Murray Benedict, *Farm Policies of the United States, 1790–1950* (New York: 20th Century, 1953).

10. Mark Drabenstott, "Do Farm Payments Promote Rural Economic Growth," Kansas City Federal Reserve's Main Street Economist, March 2005, https://www.kansascityfed.org/publicat/mse/MSE_0305.pdf.

11. For a detailed description of the PLC and ARC programs, see Vincent H. Smith, Barry K. Goodwin, and Bruce A. Babcock, *Field of Schemes: The Taxpayer and Economic Welfare Costs of Shallow-Loss Farming Programs*, American Enterprise Institute, May 30, 2012, http://www.aei.org/publication/field-of-schemes-the-taxpayer-and-economic-welfare-costs-of-shallow-loss-farming-programs/; and Vincent H. Smith, Barry K. Goodwin, and Bruce A. Babcock, *Field of Schemes Mark II: The Taxpayer and Economic Welfare Costs of Price Loss Coverage and Supplementary Insurance Coverage Programs*, American Enterprise Institute, September 12, 2012, http://www.aei.org/publication/field-of-schemes-mark-ii-the-taxpayer-and-economic-welfare-costs-of-price-loss-coverage-and-supplementary-insurance-coverage-programs/.

12. David Orden, Robert Paarlberg, and Terry Roe, *Policy Reform in American Agriculture* (Chicago: University of Chicago Press, 1999).

13. Bruce A. Babcock, *Covering Losses with Price Loss Coverage, Agricultural Risk Coverage, and the Stacked Income Protection Plan*, American Enterprise Institute, October 13, 2017, http://www.aei.org/publication/covering-losses-with-price-loss-coverage-agricultural-risk-coverage-and-the-stacked-income-protection-plan/.

14. Smith, Goodwin, and Babcock, *Field of Schemes*; and Smith, Goodwin, and Babcock, *Field of Schemes Mark II*.

15. Erik Lichtenberg, "Conservation, the Farm Bill, and U.S. Agri-Environmental Policy," *Choices* 29, no. 3 (2014).

16. White House, "2013 Economic Report of the President," https://obamawhitehouse. archives.gov/administration/eop/cea/economic-report-of-the-President/2013.

17. Julian M. Alston et al., *Persistence Pays: U.S. Agricultural Productivity Growth and the Benefits from Public R&D Spending* (New York: Springer, 2010).

18. Philip G. Pardey and Jason M. Beddow, "Revitalizing Agricultural Research and Development to Sustain US Competitiveness," Farm Journal Foundation, February 28, 2017, http://www.farmersfeedingtheworld.org/policy-briefing/.

19. Alston et al., *Persistence Pays*.

20. Michael K. Conaway, "Rural Economic Outlook: Setting the Stage for the Next Farm Bill," statement before the Committee on Agriculture, US House of Representatives, February 15, 2017.

21. Joe L. Outlaw, "Rural Economic Outlook: Setting the Stage for the Next Farm Bill," statement before the Committee on Agriculture, US House of Representatives, February 15, 2017.

22. In March 2017, the USDA reported that the area planted to cotton is likely to increase by more than 20 percent relative to the area planted to cotton in 2018, scarcely evidence of a crisis in cotton land. See US Department of Agriculture, National Agricultural Statistics Service, "Prospective Plantings Report," March 31, 2017.

23. Vincent H. Smith, "A Midterm Review of the 2014 Farm Bill," American Enterprise Institute, February 2016, http://www.aei.org/wp-content/uploads/2016/02/Midterm-Review.format.pdf.

24. Orden, Paarlberg, and Roe, *Policy Reform in American Agriculture*.

25. Smith, "A Midterm Review of the 2014 Farm Bill."

26. Seeking Alpha, "5 High Yield Stocks from the S&P 500 with Lowest Debt to Equity Ratio," January 25, 2012, http://seekingalpha.com/article/322041-5-high-yield-stocks-from-the s and-p-500-with-lowest-debt-to-equity-ratio.

27. Gardner, *American Agriculture in the Twentieth Century*.

28. D. Gale Johnson, *World Agriculture in Disarray* (New York: St. Martin's Press and New Viewpoints, 1973).

29. Christopher B. Barrett and Daniel G. Maxwell, *Food Aid After Fifty Years: Recasting Its Role* (London: Routledge, 2005).

30. Bruce L. Gardner, "The Political Economy of U.S. Export Subsidies for Wheat," in *The Political Economy of American Trade Policy*, ed. Anne Osborn Krueger (Chicago: University of Chicago Press, 1994): 291–334.

31. Johnson, *World Agriculture in Disarray*.

32. Barry Goodwin and Ashok Mishra, "Another Look at Decoupling: Additional Evidence of the Production Effects of Direct Payments," *American Journal of Agricultural Economics* 87, no. 5 (2005): 1200–10; Barry Goodwin and Ashok Mishra, "Are 'Decoupled' Farm Program Payments Really Decoupled?," *American Journal of Agricultural Economics* 88, no. 1 (2006): 73–89; and Nathan P. Hendricks and Daniel A. Sumner, "The Effects of Policy Expectations on Crop Supply, with an Application to Base Updating," *American Journal of Agricultural Economics* 96, no. 3 (2004): 903–23.

33. Gary W. Brester, *20 Years in, NAFTA Finally Sours the US Sugar Program*, American Enterprise Institute, September 4, 2014, http://www.aei.org/publication/20-years-in-nafta-finally-sours-the-us-sugar-program/; and John Beghin and Amani Elobeid, *Analysis of the*

US Sugar Program, American Enterprise Institute, November 6, 2017, http://www.aei.org/publication/analysis-of-the-us-sugar-program/.

34. Glauber and Sumner, *US Farm Policy and Agricultural Trade*.

35. Joseph W. Glauber and Patrick Westhoff, "WTO Compliance Under the 2014 Farm Bill," in *The Economic Welfare and Trade Relations Implication of the 2014 Farm Bill*, ed. Vincent H. Smith (Bingley, UK: Emerald Group Publishing, 2016): 59–74.

36. Scott Andersen and Meredith Taylor, "Brazil's Challenge to US Cotton Subsidies: The Road to Effective Disciplines of Agricultural Subsidies," *Business Law Brief*, October 2009.

37. In the United States–Upland Cotton dispute, Brazil sought compensation through actions, affecting intellectual property such as pharmaceuticals or seed patents.

38. Vincent H. Smith and Barry K. Goodwin, "The Environmental Consequences of Subsidized Risk Management and Disaster Assistance Programs," *Annual Review of Resource Economics* no. 5 (2013): 35–60; Vincent H. Smith and Joseph W. Glauber, "Agricultural Insurance in Developed Countries: Where Have We Been and Where Are We Going?," *Applied Economic Perspectives and Policy* 34, no. 3 (2012): 363–90; and Brian Davern Wright, "Multiple Peril Crop Insurance," *Choices* (2014).

39. Vincent H. Smith and Barry K. Goodwin, "Crop Insurance, Moral Hazard, and Agricultural Chemical Use," *American Journal of Agricultural Economics* 78, no. 2 (May 1996): 428–38, https://www.jstor.org/stable/1243714?seq=1#page_scan_tab_contents; and Roger Claassen, Joseph C. Cooper, and Fernando Carriazo, "Crop Insurance, Disaster Payments, and Land Use Change: The Effect of Sodsaver on Incentives for Grassland Conversion," *Journal of Agricultural and Applied Economic* 43, no. 2 (2011): 195–211.

40. Claassen, Cooper, and Carriazo, "Crop Insurance, Disaster Payments, and Land Use Change"; and Roger Claassen, Christian Langpap, and JunJie Wu, "Impacts of Federal Crop Insurance on Land Use and Environmental Quality" (selected paper, 2015 Agricultural and Applied Economics Association, San Francisco, CA, July 26–28, 2015).

41. Pardey and Beddow, "Revitalizing Agricultural Research and Development to Sustain US Competitiveness."

42. Philip G. Pardey and Vincent H. Smith, *Waste Not, Want Not: Transactional Politics, R&D Funding, and the US Farm Bill*, American Enterprise Institute, December 11, 2017, http://www.aei.org/publication/waste-not-want-not-transactional-politics-research-and-development-funding-and-the-us-farm-bill/.

43. D. Gale Johnson, *Trade and Agriculture: A Study of Inconsistent Policies* (New York: John Wiley and Sons, 1950).

2

Where the Money Goes:
The Distribution of Crop Insurance
and Other Farm Subsidy Payments

ANTON BEKKERMAN, ERIC J. BELASCO, AND VINCENT H. SMITH

Who receives what benefits from farm subsidy programs has been a focus of economics research throughout the evolution of US agricultural policy. The issue is politically controversial. However, economists have continued to examine the issue on an evidence basis, in part in response to D. Gale Johnson's call in the early 1970s that "any governmental program that involves substantial expenditures by taxpayers and consumers should be periodically evaluated."[1] In the mid and late 2000s, the findings from these evidence-based analyses led to widespread criticisms of many agricultural support programs—including the Direct Payment (DPP), Countercyclical Payment (CCP), Average Crop Revenue Election (ACRE), and Supplemental Revenue Assurance (SURE) programs—by economists, policymakers, and the media.[2]

The 2014 Farm Bill (the 2014 Agriculture Act) terminated the DPP, CCP, ACRE, and SURE programs. However, it replaced CCP and ACRE with two new initiatives, the Price Loss Coverage (PLC) and Agricultural Risk Coverage (ARC) programs. Together with the federally subsidized crop insurance program—a new Stacked Income Protection Plan (STAX) for cotton and a new Dairy Margin Protection Program—ARC and PLC comprise what is widely described as the current farm safety net. Federal expenditures on ARC, PLC, and the federal crop insurance program are estimated to have averaged $12–$14 billion per year since 2014 and are expected to be similarly funded between 2018 and 2027.[3] Further, those subsidies are targeted mainly to producers of program crops.[4] However, the Congressional Budget Office has also estimated that, between 2017 and 2027, more than

70 percent of ARC, PLC, and crop insurance payments will flow to producers of just three crops: corn, soybeans, and wheat.[5]

In light of the substantial estimated public expenditures on these new agricultural support programs, this study also follows Johnson's call to evaluate the economic equity of the 2014 Farm Bill safety-net programs.[6] We use farm-level data from the Agricultural Resource Management Survey (ARMS) to estimate distributions of subsidy payments by size of farm as measured by crop sales, and then we use these estimates to examine potential benefit-cost trade-offs for agricultural producers and taxpayers resulting from changes to the structure of current safety-net programs. We estimate that in 2014 and 2015, approximately 60 percent of total crop insurance subsidies and ARC and PLC government subsidies were paid to producers in the highest 10 percent of the crop sales distribution. Farm businesses in the top 5 percent of crop sales received nearly 40 percent of all program payments, but more than 50 percent of farms in the lower 70 percent of the crop sales distribution received no subsidy or program payments. Further, the results indicate that more stringent restrictions on existing agricultural programs and crop insurance subsidies considered here would affect only farm businesses in the top 5–7 percent of the crop sales distribution but would likely result in a 30–40 percent reduction in public expenditures.

Methods

The objective of this study is to estimate the extent to which small, medium, and large farm businesses receive subsidies under the ARC, PLC, and federal crop insurance programs. The focus is on farm size as measured by value of crop sales. We use this measure to characterize economic returns from agricultural farm operations because of both precedence[7] and other measures that may be less informative for assessing the ARC, PLC, and crop insurance programs.[8]

The analysis uses farm-level data, which are obtained from the 2014 US Department of Agriculture (USDA) ARMS, the most recent survey for which data are available. ARMS is a national survey of agricultural producers, conducted annually by the USDA National Agricultural Statistics Service. The survey collects information about farm finances, off-farm income, and household characteristics. The survey also provides information about each farm's elections with respect to enrollment in ARC and PLC programs and farm-level crop insurance expenditures.

Well-established statistical procedures are used to estimate and represent program payment and insurance subsidy receipts for a national population of farm businesses producing four commodities: corn, cotton, soybeans, and wheat.[9] First, ARMS data on farms' crop insurance coverage level and expenses are linked with the USDA Risk Management Agency (RMA) county-level premium subsidy information to estimate farm-level subsidy rates. Next, we combine farms' ARC and PLC enrollment decisions with USDA Farm Service Agency (FSA) program payments data to calculate farm-level payment receipts. All the estimates are then validated to represent the US farm population using information from the 2012 Census of Agriculture, USDA RMA Summary of Business, and USDA FSA program payment database.[10]

Distribution of Crop Insurance Subsidies and Program Payments

Figure 1 shows the average subsidy per acre[11] given to all farms in a crop sales decile and the proportion of total subsidies received by farms across the crop sales distribution. Farms in the top crop sales decile (i.e., the farms for which the value of annual crop sales ranked in the top 10 percent of crop sales values) receive 67.9 percent of all insurance premium subsidies. Additionally, subsidies per acre are 20 percent higher for farms in the top decile than for the next two deciles (70–80 percent and 80–90 percent), a consequence of higher per-acre insurance coverage levels (liabilities) that largely derive from higher per-acre sales. Figure 1 also shows that farms in the top 2 percent of crop sales receive 30.2 percent of all premium subsidy payments, at a rate of $49.89 per acre. This amount is nearly double the average for those in the top 20 percent ($25.27) and more than four times higher than the average per-acre subsidy of $12.28.[12]

Figure 2 presents the distribution of 2015 ARC and PLC payments across the weighted crop sales distribution. The data indicate that farms in the lowest 70 percent of the crop sales distribution received total payments from ARC and PLC programs that were on average approximately $2,500 per farm.

Figure 1. Crop Insurance Subsidy Payments Across Farms in the Weighted Crop Sales Distribution

Panel A. Crop Insurance Subsidy Payment Distributions by Crop Sales Deciles

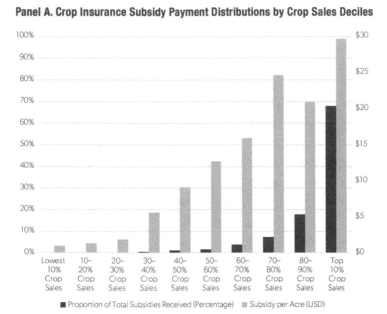

■ Proportion of Total Subsidies Received (Percentage)   ■ Subsidy per Acre (USD)

Panel B. Crop Insurance Subsidy Payment Distributions for Farms in the Top 20 Percent of Crop Sales

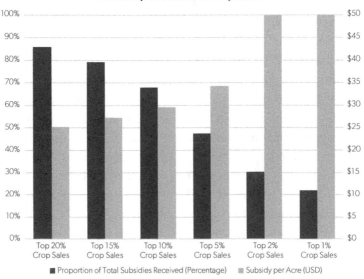

■ Proportion of Total Subsidies Received (Percentage)   ■ Subsidy per Acre (USD)

Source: Authors.

Figure 2. ARC and PLC Per-Farm and Total Payments Across Farms in the Weighted Crop Sales Distribution

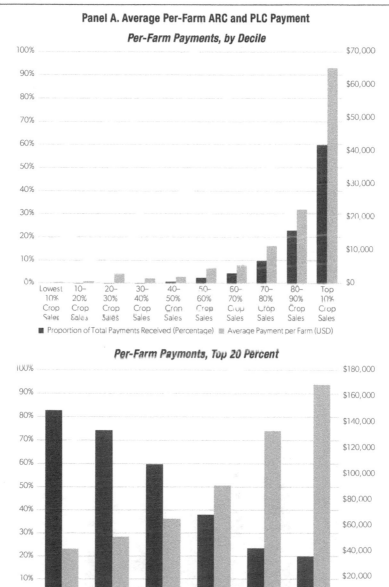

Panel A. Average Per-Farm ARC and PLC Payment

Per-Farm Payments, by Decile

■ Proportion of Total Payments Received (Percentage) ▨ Average Payment per Farm (USD)

Per-Farm Payments, Top 20 Percent

■ Proportion of Total Subsidies Received (Percentage) ▨ Average Payment per Farm (USD)

Source: Authors.

Figure 2. ARC and PLC Per-Farm and Total Payments Across Farms in the Weighted Crop Sales Distribution *(continued)*

Panel B. Total ARC and PLC Payment Expenditures

Total Payments, by Decile

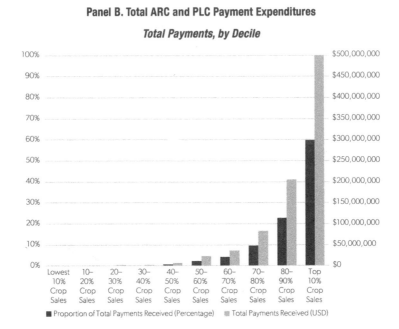

■ Proportion of Total Payments Received (Percentage)   ▨ Total Payments Received (USD)

Total Payments, Top 20 Percent

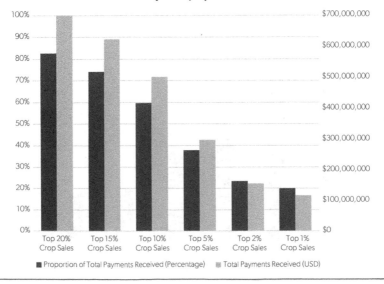

■ Proportion of Total Payments Received (Percentage)   ▨ Total Payments Received (USD)

Source: Authors.

In contrast, farms in the top decile received average payments of $65,022 per farm.[13] In total, farms in the top 10 percent of crop sales received an estimated 58.3 percent of all ARC and PLC payments made to corn, soybean, and wheat producers in 2015. Figure 2 also shows that the overwhelming majority of those payments are concentrated in the top 20 percent of the crop sales distribution. In 2015, 82.1 percent of all ARC or PLC subsidies were paid to those farms. The average ARC and PLC subsidy payment for farms in the top fifth percentile was approximately $91,000, farms in the top 2 percent received average payments of $133,000, and farms in the top 1 percent of crop sales received average payments of $169,000, accounting for nearly 14 percent of all payments. In total, farms in the top 5 percent of the crop sales distribution received close to the same amount ($299 million) of ARC and PLC payments as all the payments received by the bottom 90 percent ($358 million).

Figure 3 shows farm-level receipts of the sum of ARC, PLC, and crop insurance premium subsidies estimated to have been received by farms in 2015.[14] The total estimated payments to farms in the top 10 percent of the crop sales distribution were nearly $3 billion. The top 20 percent received nearly $4 billion in program and subsidy payments, of which nearly half was paid to the top 5 percent of farms. The results presented in Figure 3 also show that farms for which crop sales are in the bottom 80 percent of the sales distribution received only 18.1 percent of total ARC, PLC, and crop insurance subsidy payments, approximately equal to the total payments received by farms in the top 2 percent.

Figure 4 shows the distribution of farms that received payments from each of the different programs in 2015. Fewer than 15 percent of farms in the bottom 40 percent of the crop sales distribution were recipients of any subsidy related to ARC, PLC, or crop insurance. Moreover, more than half the farms in the bottom 70 percent of the crop sales distribution received no payments or subsidies. Conversely, 51.5 percent of farms in the top 20 percent of crop sales received payments from at least one program, and 8.8 percent of those farms received payments from two of the three possible sources. This suggests that not only do corn, soybean, and wheat farms with large market sales have a better than 50 percent chance of receiving a government payment in 2015 but also, as a group, their share of total program payments will almost certainly be larger than the share of those

Figure 3. ARC, PLC, and Crop Insurance Subsidy per Farm and Total Payments Across Farms in the Weighted Crop Sales Distribution

Panel A. Proportion of Farms Receiving Payments, Crop Sales Deciles

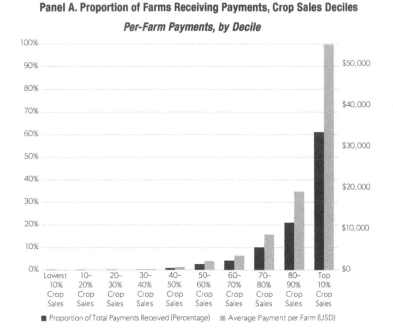

Per-Farm Payments, by Decile

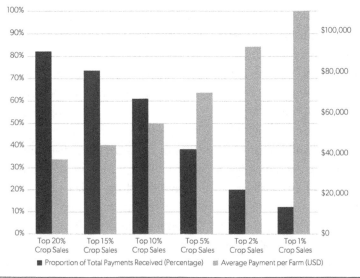

Per-Farm Payments, Top 20 Percent

Source: Authors.

Figure 3. ARC, PLC, and Crop Insurance Subsidy per Farm and Total Payments Across Farms in the Weighted Crop Sales Distribution *(continued)*

Panel B. Proportion of Farms Receiving Payments, Farms in the Top 20 Percent of Crop Sales

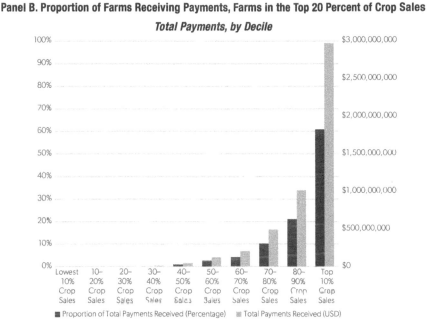

Total Payments, by Decile

■ Proportion of Total Payments Received (Percentage)   ▨ Total Payments Received (USD)

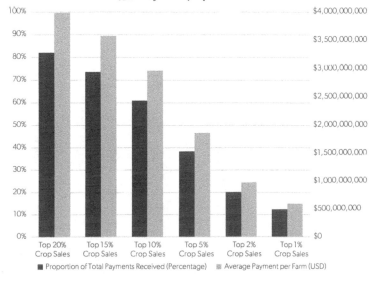

Total Payments, Top 20 Percent

■ Proportion of Total Payments Received (Percentage)   ▨ Average Payment per Farm (USD)

Source: Authors.

Figure 4. Proportion of Farms Receiving Payments from ARC, PLC, or Crop Insurance Subsidies Across Farms in the Weighted Crop Sales Distribution

Panel A. Proportion of Farms Receiving Payments, Crop Sales Deciles

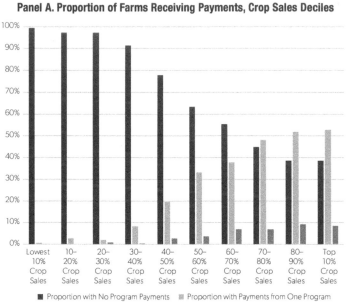

Panel B. Proportion of Farms Receiving Payments, Farms in the Top 20 Percent of Crop Sales

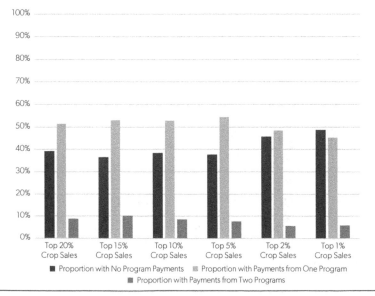

Source: Authors.

payments received by the vast majority of other farms. And while future payment probabilities would depend on relative market prices and farms' coverage-level choices, the distributional characteristics of payments is likely to be roughly similar.

Analysis of Policy Changes on Payments Across the Farm Distribution

The data indicate that producers who receive the majority of total ARC and PLC programs and crop insurance subsidy payments also own the largest farms, generate the highest crop sales revenues, and have the highest amounts of wealth. However, these farms are also generally the least vulnerable to adverse shocks in production and market prices.[15] While subsidized agricultural programs do aid these producers in addressing financial challenges during unfavorable periods, a significant proportion of these payments may not be required to help these farms bridge periods of financial downturns. The burden of these excess payments falls on US taxpayers.

We investigate the effects on agricultural producers and taxpayer savings from expanded limits on government program payments and subsidies. Specifically, we consider four potential policy proposals:[16]

- Introducing caps of $30,000, $40,000, and $50,000 on crop insurance subsidies;

- Reducing the total amount of ARC and PLC payments to a maximum of $125,000 per farm;

- Limiting the sum of ARC, PLC, and crop insurance subsidy payments to $250,000 (the current per-farm limit on ARC and PLC payments); and

- Limiting the sum of ARC, PLC, and crop insurance subsidy payments to $125,000.

Table 1 presents estimates of the impact of imposing a cap of $40,000 on insurance premium subsidies. If this cap had been in effect in 2014, total

Table 1. Hypothetical Incidence of Proposed Insurance Subsidy Cap

Crop Sales Percentile	Average Payment Reduction per Farm (USD)	Total Payment Reduction (Million USD)	Proportion of Farms Affected in Percentile Group	Average Subsidies per Farm (USD)	Percentage of Payment Reduction as a Proportion of Total Subsidies
		$40,000 Cap on Crop Insurance Subsidies per Farm			
0–30%	$0.80	$0.2	0.01%	$87.00	0.88%
30–40%	$6.80	$0.5	0.02%	$482.70	1.41%
40–50%	$68.90	$5.1	0.30%	$1,312.10	5.25%
50–60%	$126.60	$9.4	0.41%	$2,116.80	5.98%
60–70%	$754.30	$55.8	1.19%	$4,373.90	17.25%
70–80%	$576.60	$42.7	2.10%	$7,625.30	7.56%
80–90%	$2,474.00	$183.0	9.58%	$15,991.30	14.47%
Top 20%	$13,167.90	$1,947.9	22.84%	$31,043.40	42.42%
Top 15%	$17,001.10	$1,885.9	28.32%	$37,173.30	45.73%
Top 10%	$23,857.00	$1,764.9	36.09%	$46,089.30	51.76%
Top 5%	$35,815.80	$1,323.8	43.87%	$59,212.30	60.49%
Top 2%	$55,991.00	$827.4	45.66%	$77,216.90	72.51%
Top 1%	$77,937.30	$575.8	41.93%	$96,491.20	80.77%
All	$2,347.10	$2,016.4	4.97%	$7,824.60	30.00%

Source: Authors.

payment reductions would have been $2.02 billion (42 percent of all premium subsidy outlays), but it would have reduced premium subsidies for only 4.97 percent of farms.[17] The affected farms would have experienced an average reduction of $13,168 in premium subsidies, and approximately 77 percent of savings would have come from lower payments made to farms that received more than $100,000 in premium subsidies in 2014. Under a lower $30,000 cap, total taxpayer savings in 2014 would have been approximately $2.51 billion (43.2 percent of total 2014 subsidies), while a higher subsidy cap of $50,000 would have resulted in $1.74 billion in savings (30 percent of total 2014 subsidies). The majority of savings would be realized by reducing payments to corn and soybean producers. Depending on the cap amount, reductions in payments to producers of these commodities would account for 59 percent and 61 percent of savings; wheat and cotton producers would have experienced an approximately 33 percent reduction in 2014 subsidy payments.

Table 2 summarizes the distributional impacts from limits on combined ARC and PLC payments. The table presents results only for farms in the top 20 percent of crop sales because such limits would not affect nearly any farm in the bottom 80 percent. For example, a $125,000 cap on ARC and PLC payments would affect 17.2 percent of all farms enrolled in the programs. Of these, 40 percent (6.9 percent of all farms) are in the top 1 percent of crop sales, and 65 percent are in the top 2 percent of the crop sales distribution. In addition, the overwhelming majority of the reduction in ARC and PLC payments (99 percent) would result from payment reductions to farms in the top 10 percent of the crop sales distribution. Had a $125,000 cap existed in 2015, total savings in government spending on payments to corn, soybean, and wheat producers would have been approximately $70 million, and approximately $64 million of those savings would be realized by reducing payments to farms in the top 5 percent of the crop sales distribution.

Imposing a $250,000 per-farm cap on the sum of ARC, PLC, and crop insurance subsidy payments would result in the general patterns described above, but the estimated level of savings would be nearly four times larger; that is, $273 million. Two-thirds of those savings would result from reducing payments to farms in the top 1 percent of the sales distribution, and nearly 80 percent of savings—more than $217 million—would come from reductions in payments to the top 2 percent of farms in the crop sales distribution.

Finally, Table 2 presents the estimated savings and affected farms resulting from the policy that places a $125,000 ceiling on the combined ARC, PLC, and crop insurance premium subsidies. This policy would not affect farms below the median of crop sales and would affect only 3 percent of farms with crop sales between the 50th and 90th percentiles of the crop sales distribution. For these farms, the average reduction in ARC, PLC, and premium subsidy payments would be $70. For farms in the top 10 percent of crop sales, the average per-farm payment reduction would be approximately $25,600, resulting in total savings of nearly $650 million in government outlays. This represents more than 95 percent of the total savings that would have occurred with a $125,000 cap on total program payments and subsidies in 2015.

Table 2. Hypothetical Incidence of Proposed ARC, PLC, and Insurance Subsidy Caps, 2015 Crop Year

Crop Sales Percentile	Average Payment Reduction per Farm (USD)	Total Payment Reduction (Million USD)	Proportion of Farms Affected in Percentile Group
$125,000 Cap on ARC and PLC Payments			
80–90%	$8.96	$0.62	0.03%
Top 20%	$511.17	$70.21	0.78%
Top 15%	$681.55	$70.21	1.04%
Top 10%	$1,013.49	$69.59	1.53%
Top 5%	$1,874.39	$64.39	2.80%
Top 2%	$3,828.66	$52.61	4.29%
Top 1%	$6,812.60	$46.79	6.88%
$250,000 Cap on ARC, PLC, and Crop Insurance Subsidies			
80–90%	$3.46	$0.24	0.01%
Top 20%	$1,987.43	$272.97	1.04%
Top 15%	$2,649.88	$272.97	1.39%
Top 10%	$3,971.88	$272.73	2.07%
Top 5%	$7,738.32	$265.83	3.76%
Top 2%	$15,851.82	$217.84	6.12%
Top 1%	$26,227.88	$180.13	9.08%
$125,000 Cap on ARC, PLC, and Crop Insurance Subsidies			
50–60%	$4.13	$0.28	0.02%
60–70%	$18.00	$1.26	0.04%
70–80%	$44.63	$3.07	0.15%
80–90%	$211.86	$14.55	0.72%
Top 20%	$4,838.06	$664.50	4.50%
Top 15%	$6,369.12	$656.09	5.75%
Top 10%	$9,465.43	$649.95	8.27%
Top 5%	$16,662.35	$572.39	11.87%
Top 2%	$30,249.28	$415.70	17.75%
Top 1%	$46,328.95	$318.18	22.62%

Note: The scenarios are based on realized 2015 ARC and PLC payments and approximate 2015 crop insurance subsidy rates. Affected farms are those that received payments or subsidies in 2015 but would not have under each hypothetical cap scenario. Total payment reduction represents the value of expenditures that were distributed as program payments or crop insurances subsidies in 2015 but would have not been distributed under each hypothetical cap scenario. Only crop sales percentiles in which farms would have been affected are presented.
Source: Authors.

The above estimates have two caveats. First, changes to program structure and payment caps may create opportunities for farm businesses to restructure their operations and change program enrollment and crop insurance coverage-level decisions. For example, large farms may reorganize as a group of smaller farm businesses, each of which is eligible to receive the maximum amount allowed by a payment cap. Alternatively, if farm structure reorganization is not an optimal strategy in response to caps on crop insurance premium subsidies, a farm may re-optimize by reducing its crop insurance and other risk-management program or altering its production and management strategies. These behavioral adjustments would affect the amount of program outlays and potential savings relative to the estimates presented above. However, the impacts on program payments to farm businesses across the crop sales distributions would likely remain similar because, as we show, the proposed payment caps would have no or minimal impacts on the vast majority of operations.

Conclusion

In the early 1970s, Charles Schultze and Russell Martin Lidman reported that the largest 4–7 percent of all farms received more than 40 percent of agricultural price support program benefits, while farms in the lowest 40 percent of the sales distribution received less than 7 percent.[18] More than 40 years later, the evidence presented in this study indicates that surprisingly little has changed, even though substantial adjustments have been made to farm subsidy programs. In fact, as farm sizes have continued to increase and agricultural production has become more consolidated, program payments have also become more concentrated.[19] The persistence of these distributional impacts raises important questions about the inconsistency between the major rationale for farm safety-net programs—that they exist to protect all agricultural producers against production, price, and income risks—and the observed outcomes from those programs.

If the objective of cost-effective farm safety-net policies is to ensure a stable food supply by helping all farms manage otherwise volatile revenues, then the current programs do not direct taxpayer funds in ways that effectively protect the farm operations most vulnerable to such shocks. Market forces have provided incentives for farm operations to consolidate and rec-ognize economies of scale and scope. However, we show that those farms are also most likely to be the largest beneficiaries of the three major farm programs, even though these farms are likely to be the least vulnerable to shocks that hurt their revenues and costs.[20]

Policies that limit payments could help reduce the disproportionate allo-cation of agricultural program benefits to farms that generally need less help managing financial risks. We show that policies capping crop insurance sub-sidies and ARC and PLC benefits could result in substantial reductions in federal outlays without any adverse implications for 90 percent (and in some cases, more) of US farms.

Notes

1. D. Gale Johnson, *Farm Commodity Programs: An Opportunity for Change* (Washing-ton, DC: AEI Press, 1973), 21.

2. John Antle and Laurie Houston, "A Regional Look at the Distribution of Farm Program Payments and How It May Change with a New Farm Bill," *Choices* 28, no. 4 (2013), http://www.choicesmagazine.org/UserFiles/file/cmsarticle_339.pdf; and David Orden and Carl Zulauf, "Political Economy of the 2014 Farm Bill," *American Journal of Agricultural Economics* 97, no. 5 (2015): 1298–311.

3. Congressional Budget Office, "CBO's June 2017 Baseline for Farm Programs," 2017, https://www.cbo.gov/sites/default/files/recurringdata/51317-2017-06-usda.pdf.

4. Crops eligible for PLC and ARC payments include barley, chickpeas, corn, dry peas, grain sorghum, lentils, oats, peanuts, rice soybeans, wheat, and a wide range of minor oilseed crops including canola, crambe, flaxseed, mustard, rapeseed, safflower, sesame seeds, and sunflower. More than 130 crops are eligible for federal crop insurance subsidies. See Anton Bekkerman, Eric J. Belasco, and Vincent H. Smith, "Does Size Mat-ter? Distribution of Crop Insurance Subsidies and Government Program Payments Across US Farms" (working paper, Montana State University Center for Regulation and Applied Economic Analysis, 2017), https://www.agri-pulse.com/ext/resources/pdfs/Smith-distributions-paper-october-2017.pdf.

5. In 2017, corn, soybeans, and wheat together received $4.458 billion in crop insur-ance premium subsidies, 73 percent of the total amount of $6.07 billion in premium subsidies paid to all 130 or more crops in the program. In 2016, ARC and PLC pay-ments for all crops amounted to $5.283 billion, of which corn ($3.752 billion), wheat ($756 billion), and soybeans ($328 billion) received 85 percent ($4.502 billion). Con-gressional Budget Office, "CBO's June 2017 Baseline for Farm Programs."

6. Johnson, *Farm Commodity Programs*.

7. James D. Johnson and Sara D. Short, "Commodity Programs: Who Has Received

the Benefits?," *American Journal of Agricultural Economics* 65, no. 5 (1983): 912–21.

8. We do also check the robustness of the crop sales measure by conditioning program and subsidy receipts on other possible economic status measures, including wealth, total farm acreage, or gross income from sales. The results are qualitatively nearly identical.

9. These four commodities accounted for 74 percent of total crop insurance liabilities between 2014 and 2016. For analyzing ARC and PLC program payments, we consider only corn, soybeans, and wheat, because cotton producers are ineligible for ARC and PLC.

10. A full description of the data, estimation, and validation procedures is presented in Bekkerman, Belasco, and Smith, "Does Size Matter?"

11. The average per-acre subsidy figures are computed based on the entire percentile, including those who did not receive any subsidies. When we compute averages that include only those who receive payments in each percentile range, the shape of the distribution is similar, albeit with higher rates.

12. When we compute average per-acre subsidies by excluding those who did not receive any premium subsidy payments in each percentile range, the top 20 percent received $32.59 per acre, while the top 2 percent received an average subsidy of $77.07 per acre, which is still more than double the top 20 percent.

13. When we compute average payment per farm with only those farms that receive a payment, the bottom 70 percent received an average payment of $3,422, while those in the top 10 percent received an average payment of $69,038.

14. The most recently available ARMS data do not report 2015 crop insurance election and insured acres information. As such, each farm's crop insurance premium subsidies are assumed to be those they would have received if, in 2015, each farm's crop insurance coverage level and out-of-pocket payments were approximately the same as those that were actually observed for 2014. There is only marginal inter-year variability between coverage levels and insured acres for producers of the four major row crops, and projected prices were also relatively similar in 2014 and 2015. The projected price for revenue protection policies was $4.62 per bushel in 2014 and $4.15 per bushel in 2015 for corn, $11.36 per bushel in 2014 and $9.73 per bushel in 2015 for soybeans, and $7.02 per bushel in 2014 and $6.30 per bushel in 2015 for wheat. See US Department of Agriculture, Risk Management Agency, "Informational Memorandum: PM-14-041," September 16, 2014; and US Department of Agriculture, Risk Management Agency, "Informational Memorandum: PM-15-013," March 3, 2015. Implied price volatility between 2014 and 2015 also remained relatively similar during the three-month period preceding the crop insurance closing date for each crop: For corn, price volatility was 20.12 in 2014 and 24.06 in 2015; for cotton, 21.62 and 22.08; for soybeans, 19.03 and 21.62; and for wheat, 24.39 and 27.75. While these prices are similar, we do acknowledge that using 2014 ARMS data to approximate crop insurance subsidy payments in 2015 would likely marginally overestimate premium subsidies. However, because projected prices and price volatilities between 2014 and 2015 changed by only 11–15 percent, the potential upward bias is expected to be minimal. Moreover, the relative allocation of subsidy payments across the distribution of farms is not likely to change because all farmers face the same price elections.

15. Bryan Schurle and Mike Tholstrup, "Farm Characteristics and Business Risk in Production Agriculture," *North Central Journal of Agricultural Economics* 11, no. 2 (1989): 183–88; Barry M. Purdy, Michael R. Langemeier, and Allen M. Featherstone, "Financial Performance, Risk, and Specialization," *Journal of Agricultural and Applied Economics* 29, no. 1 (1997): 149–61; and Peter J. Barry, Cesar L. Escalante, and Sharon K. Bard, "Economic Risk and the Structural Characteristics of Farm Businesses," *Agricultural Finance Review* 61, no. 1 (2001): 74–86.

16. A $40,000 cap on per-farm crop insurance premium subsidies was included in the Assisting Family Farmers Through Insurance Reform Measures Act, first introduced by Sens. Jeff Flake (R- AZ) and Jeanne Shaheen (D-NH) and Reps. Ron Kind (D-WI) and Jim Sensenbrenner (R-WI) in 2015 and reintroduced in 2017. The act would limit the total value of crop insurance subsidies to $40,000 per person each year and end subsidies for those with an adjusted gross income of more than $250,000.

17. Our analysis assumes that all caps are instituted after farms made their crop insurance and ARC and PLC allocation decisions. Farmers' knowledge of payments caps could lead to re-optimization of enrollment and coverage-level decisions, which would alter the amount of program outlays and potential savings.

18. Charles L. Schultze, *The Distribution of Farm Subsidies: Who Gets the Benefits?* (Washington, DC: Brookings Institution, 1971); and Russell Martin Lidman, "The Distributional Implications of Agricultural Commodity Programs," University of Wisconsin, Institute for Research on Poverty, 1972.

19. James Michael MacDonald, Penni Korb, and Robert A. Hoppe, *Farm Size and the Organization of US Crop Farming*, US Department of Agriculture, 2013, https://www.ers. usda.gov/webdocs/publications/45108/39359_err152.pdf?v=41526.

20. Schurle and Tholstrup, "Farm Characteristics and Business Risk in Production Agriculture"; Purdy, Langemeier, and Featherstone, "Financial Performance, Risk, and Specialization"; and Barry, Escalante, and Bard, "Economic Risk and the Structural Characteristics of Farm Businesses."

Section II

Multi-Commodity Farm Subsidy Program

3

The US Federal Agricultural
Insurance Program: Time for Reform?

VINCENT H. SMITH, JOSEPH W. GLAUBER,
AND BARRY K. GOODWIN

Once criticized and recommended for elimination, over the past 35 years the federal crop insurance program has become the largest and one of the most popular subsidy programs among farmers. Currently, close to 300 million acres are enrolled in the program, with an estimated participation rate of about 85 percent of eligible area and a total liability (coverage in force) of $100 billion. Federally subsidized insurance is now available for more than 130 crops, with modest coverage also available for livestock and dairy producers.

The program has expanded from products that offer limited coverage on a farm's crop yields to policies that insure producers' gross revenues, indemnify yield losses at the harvest price when it is higher than at planting time, and provide supplemental policies that allow producers to recapture a portion of the base policy's deductible when losses are widespread in a county. By any measure, federal crop insurance has become a centerpiece of the suite of US federal farm programs, one that requires annual average subsidies in excess of $8 billion.

The program's current popularity among farmers and farm state legislators stands in sharp contrast to its status 40 years ago. Before the 1980 Federal Crop Insurance Act, the program operated on a limited basis with coverage offered for a limited number of crops in a limited number of counties.[1] The 1980 act recast crop insurance as a primary means of protecting producers against natural disasters. To encourage participation, standing disaster programs were eliminated, producers were offered subsidies covering up to 30 percent of premium costs, and private companies were enlisted to actively sell insurance coverage to producers (as opposed to the more passive way it had been offered previously through United States Department of Agriculture (USDA) county offices).

After the 1980 act was passed, the program rapidly expanded in county and crop coverage but not in participation, which remained modest. When a widespread drought struck the Midwest and Northern Great Plains in 1988, only 25 percent of the area eligible for coverage was enrolled nationwide, prompting large ad hoc disaster assistance from Congress. Many perceived the crop insurance program as a failure, so much so that the George H. W. Bush administration recommended eliminating the program and returning to a standing disaster program as part of its 1990 Farm Bill proposal.

Instead, Congress passed additional legislation in 1994 and 2000 that increased premium subsidy rates to an average of more than 60 percent of the premium costs. Participation then expanded. Producers enrolled more of their crop area in the program, and many chose higher levels of insurance coverage. As a result, by 2015 average coverage levels were more than 70 percent of expected yields or revenues. Penetration levels for crop insurance have been sufficiently high to obviate the need for supplemental disaster assistance. As an example, consider the 2012 drought, which was a weather event widely viewed as more severe than the 100-year drought that struck the Midwest and Northern Great Plains in 1988. Crop insurance indemnities in 2012 totaled more than $17 billion, but in contrast to 1988, Congress refrained from passing ad hoc legislation.

Perhaps the greatest testament to the federal crop insurance program's popularity is that the program was sheltered from budget cuts in the 2014 Farm Bill when other programs, such as the Direct Payment and Countercyclical Payment Programs, were terminated or, like the Supplemental Nutrition Assistance Program and Conservation Reserve Program (CRP), were reduced in scope. In contrast, Congress added new insurance programs, such as the Supplemental Coverage Option and a cotton-specific program known as the Stacked Income Protection Plan, and mandated the development of new revenue insurance policies for peanut producers and margin insurance for rice producers.

Crop insurance will continue to be a major focus in farm bill legislation. With an expected annual budget of almost $8 billion, the initiative will likely remain the largest farm program in federal government spending. Since the mid-2000s, Republican and Democrat administrations have proposed cutting premium subsidies or reducing delivery costs in their annual budget submissions, but Congress has rejected those calls. With tighter federal budgets on the horizon, crop insurance will likely receive renewed scrutiny.

In addition, the program has been criticized for providing subsidized coverage for risks that arguably are better managed by private-sector products. Under the Federal Crop Insurance Act, approved insurance products are not supposed to crowd out products already available in commercial markets. Despite this mandate, the most popular insurance product, revenue insurance, offers subsidized price protection in the event of yield loss—coverage that is readily available through well-established organized private futures and options market exchanges.

Understandably, such heavily subsidized coverage is popular with producers, but it is costly and arguably, because of subsidies, serves as a vehicle for providing price support to corn, cotton, wheat, and other major row crops rather than serving as a safety-net protection for farmers. Moreover, heavily subsidized crop insurance has been shown to affect crop choice and production practices and lead to shifting highly erodible lands from pasture and grazing to crop production. Those impacts have generated environmental and trade concerns.

Lastly, the delivery system for the federal crop insurance program needs to be reevaluated. One of the goals of the 1980 act was to privatize delivery to the maximum extent possible. In response, the federal crop insurance program created incentives to encourage that shift.[2] Private companies have taken on some underwriting risks, but delivery costs are large and account for about one-third of the total expected outlays for crop insurance over the next 10 years. The crop insurance industry has defended those costs, arguing that expenses have outstripped reimbursements and that profitability measures in the crop insurance industry lag comparable measures faced by other property and casualty lines of insurance. Others have advocated more competition among companies by allowing companies to compete directly on rates.[3]

The Evolution of the Federal Crop Insurance Program

The federal crop insurance program's evolution from a relatively small-scale, low-cost component of US farm subsidy initiatives to the most expensive

Figure 1. Total Acres Insured and Estimated Program Participation Rates, 1981–2014

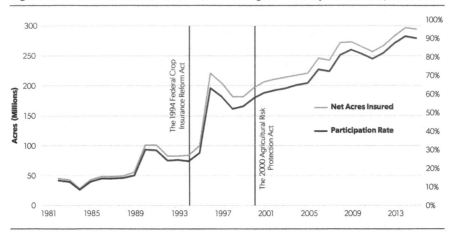

Source: The annual data on insured acres were obtained from the USDA Risk Management Agency, and program participation rates were computed by the authors using USDA National Agricultural Statistics Service annual data on total area planted to crops.

subsidy program available to US farmers can be traced back directly to the 1980 Federal Crop Insurance Act. In 1980, farmers insured 45 million acres (13 percent of total crop acres) through a program that offered coverage for 29 crops under one type of insurance policy, yield insurance. (See Figures 1 and 2, which present data on insured acres, program participation rates, numbers of crops covered, and numbers of county-based programs for specific crops.) By 2015, farmers were insuring 295 million acres through separate programs for more than 130 agricultural commodities under more than 20 different types of yield, revenue, margin, whole farm, and other insurance programs.

Government spending on crop insurance subsidies also increased as participation rose because of higher premium subsidy rates that substantially reduced farmers' costs of acquiring coverage (Figure 3). In 1981, federal crop insurance program subsidies were $84 million; by 2014, those expenditures had increased by more than 80-fold to $7 billion in 2014 and accounted for more than 30 percent of total federal spending on farm subsidy programs. In 2012, at their peak, subsidy outlays were $13 billion, accounting for about 50 percent of total federal spending on farm subsidies. Those outlays are expected to average $7.7 billion annually over the next 10 years.[4]

Figure 2. Numbers of County Programs and Covered Crops, 1981–2014

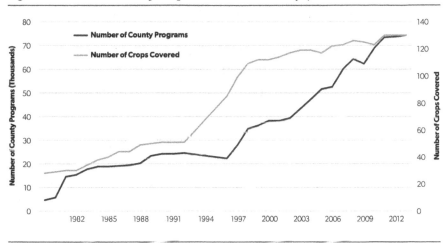

Source: US Department of Agriculture, Risk Management Agency.

Figure 3. Government Expenditures on Premium Subsidies and Administration and Operations Subsidies, 1981–2015 ($ Millions)

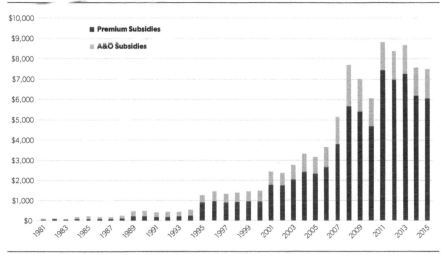

Source: US Department of Agriculture, Risk Management Agency.

Before 1980, government subsidies had been limited largely to funding administrative and operating (A&O) expenses,[5] although there were relatively short multiyear periods when indemnities persistently exceeded farmer-paid premiums and the government served as reinsurer. Premium rates that farmers paid were supposed to be actuarially fair; that is, on average, farmers' payments into insurance pools were to cover the indemnity payments they received.

However, the 1980 Federal Crop Insurance Act explicitly mandated that farmers receive premium subsidies. The targeted premium subsidy rate was 30 percent, so beginning with the 1981 crop year, on average farmers would pay only 70 percent of the actuarially fair premium.[6] The argument for introducing a 30 percent premium rate subsidy was as follows. In the 1970s, Congress had responded to successive appeals for help from farm groups through standing disaster assistance payments. Those payments were direct transfers from taxpayers to farmers, providing the agricultural sector with around $700 million a year during that decade,[7] and they involved no contributions by farmers. Thus, it was claimed, providing farmers with an incentive to participate in the crop insurance program would (1) allow Congress to ignore requests for disaster aid funds and (2) result in farmers providing a substantial share of the funds that would be distributed when they experienced substantial crop losses.

Neither of these assertions turned out to be correct. Participation in the federal crop insurance program had been modest before 1980, partly because of geographic constraints on available coverage and the limited number of crops for which federally subsidized crop insurance was available. However, the main causes of low participation rates were related to adverse selection issues—rates were set based on expected countywide average losses, and many farmers had much lower expected losses[8]—and the availability of much less expensive ways of managing production risks.[9]

The 30 percent premium subsidy the 1980 legislation introduced was too small to have much effect on participation. And the program's rapid expansion in geographic coverage and number of covered crops, illustrated in Figure 2, also did not have any measurable impacts. Participation in the federal crop insurance program remained less than 30 percent of the area eligible for coverage until 1989 and only increased then because of a requirement that farms without insurance coverage would not be eligible for any disaster aid payments (Figure 1). As a result, Congress continued to allocate substantial funds for ad hoc disaster assistance throughout and well beyond the 1980s. By the end of the 1980s, participation in the federal crop insurance program had failed to increase substantially, and ad hoc disaster aid payments continued to be a burden for Congress. Farm and insurance industry lobbies therefore pushed for increased subsidies and found sympathetic ears among senators and representatives from farm states. They were successful in obtaining increased taxpayer funds through the provisions of the 1994 Federal Crop Insurance Reform Act (CIRA), which increased premium subsidy rates to an average of about 40 percent.

In addition, in the early 1990s farm interest groups had been seeking an expanded array of insurance products. Two themes dominated discussions over crop insurance products at that time. First, many farm groups argued that their members needed cost of production insurance. However, until a margin insurance program was approved on a pilot or quasi-experimental basis by the Federal Crop Insurance Corporation (FCIC) Board in 2015, their lobbies were unsuccessful in achieving that goal.

From a public policy perspective, their failure was a positive outcome. It is essentially impossible to meaningfully estimate the actual costs of production of any business, never mind a farm where household and production-related outlays are typically inextricably intertwined. Moreover, insuring a farmer's actual costs of production encourages moral hazard and even fraudulent behavior by discouraging farmers from minimizing those costs. When, eventually, the USDA Risk Management Agency (RMA) offered a margin insurance product in 2015, the product was based on futures prices for crops and inputs and not on actual farm-specific expenditures, thus mitigating some of the moral hazard concerns.

The second theme was a push for revenue insurance products. Up to 1994, farmers' estimated expected per-acre yields had been insured. Now farm interest groups sought insurance against reductions in per-acre revenues. Such insurance was authorized by the 1994 CIRA and introduced for crops such as corn, for which viable futures markets existed, or for crops whose prices were closely linked to those of other crops with futures markets (for example, barley). By 1997, revenue insurance products had been created for major commodities such as corn, soybeans, and wheat and for smaller acre crops such as barley, and they were relatively heavily used.

With the 1994 CIRA-mandated increases in premium subsidies and the expanded portfolio of products for the most heavily insured crops, participation in the federal crop insurance program modestly increased between 1994 and 2000. By 1997, farmers insured about 60 percent of the crop area eligible for coverage (Figure 1), and coverage levels remained low, with many insuring only at the lowest catastrophic level. However, as part of its response to low prices for major row crops such as corn and wheat that began in 1998, Congress passed supplemental legislation, which provided additional premium subsidies for the 1999 and 2000 crops, and then, in 2000, passed the Agricultural Risk Protection Act (ARPA), which further expanded premium subsidies for farmers.

The new schedule of subsidies resulted in farmers receiving subsidies that average 62 percent of the estimated actuarially fair premium rates. In response, since the early 2000s, farmers have increased their participation in the federal crop insurance program to the extent that between 85 and 90 percent of the crop area eligible for insurance is covered. This is not a surprise. The average risk-neutral farmer can expect to receive more than $2 back for every dollar he or she spends buying federal crop insurance; risk-averse farmers enjoy even larger benefits.

The 2000 ARPA also included an important feature through which the price risk associated with a Harvest Price Option (HPO) endorsement to revenue insurance would be subsidized. The HPO, originally made available to farmers in 1996, works as follows. A standard revenue contract establishes the expected revenue per acre for a farm at the time coverage is purchased (just before a farmer plants the crop) by multiplying the farm's expected yield based on the farmland's actual production history (APH) with the price expected for the crop at harvest time, several months later.

The HPO endorsement increases the price at which production losses will be valued when, between planting time and harvest time, crop prices have increased. Expanding the premium subsidy to the HPO in 2000 resulted in a rapid shift into revenue insurance, and since 2002 about 70 percent of all subsidized crop insurance coverage has been in revenue insurance, including the HPO. A recent Congressional Budget Office (CBO) analysis[10] reported that ending the HPO subsidy would reduce taxpayer outlays on the federal crop insurance program by about $1.9 billion annually, almost 25 percent of total estimated federal spending on the program.

Figure 4. Total Annual Government Expenditures on the Federal Crop Insurance Program ($ Billions)

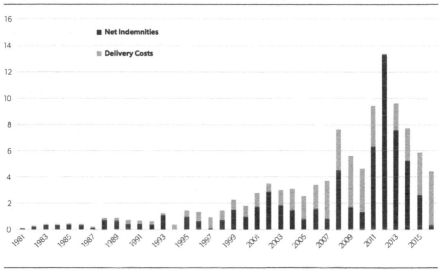

Source: US Department of Agriculture, Risk Management Agency.

Information on government expenditures on the federal crop insurance program is presented in Figure 3 for 1980–2015. These data include expenditures on explicit premium subsidies (the share of total payments into the insurance pools the federal government made on the farmers' behalf) and subsidy payments to the insurance companies for administration and operations costs. Government outlays also include expenditures by the government agency that manages the crop insurance for research, product development, personnel, and other cost items, such as computers and facilities. Those costs currently amount to about $100 million a year. Total annual government expenditures on the program are presented in Figure 4. These expenditures include all delivery costs (A&O subsides and expenditures on RMA and FCIC operations) and net indemnity payments by the government (total indemnities minus the sum of producer premium payments and any underwriting losses shred by the private insurance companies). Government net indemnity payments may exceed or fall short of premium subsidies in any given year because of year-to-year unpredictable differences in actual indemnifiable losses.

The information on annual program costs presented in Figures 3 and 4 provides an additional set of measures of the growth of the US crop insurance program. From small beginnings in 1981, when total government premium and A&O subsidies amounted to $54 million, those subsidies increased to a maximum of $8.8 billion in 2011, moderated a little to $7.5 billion in 2015, and were forecast by the CBO to average about $8.5 billion a year over the next 10 years.[11] Premium subsidies increased as program participation expanded modestly between 1981 and 1995, and the number of crops covered also expanded, with costs rising from $54 million in 1981 to $200 million in 1993 at an average annual growth rate of 12.6 percent. However, over the period, the subsidies for A&O outlays rose more rapidly, increasing from $4 million in 1981 to $34 million in 1983, as private companies began to market subsidized crop insurance products, and then to $234 million by 1993 at an annual average growth rate of 19.1 percent between 1983 and 1993.

Spending on premium subsidies increased more rapidly between 1994 and 2000, rising from $255 million to $951 million at an annual growth rate of 10 percent, as participation increased in response to the higher premium subsidy rates introduced in 1994. Expenditures on A&O subsidies also increased, almost doubling from $282 million in 1994 to $552 million in 2000, but at a slower rate than premium subsidies because A&O subsidy rates were reduced from 33 percent of total premiums in 1993 to 31 percent in 1995 and 27 percent in 1997.

After 2000, when premium subsidies increased to an average of 62 percent and were extended to the HPO, premium subsidies rose quickly, increasing from $951 million in 2000 to $2.7 billion in 2006, largely because of expanded participation but also because prices for crops such as corn and wheat began to increase. They then surged, rising to $7.3 billion in 2013, largely because of increases in crop prices, as liability is essentially proportional to crop prices for any given crop insurance contract.

Since then, as prices for the most heavily insured crops have moderated, premium subsidies have also moderated, falling to $6.1 billion in 2015. Subsidies for company A&O expenses also increased rapidly and at a somewhat similar rate to increases in premium subsidies between 2000 and 2008 because payments were proportional to total premiums, as to a large extent were premium subsidies. However, after 2010, A&O payments became subject to an effective cap of about $1.4 billion as members of Congress became concerned about the total revenues earned by the companies relative to the number of policies being serviced.[12]

Premium Rates and Crop Insurance Program Participation

An important characteristic of crop insurance programs around the world is that significant premium subsidies are required to induce farmers to participate in them. This has proved true across a wide range of programs, including highly developed programs such as those found in the US and other developed countries and new programs intended to help subsistence farmers in parts of Latin America, Asia, and Sub-Saharan Africa. At first glance, this seems to be a paradox in that conventional theories of producer behavior under risk typically assert that risk-averse agents will fully insure at actuarially fair premium rates. However, a wide range of willingness-to-pay studies indicate that farmers are unwilling to pay much at all for risk protection through crop insurance,[13] and adverse selection issues are almost impossible to solve through product design. Thus, farmers must be paid to buy crop insurance if any measurable degree of participation is to be obtained.

Figure 5 summarizes the development of the US federal crop insurance program over the past 35 years. It presents the annual average loss ratio (the ratio of indemnities to premiums), the implicit premium subsidy rate (the ratio of premium subsidies to total premium), and a measure of total program participation (given by total enrolled acreage as a proportion of acreage in 2016). Several points are notable. First, participation tracks premium subsidies closely. The impacts of the increased subsidy the 1994 CIRA mandated were substantial. Acreage enrolled in the program increased significantly in 1995. However, 1995 is unique in that, under a provision of the 1994 act, participation in the program was required for a farm to be eligible for other agricultu~ efits. This requirement, which proved to be unpopular w quickly rescinded, and a large decrease in acreage enroll occurred in 1996. Participation in total acreage increase decades that followed.

Figure 5. Summary Statistics for the US Federal Crop Insurance Program

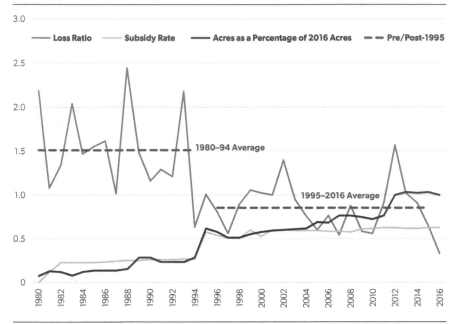

Source: Annual data obtained from the US Department of Agriculture, Risk Management Agency. Summary statistics computed by the authors.

Another fact, not immediately obvious from Figure 5, is that the nature of coverage shifted significantly throughout the late 1990s and 2000s. Revenue coverage was introduced in 1996 and quickly became the most prominent form of insurance. Figure 6 illustrates the proportion of total liability in the federal crop insurance program that is accounted for by revenue coverage. Increases in participation over the 1995–2005 period reflect the increasing availability of revenue coverage, which has proved to be preferred by farmers.

Finally, the actuarial performance of the program, defined as the program's overall total loss ratio, appears to have improved as subsidies were increased and participation levels rose. In the early 1980s, acres enrolled in the program were about 12 percent of the 2016 levels. Over that 36-year period, in terms of the program's total loss ratio, the program's actuarial performance appears to have improved. From 1981 to 1994, the gross loss io (defined as total indemnities divided by total premiums collected,

Figure 6. Proportion of Liability in Revenue Coverage

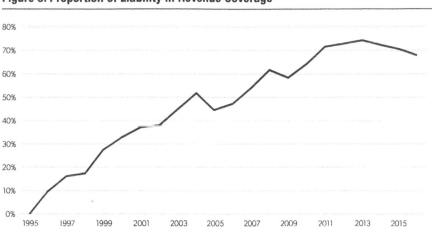

Source: US Department of Agriculture, Risk Management Agency.

including premium subsidies) averaged 154 percent. Since then, the total loss ratio has averaged about 82 percent. However, as shown in Figure 7, producer loss ratios, defined as indemnities paid divided by producer-paid premiums, did not substantially change. Throughout the entire period, on average producers have received about $2.20 in indemnities for every dollar paid in premiums. A clear implication is that, when participation rates were low, only the individuals whose premium rates were underpriced were choosing to insure their crops, but when increases in subsidies and changes in the types of offered insurance products triggered increased participation, the actuarial performance of the program, as measured by the total loss ratio, improved.[14]

This is consistent with the death spiral of adverse selection. Decreases in the cost of insurance to purchasers of coverage expand the insured pool and, relative to total payments into the pool from all sources (farmers and the federal government), simultaneously lower the overall risk of the pool. The historical data certainly suggest that participation is responsive to farmer-paid premiums and that lower-risk individuals will likely have a more elastic response to changes in premium rates.

These figures reflect some of the basic challenges associated with determining producer responses to changes in premium rates. The program has

Figure 7. Total and Producer Loss Ratios, 1981–2015

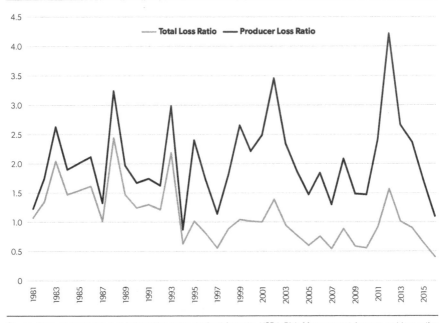

Source: Data on premiums and indemnities were obtained from the USDA Risk Management Agency, and loss ratios were computed by the authors.

undergone significant changes over its history. The revenue coverage that is so prominent today was not available before 1995. It is also the case that many other institutional factors have changed over time in ways that have affected participation in the programs. Production technologies have undergone significant changes. These changes include genetic modification, precision planting, and harvesting methods, as well as the development of improved inputs such as pesticides, herbicides, and fungicides. Such technological advances have certainly affected the risk that underlies crop production.

The demand for crop insurance and the response to premium rate changes have been frequent topics of empirical research. Barry Goodwin found that higher-risk farmers had a much less elastic demand than lower-risk farmers, again confirming the potential for a death spiral from adverse selection.[15] Richard Just, Linda Calvin, and John Quiggin found that risk aversion does not appear to be a significant factor influencing insurance demand.[16] In subsequent work, Goodwin, Monte Vandeveer, and John Deal, as well as Erik O'Donoghue, confirmed that demand is responsive to premium changes and that increasing premium subsidies will increase participation in the program.[17]

Further, O'Donoghue and Sarah Tulman present a summary of research that has attempted to estimate an elasticity of insurance demand. They note that nearly all existing research, including research from the early years of the modern program, tended to find relatively inelastic responses to premium (and thus to subsidies). They also find inelastic responses to premium changes, with elasticities of demand falling between –0.1 and –0.8. They do find a more elastic demand for soybeans in some specifications.[18]

The elasticity of demand will play an important role as farmers react to any changes in the federal crop insurance program under the upcoming farm bill.[19] The consensus of the empirical literature seems to be that responses to premium changes are inelastic, potentially suggesting that policy changes that reduce premium subsidies will decrease participation, although in an inelastic fashion. This may suggest that policy changes that reverse some of the large subsidy increases that affected crop insurance after 1995 may not necessarily lead to participation levels like those observed in the 1980s.

However, it is important to emphasize just how much the program has changed since then, potentially making existing research of limited relevance to understanding future program changes. Farmers have shown an obvious preference for revenue protection (with the harvest price replacement option). If subsidies on the higher risk associated with the HPO were reduced or eliminated, as some policy observers have predicted, participation levels in revenue insurance could drop substantially and shift back to pre-2000 levels. As Goodwin, Vincent Smith, and Alan Baquet showed, reductions in subsidy rates that shift some farmers from having positive net expected returns to negative net expected returns from crop insurance could reduce participation in the program substantially, even though overall demand appears to be relatively price inelastic.[20] For example, if subsidies were rolled back to pre-1994 levels at about 30 percent of the actuarially fair premium, participation rates seem likely also to drop back, perhaps to pre-1994 levels.

Effects of Premium Subsidies on Farm-Level Production Decisions

The growth of the crop insurance program has led to concerns that premium subsidies are distorting cropping decisions and encouraging production in marginal areas. Empirical work has focused primarily on the effects of the US crop insurance program on planted areas and the effects of insurance on input use. Early research by JunJie Wu suggested that farms that purchased insurance were more likely to produce soybeans and less likely to produce forage crops, which, in turn, Wu argued would lead to increased chemical use.[21]

Edwin Young, Vandeveer, and Randall Schnepf found that planted acreage for major field crops was only 0.4 percent higher due to subsidized insurance. Increased plantings of wheat and cotton accounted for about three-fourths of the increase.[22] Goodwin, Vandeveer, and Deal examined midwestern corn and soybean producers and wheat and barley producers in the Northern Plains and found that a 30 percent decrease in premium costs were likely to increase barley acreage by about 1.1 percent and corn acreage by less than 0.5 percent.[23] Soybean and wheat acreage responses were statistically insignificant.

Several studies have examined the effects of crop insurance on broader land-use patterns such as conversion of pastureland to cropland. Ruben Lubowski et al. concluded that the increase in crop insurance subsidies changed land use measurably, but modestly.[24] The change in premium subsidies in the mid-1990s was estimated to have increased cultivated cropland area in 1997 by 2.5 million acres, or 0.82 percent, with the bulk of this land (1.8 million acres) coming from uncultivated crops and pasture. That estimate rose by about 380,000 acres when shifts from forests, range, and CRP land were included. Lubowski, Andrew Plantinga, and Robert Stavins concluded that government payments caused a 2 percent increase in planted area between 1982 and 1997.[25] However, this increase was more than offset by land put into the CRP. The analysis did not differentiate between insurance payments and other price and income support payments.

Some recent analyses have focused on land use in the Northern Plains states, in particular the so-called Prairie Pothole Region, where conversion of pasture and rangeland to cropland over the past 20 years is evident. Studies by Roger Claassen et al. and Claassen, Joseph Cooper, and Fernando Carriazo found evidence that crop insurance increased the conversion of grassland to cropland, although the impacts were generally small.[26] Hongli Feng, David Hennessy, and Ruiqing Miao found that over the period 1986 to 2011, higher crop insurance participation contributed to a reduction in acres offered under the CRP.[27] Similar results from Miao, Hennessy, and Feng suggest that 3 percent of insured land in the Prairie Pothole Region would have remained as grassland if there had been no crop insurance subsidies.[28] More recently, Ethan Ligon analyzed the impact of crop insurance on specialty crops and concluded that the introduction of crop insurance had a large and positive impact on tree crops but a negligible impact on non-tree crops.[29]

Goodwin and Smith have questioned whether the results of earlier studies are still relevant given that subsidy levels are much higher now than when the earlier research was conducted and that revenue policies have largely replaced yield coverages.[30] For example, the Goodwin, Vandeveer, and Deal study examined the effects of insurance subsidies over 1986–93,[31] before enactment of major legislation in 1994 and 2000—which dramatically increased subsidy levels—and before the introduction of revenue insurance.[32] In 1993, government subsidies as a percentage of total premium costs averaged 25 to 27 percent for the crops examined in the study compared to 60 to 63 percent for those crops in 2014. Average subsidies ranged from $1.33 to $2.12 per acre in 1993, compared with $15.12 to $27.70 per acre in 2014.

Recent studies by Cory Walters et al. and Claasen, Christian Langpap, and Wu find negligible effects of crop insurance on land use, although the latter reported more significant impacts on crop choice and crop rotation.[33] Jisang Yu, Smith, and Sumner also found significant effects on area, although the effects were small.[34] Yet, while the levels of support for insurance products have increased substantially, the relative share of subsidies across crops has remained largely the same, at least for those crops that are offered similar types of insurance products. With improvements in rate making due in part to the wealth of farm-level data, premium rates are more in line with underlying risks, which means that relative rates should not favor one insured crop over another.[35] Further, since price elections for most of the major row crops are based on futures market prices, per-acre premiums (and subsidies) tend to be correlated with harvest price expectations.

While the general findings from this body of research may appear mixed, several broad conclusions can be drawn. Studies have mostly indicated that crop insurance subsidies have a significant but small effect on the extensive margin; that is, insurance tends to have a positive but small impact on conversion of nonagricultural land to cropland.

Crop insurance likely has larger impacts on crop choice when insured crops compete against uninsured crops or when crops for which revenue products are available compete against crops for which only yield products are available.[36] Such distortions may become even larger as new products, such as margin insurance and supplemental coverage, are developed, particularly if those products are not widely available across crops.

Lastly, the evidence on the impact of crop insurance on input use is related, in part, to the program's effects on crop choice. To the degree that crop insurance shifts plantings toward more input-intensive crops, aggregate input usage may be affected. However, studies of the effects of moral hazard on input usage suggest small impacts that are largely statistically insignificant.

Crop Insurance Moral Hazard Incentives: Input Use and Prevented Planting

The vulnerability of federal crop insurance programs to moral hazard behaviors remains an important issue. Moral hazard behaviors occur when agents alter their behavior in ways that change risks of loss after they purchase insurance coverage. Several characteristics of the underwriting provisions of the federal program may actually exacerbate concerns about moral hazard. The ability to insure separately individual units or areas of planted crops in a farm rather than an aggregate unit (the whole farm) has been identified as a possible avenue for cheating because it may be difficult to assign production to a given field, which may be insured individually. Smith and Goodwin found a significant difference in the production practices of Kansas wheat growers who purchased crop insurance relative to their neighbors who did not. Their results suggest that wheat growers with insurance tended to spend about 30 percent less per acre on fertilizer and chemical inputs.[37]

One feature of the all-risk coverage the US federal crop insurance program provides pertains to coverage for prevented planting. This coverage provides indemnity payments if a producer is unable, because of covered perils, to plant the crop before the final planting deadline. Prevented planting coverage was included in the provisions of the 1994 CIRA. Indemnity payments are generally set at 60 percent of the coverage for a planted crop, and producers are offered the opportunity to buy up this level of coverage at subsidized premium rates.

A 1996 study by the USDA Economic Research Service (ERS) measured preplanting costs and compared them with the basic level of coverage offered under the federal plan.[38] This evaluation used farm-level cost and returns surveys. The ERS study concluded that prevented planting indemnity payments were far higher than actual preplanting costs. The extent of overpayment varied across crops, with cotton growers receiving the highest payments in excess of actual preplanting costs. That producers can buy this coverage at a heavily subsidized rate suggests that prevented planting payments may significantly exceed actual losses. The potential for distortions is obvious. Further, that the total premium is subsidized at a rate exceeding 60 percent suggests even greater returns to a farmer making a prevented planting claim.

Another aspect of prevented planting coverage may result in additional distortions to behavior. Under a regular claim for lost production, a farmer's APH yield for insurance purposes is reduced to account for the loss. The APH yield is determined by the average of the previous 4–10 years of yield histories. In a prevented planting claim, no penalty to APH is applied. That an indemnity today can mean lower coverage tomorrow certainly is relevant to growers' insurance and claim decisions. Excluding years with prevented planting payments from the history makes prevented planting claims only more attractive to growers.

The way in which prevented planting is designed and managed clearly creates the potential for unnecessary claims to be paid. Farmers receive a payment, made even more attractive by large premium subsidies, that substantially exceeds the actual losses they may suffer. Monitoring preplanting costs, many of which are difficult to identify and observe in farm records, may be challenging. Thus, the potential for claims to be made even if no crop was intended to be planted seems substantial. Price changes early in the insurance cycle (after the sign-up deadline but before the crop is planted) may also distort producer decisions regarding planting versus taking a prevented planting payment.

Figure 8. Prevented Planting Indemnity Payments, 2009–17

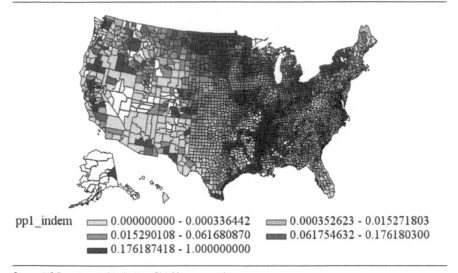

ppl_indem	▭ 0.000000000 - 0.000336442	▭ 0.000352623 - 0.015271803
	▬ 0.015290108 - 0.061680870	▬ 0.061754632 - 0.176180300
	▬ 0.176187418 - 1.000000000	

Source: US Department of Agriculture, Risk Management Agency.

Prevented planting provisions of the federal program were recently reviewed by the USDA's Office of the Inspector General (OIG). The study found that the agency had paid about $4.6 billion in claims to producers who filed claims for being prevented from planting their crops. The review also noted that the payment rates, which were intended to cover all pre-planting costs in a conservative manner, are set too high. That producers making a prevented planting claim do not have their APH adjusted *unless* they plant a second crop also serves as a disincentive to plant a crop in the first place rather than take the claim. The report notes that only 0.1 percent of producers receiving a prevented planting indemnity replanted a second crop on the prevented planting acres.

The OIG review also notes that loss adjustors appeared to violate documentation requirements when assessing prevented planting claims. The OIG reviewed 192 policy claims and found that *none* of those claims included the required documentation and support for the claim. In no case did the loss adjustment records document that the acres claimed would have normally been available for planting. The report notes that the current program

Figure 9. Aggregate Loss Ratios, 2000–16

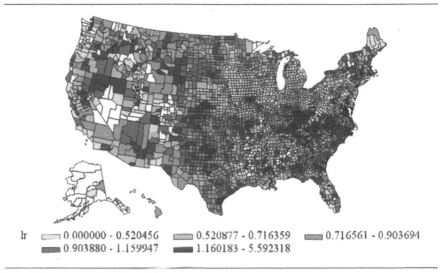

lr
- 0.000000 - 0.520456
- 0.903880 - 1.159947
- 0.520877 - 0.716359
- 1.160183 - 5.592318
- 0.716561 - 0.903694

Source: US Department of Agriculture, Risk Management Agency.

guidelines and standards for documenting prevented planting are not practical or workable. It also notes that a workable plan would require loss adjustors to be familiar with the weather history of a specific area to make a determination of what "normal" planting conditions are.

It is interesting to consider patterns of prevented planting losses. We used the RMA's cause-of-loss database, which is available from 2010 to 2016, to evaluate the prominence of prevented planting indemnity payments. Figure 8 presents the shares of total indemnities for all crops and insurance plans at the county level accounted for by prevented planting claims. In some areas, such as the upper Great Plains and the Mississippi Delta, a high proportion of total indemnities are paid for prevented planting.

In contrast, the middle Great Plains and Texas appear to have relatively fewer prevented planting claims. Figure 9 presents the average loss ratio across all crops and plans at the county level. The information in Figure 9 illustrates that considerable heterogeneity exists in the actuarial performance of the federal crop insurance program and in the returns to insurance f different producers. The share of indemnities paid as prevented pla claims does not appear to be highly correlated with the overall loss ratio. Areas with the highest loss ratios, such as central Texas and the southeastern US, appear to have a lesser degree of prevented planting claims as compared with total indemnities.

The moral hazard implications associated with prevented planting insurance in the federal program remain an important area of ongoing research. Weather conditions should explain prevented planting losses. If prices or other factors not related to planting conditions affect prevented planting payments, then moral hazard may exist.

The Agricultural Insurance Delivery System

The 1980 Federal Crop Insurance Act included a provision to privatize the delivery of federal crop insurance policies that had considerable long-term political implications and resulted in substantial costs for taxpayers. Lobbying by some relatively small insurance companies already offering specific peril coverage against crop losses from hail and fire contributed to including a mandate to shift delivery of federal crop insurance policies through the private sector instead of through the USDA FCIC.[39] In addition, both Congress and the Carter administration argued that private-sector delivery would be more effective in boosting program participation than under a government-agency-based system.

While participation rates have exceeded those envisioned by the 1980 act, that growth has been largely due to increased premium subsidies. Private-sector delivery has proved increasingly costly, as illustrated in Figure 10, which shows the revenues received by the crop insurance industry from the federal program over 1980–2014. Projected costs for 2018–27 are $2.3 billion annually and account for about 34 percent of total federal crop insurance expenditures.[40]

In fact, a series of US Government Accountability Office (GAO) reports identified several inherent accountability and efficiency problems associated with allowing private crop insurance companies to manage and disburse government funds throughout the 1980s and 1990s.[41] Those reports consistently noted that the private-sector delivery system was more costly than the public system it replaced, a finding in some ways

Figure 10. Insurance Company Revenue Streams, 1980–2014 ($ Millions)

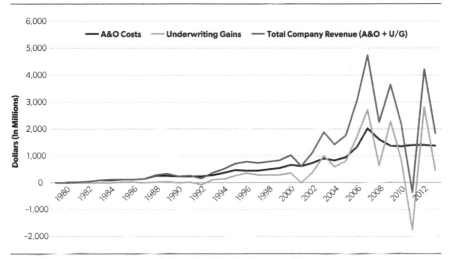

Source: The authors, based on data obtained from the USDA Risk Management Agency.

confirmed in the mid-2000s by Olivier Mahul and Charles Stutley. In their analysis of approximately 80 countries, the US federal crop insurance program ranked as having the delivery system with, by a substantial margin, the highest costs.[42]

One reason why the US delivery system is so expensive is that the insurance industry and farm interest groups have incentives to lobby cooperatively for the program in ways that benefit both groups.[43] Bruce Babcock, for example, showed that crop insurance agents make substantially more than their counterparts in other lines of insurance business, suggesting that substantial economic rents (excess payments over the amounts needed to ensure the services are provided) are accruing to the industry as a whole.[44] Smith, Glauber, and Robert Dismukes also provide econometric evidence that substantial rents accrue to the crop insurance industry.[45] Belasco and Smith pointed out that in 2015 crop insurance companies were paid about $1 billion (adjusting for any inflation effects) more than they received in 2006 while servicing slightly fewer insurance policies.[46] Glauber noted that for every dollar of subsidy paid to farmers over the previous decade, insurance companies received 47 cents.[47]

The insurance industry has also consistently claimed that the rates of return they obtain from their federal crop insurance books are unacceptably low, compared with other lines of business such as property and casualty, given the amount of risk they take on.[48] However, the Standard Reinsurance Agreement (SRA) under which they operate requires them to take on only a small part of the risk of losses. As shown in Figure 11, the federal government disproportionately funds most of the annual losses that occur (when indemnities exceed the total premiums paid into the national insurance pool) and receives relatively little in the way of annual underwriting gains (when total premium exceeds total indemnities). For example, in 2012, when total underwriting losses exceeded $6.4 billion, the government funded about 80 percent ($5.1 billion) and the companies only about 20 percent ($1.3 billion) of those losses.

In contrast, in 2013, when the federal crop insurance program experienced a net underwriting loss of $265 million, the companies enjoyed net underwriting gains of $646 million. Meanwhile, the federal government had to pay out an additional $911 million (over and above premium subsidies) to "cover" both the program's net underwriting losses and the companies' net underwriting gains on their "share" of the book of business. This indicates that the companies operate in a relatively risk-free environment under their current SRA with the federal government and casts doubt on company claims that their underwriting gains, while positive and over the long run consistently substantial, are too low.

Finally, insurance companies and insurance agents have strongly opposed several commonsense initiatives that would substantially reduce delivery costs. For example, most farmers could simply renew their annual crop insurance coverages by signing up online, eliminating the need for the majority of the services provided by crop insurance agents. However, current legislation prohibits farmers from doing just that.

One approach to reducing delivery costs and premium subsidy costs, as Glauber suggests,[49] would be to permit companies to compete for farmers' federally subsidized crop insurance policies through limited premium rate (price) competition. However, given that the federal government is almost surely likely to be liable for any costs associated with company failures and defaults on indemnity payments, moral hazard issues associated with the government's reinsurance role would need to be addressed.

Figure 11. Company and Government Shares of Net Underwriting Gains in the Federal Crop Insurance Program, 1992–2016 ($ Million)

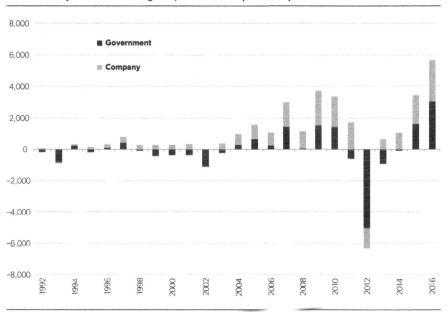

Source: The authors, based on data obtained from the USDA Risk Management Agency.

An alternative is to simplify the portfolio of crop insurance products offered to individual farm-yield policies and area-based index products and revert to a publicly managed delivery system in which there is no need for insurance companies to play any role in selling and servicing publicly funded agricultural insurance policies.

The US Crop Insurance Program and US World Trade Organization Commitments

Crop insurance subsidies, like other agricultural subsidies, are also subject to discipline under the World Trade Organization (WTO) rules on agricultural domestic support, and there is empirical evidence of program impacts on land-use decisions and crop production. The United States has notified crop insurance subsidies as amber box subsidies under the WTO

Agreement on Agriculture.[50] Premium subsidies are currently notified on a product-specific basis.[51] Subsidies to a commodity are included in the Aggregate Measurement of Support (AMS) if the total value of subsidies to a given commodity exceeds 5 percent of the value of production of that commodity; otherwise, they are considered de minimis and not included in the AMS. Most crop insurance subsidies are de minimis because they do not exceed the 5 percent threshold. In 2014, for example, US crop insurance subsidies exceeded $6.2 billion, of which approximately 70 percent was reported as de minimis.

In addition, the US crop insurance program could be vulnerable in the WTO under the Subsidies and Countervailing Measures Agreement. Brazil challenged US crop insurance subsidies for cotton as part of the United States–Subsidies on Upland Cotton dispute, arguing that the subsidies depressed prices in world markets by encouraging US cotton production. While the panel in the US–Upland Cotton case rejected that argument for crop insurance subsidies, some argue that the case provides a template for future WTO litigation.[52]

The Current Legislative Debate

As is true for many agricultural programs, the considerable taxpayer outlays that the federal crop insurance program demanded are drawing more attention and scrutiny, even outside the agricultural policy arena. Although the approximately $8 billion spent on the program annually is modest by Washington standards, that many of the program's beneficiaries are wealthy individuals with high incomes has raised questions regarding the necessity of subsidized crop insurance.

Much of this scrutiny is reflected in the March 2015 GAO report "Crop Insurance: Reducing Subsidies for Highest Income Participants Could Save Federal Dollars with Minimal Effect on the Program."[53] In a series of related reports, the GAO evaluated the potential savings and impact on farmers of means testing and subsidy caps on crop insurance subsidies. These reports repeatedly emphasize several findings.

The program directs subsidies to a small but wealthy segment of the US public, as also shown by Bekkerman, Belasco, and Smith in Chapter 2.

Total subsidy amounts are essentially unlimited, resulting in a significant concentration of benefits among a small number of big growers. The delivery system, through what is typically termed a "public-private" partnership, is costly and directs significant benefits to private insurance companies through a favorable reinsurance agreement that limits risk, guarantees returns, and covers A&O costs through subsidies. Finally, the reports have noted that the harvest price replacement feature (widely known as the HPO) inherent in the vast majority of insurance contracts can result in farmers earning more with a significant yield loss than they would had a full crop been made.

These GAO reports reflect only a part of the increased scrutiny that the federal program has received. Popular press articles have picked up on many of the themes developed in these reports and have illuminated that highly subsidized crop insurance that results in expected returns in excess of $2 for every dollar paid by a farmer may have perverse distortions and impacts on farmer behavior, realized risk, and taxpayer expenditures.

This scrutiny has resulted in legislation being introduced to limit subsidies and reform the program to ease the taxpayers' burdens. Sens. Jeff Flake (R-AZ) and Jeanne Shaheen (D-NH) and Reps. Ron Kind (D-WI) and Jim Sensenbrenner (R-WI) introduced the Assisting Family Farmers Through Insurance Reform Measures (AFFIRM) Act in 2015. The act proposed to cut the costs of the program through a number of reforms, leading its proponents to argue it would save $24 billion.

The act would lower the SRA rate of return from 14.5 percent to 8.9 percent, saving taxpayers an estimated $3 billion. It would eliminate restrictions in the 2014 Farm Bill that prohibit the USDA from achieving savings when it renegotiates the SRA. Perhaps most significantly, it would eliminate the HPO feature of revenue insurance, which its sponsors argue would save $19 billion. Finally, it would limit the total value of crop insurance subsidies to $40,000 per person each year and end subsidies for those with a gross income of more than $250,000.

The House and Senate Agriculture Committees quickly buried the bill, but it was reintroduced in May 2017 and again referred to the co___ where it is now subject to debate. Cynics may see little prob___ islation actually making such changes, but the legislative a___ the greater scrutiny and increased focus on cutting crop insu___

President Donald Trump's 2017 budget contained nearly all the AFFIRM Act reforms. The administration's proposal includes a $40,000 per farmer cap on subsidies, eliminating subsidies for the harvest price replacement component of revenue insurance contracts and binding limits on subsidies that would eliminate eligibility for subsidies for farmers with more than $500,000 in adjusted gross annual income.

The likelihood that such changes will be implemented is low. To quote a familiar adage, "The president proposes but Congress disposes." The Agriculture Committees remain powerful, and crop insurance is a farm subsidy program centerpiece. However, that such reforms are being considered suggests that crop insurance may not be immune from significant changes in the upcoming farm bill.

Conclusions

Since 1980, and especially since 1994, the federal crop insurance program has expanded to become a major source of government subsidies for farmers who raise crops. The main driving force behind that growth has been premium subsidies paid to farmers, which have increased from 0 percent of the estimated actuarially fair premium in 1980 to an average of more than 60 percent today. Those subsidies are expected to average more than $6 billion a year over the next 10 years.

At the same time the government pays a substantial direct subsidy to the private crop insurance companies that sell and service the policies purchased by farmers and also allows them to collect substantial underwriting gains through an SRA that favors the companies. On an industry-wide basis, the current delivery system is costing taxpayers an additional $2.5 billion a year. Farmers are contributing about $3.6 billion a year to the total cost of the entire program, which amounts to an annual average of around $12 billion. Thus, farmers are paying 30 percent of the total cost of their crop insurance, and taxpayers are paying the remaining 70 percent.

In addition, the subsidies that flow to farmers are neither capped on a per-farm basis nor targeted to small farms operated by low-income households. Estimates by Bekkerman, Belasco, and Smith, for example, indicate that since 2007 more than 50 percent of all crop insurance subsidies have flowed to the top 10 percent of farms (in terms of sales), which on a per-farm basis have an average net worth in excess of $6 million.[54]

The federal crop insurance program also provides farmers with incentives to waste resources through moral hazard behaviors and reallocating land between crops and pasture and among crops, often with adverse environmental impacts, especially in areas where lands are fragile and subject to soil erosion. Those areas are a prime target for federal conservation programs such as the CRP, so the federal crop insurance program provides incentives that directly conflict with other federal programs' objectives, as discussed by Smith and Goodwin.[55] In addition, the production effects of the program make the program problematic with respect to US commitments under the WTO.

In summary, the federal crop insurance program is expensive, encourages farmers to waste resources, disproportionately targets large and successful farm operations that have no need of federal assistance, and has the potential to engage the US in WTO disputes over the trade impacts of US agricultural policy. Given those problems, what is the best alternative? Some would argue that the program should be eliminated,[56] but the political reality is that the program remains popular with farmers, insurance companies, and farm state legislators.

One viable alternative is to replace the entire crop insurance program with a "no cost to farmers" disaster aid program based on indexes of plant growth constructed for each covered crop. The crops would include traditional farm subsidy "program" crops such as corn, wheat, cotton, barley, peas and lentils, sorghum, soybeans, and other oilseeds. However, the program would also cover crops not historically included in major subsidy programs such as fruits, vegetables, nuts, and forages.

The federal budget savings could be substantial, in the order of $4–$5 billion a year. Moral hazard effects would largely be obviated, and incentives for changing crop mix and shifting land into crop production would be mitigated. Basis risks, the risks that farmers suffering losses will not be paid and that farmers with no losses will be indemnified, could be substantial if the indexes that trigger payments are poorly designed and applied to relatively large geographic areas such as counties.[57] However, complex weather indexes can be established that apply to relatively small areas (e.g., 12-mile-square or 8-mile-square grids) that substantially reduce those risks.

If the crop insurance program is continued, we recommend that the HPO be terminated, with a potential savings in taxpayer outlays of close to $2 billion.[58] Successive administrations have proposed this policy change, but farm state legislators have resisted implementing the initiative. Under the HPO, farmers are allowed to value crop losses at the harvest time price if it is higher than the price at which they originally insured their crops at planting time.

The CBO has recently estimated that eliminating HPO would save $1.9 billion annually over fiscal years 2018–27.[59] Babcock estimated that in 2012 the HPO increased payments to farmers for losses by about $6 billion and enabled many corn and soybean farmers in states such as Iowa to enjoy higher revenues than they had anticipated when planting their crops, even though they experienced relatively low yields.[60]

The HPO can perhaps best be described as gold-plated insurance, most of which is paid for by the taxpayer and not the farmer. In addition, as discussed above, the HPO provides subsidized price protection that could be obtained from the private sector using futures and options markets, and Congress has mandated that the federal crop insurance program is not supposed to provide products that compete with private-sector services.

Other proposals for reform of the crop insurance program have included rolling back premium subsidies to pre-2000 or pre-1994 levels to somewhere between 30 percent and 50 percent of estimated actuarially fair premiums instead of their current levels that average more than 60 percent. These changes would generate substantial reductions in expenditures and, over time, would likely reduce participation, in both insured acres and coverage levels. The challenge would then be to prevent farm groups from double dipping via congressionally authorized ad hoc disaster aid programs, as was the case before 2000, because more farmers would have no crop insurance protection, even though the decision not to have coverage would have been their choice.

In a similar vein, many observers have proposed capping annual premium subsidies on a per-farm basis at amounts ranging from $10,000 to $50,000 per farm. Smith has noted that farmers have successfully redefined the structure of their operations to evade subsidy payment limits but argued that if the limits are sufficiently draconian, then they would be more difficult and costly to evade.[61]

However, draconian limits on premium subsidies will likely have little appeal for members of the House and Senate Agriculture Committees who play a dominant role in establishing agricultural subsidy policies. One alternative that Babcock, among others, proposed is to limit coverage levels receiving subsidies to no more than 70 percent of expected revenues or yields.[62] Given that many farmers currently insure their crops at much higher coverage levels, such a limit would likely generate substantial savings in government spending, reduce crop production and moral hazard incentives, and make the US crop insurance program more in line with WTO green box criteria and likely less vulnerable to challenge.

As previously discussed, the US crop insurance delivery system is expensive. One option would be to shift delivery from the private sector back to USDA Farm Service Agency county offices, especially if the program were simplified, and involve only yield insurance or revenue insurance without the HPO. But that approach provides yet another rationale for continuing the extensive bureaucracy associated with federal agricultural programs that results in the USDA operating farm service offices in almost every county in the country.

Another set of options involves changing the rules under which the insurance companies operate, as Glauber has suggested.[63] One way to reduce delivery costs would be to require the companies to bid competitively with one another for A&O subsidies. An alternative, which is not mutually exclusive, would be to allow them to compete with one another on premiums. For example, many farmers could easily sign up for coverage online, sharply reducing delivery costs. Allowing companies to compete on price would encourage them to adopt cost-saving innovations such as online sign-up protocols with benefits for farmers and taxpayers (because lower premiums mean lower subsidies at a given premium subsidy rate) and at least a small reduction in the economic waste associated with the program.

Finally, given the problems that have been identified with prevented planting insurance—including overpayment for losses and unsubstantiated claims—the federal government should get out of the business of offering and subsidizing prevented planting insurance. Alternatively, farmers could access prevented planting insurance but be required to pay the full commercial cost of the coverage, including administrative costs and training costs for loss adjusters, and face substantial penalties for unjustified claims.

Notes

1. The growth of the program has been well-documented elsewhere. Randall A. Kramer, "Federal Crop Insurance: 1938–82," *Agricultural History* 57 (1983): 181–200; Barry K. Goodwin and Vincent H. Smith, "Private and Public Roles in Providing Agricultural Insurance in the United States," in *Public Insurance and Private Markets*, ed. Jeffrey Brown (Washington, DC: AEI Press, 2010), 173–209; Joseph W. Glauber, "Crop Insurance Reconsidered," *American Journal of Agricultural Economics* 86, no. 6 (2004): 1179–95; and Joseph W. Glauber, "The Growth of the Federal Crop Insurance Program, 1990–2011," *American Journal of Agricultural Economics* 95, no. 2 (2013): 482–88.

2. Vincent H. Smith and Michael R. Kehoe, "An Economic Analysis of Alternative Marketing Systems for Crop Insurance" (working paper, Montana State University Department of Agricultural Economics and Economics, 1995).

3. Joseph W. Glauber, "Crop Insurance and Private Sector Delivery: Reassessing the Public-Private Partnership," Taxpayers for Common Sense, December 14, 2016, http://www.taxpayer.net/library/article/crop-insurance-and-private-sector-delivery.

4. Congressional Budget Office, "CBO's January 2017 Baseline for Farm Programs," January 24, 2017, https://www.cbo.gov/sites/default/files/recurringdata/51317-2017-01-usda.pdf.

5. Barry K. Goodwin and Vincent H. Smith, *The Economics of Crop Insurance and Disaster Relief* (Washington, DC: AEI Press, 1995); and Bruce L. Gardner and Randall A. Kramer, "Experience with Crop Insurance Programs in the United States," in *Crop Insurance for Agricultural Development: Issues and Experience*, eds. Peter Hazell, Carlos Pomareda, and Alberto Valdes (Baltimore, MD: Johns Hopkins University Press, 1986).

6. The 30 percent subsidy was offered for insurance coverage levels up to 65 percent. Producers could purchase additional coverage up to 75 percent but for no additional subsidy.

7. Goodwin and Smith, *The Economics of Crop Insurance and Disaster Relief*.

8. Barry K. Goodwin, "An Empirical Analysis of the Demand for Multiple Peril Crop Insurance," *American Journal of Agricultural Economics* 75, no. 2 (1993): 425–34; and Vincent H. Smith and Alan E. Baquet, "The Demand for Multiple Peril Crop Insurance: Evidence from Montana," *American Journal of Agricultural Economics* 78, no. 1 (1996): 75–83.

9. Brian D. Wright and Julie A. Hewitt, "All Risk Crop Insurance: Lessons from Theory and Experience," in *Economics of Agricultural Crop Insurance: Theory and Evidence*, eds. Darell L. Hueth and William H. Furtan (Boston: Kluwer Academic Publishers, 1994), 73–109.

10. Congressional Budget Office, "CBO's January 2017 Baseline for Farm Programs."

11. Congressional Budget Office, "CBO's January 2017 Baseline for Farm Programs."

12. Glauber, "The Growth of the Federal Crop Insurance Program, 1990–2011"; and Barry K. Goodwin and Vincent H. Smith, "What Harm Is Done by Subsidizing Crop Insurance?," *American Journal of Agricultural Economics* 95, no. 2 (2013): 489–97.

13. Vincent H. Smith and Joseph W. Glauber, "Agricultural Insurance in Developed Countries: Where Have We Been and Where Are We Going?," *Applied Economic Perspectives and Policies* 34, no. 3 (2012): 360–90.

14. See, for example, Goodwin, "An Empirical Analysis of the Demand for Multiple

Peril Crop Insurance"; and Goodwin and Smith, "What Harm Is Done by Subsidizing Crop Insurance?"

15. Goodwin, "An Empirical Analysis of the Demand for Multiple Peril Crop Insurance."

16. Richard E. Just, Linda Calvin, and John Quiggin, "Adverse Selection in Crop Insurance: Actuarial and Asymmetric Information Incentives," *American Journal of Agricultural Economics* 81, no. 4 (1999): 834–49.

17. Barry K. Goodwin, Monte L. Vandeveer, and John L. Deal, "An Empirical Analysis of Acreage Effects of Participation in the Federal Crop Insurance Program," *American Journal of Agricultural Economics* 86, no. 4 (2004): 1058–77; and Erik O'Donoghue, "The Effects of Premium Subsidies on Demand for Crop Insurance," US Department of Agriculture, Economic Research Service, 2014.

18. Erik J. O'Donoghue and Sarah A. Tulman, "The Demand for Crop Insurance: Elasticity and Effects of Yield Shocks" (selected paper, 2016 Agricultural & Applied Economics Association, Boston, MA, 2016).

19. Estimates of changes in federal expenditures are contingent with estimates of elasticities of demand.

20. Goodwin, "An Empirical Analysis of the Demand for Multiple Peril Crop Insurance"; and Smith and Baquet, "The Demand for Multiple Peril Crop Insurance."

21. JunJie Wu, "Crop Insurance, Acreage Decisions, and Nonpoint-Source Pollution," *American Journal of Agricultural Economics* 81, no. 2 (May 1999): 305–20.

22. C. Edwin Young, Monte L. Vandeveer, and Randall D. Schnepf, "Production and Price Impacts of US Crop Insurance Programs," *American Journal of Agricultural Economics* 83, no. 5 (December 2001): 1196–203.

23. Goodwin, Vandeveer, and Deal, "An Empirical Analysis of Acreage Effects of Participation in the Federal Crop Insurance Program."

24. Ruben N. Lubowski et al., "Environmental Effects of Agricultural Land-Use Change—The Role of Economics and Policy," US Department of Agriculture, Economic Research Service, 2006.

25. Ruben N. Lubowski, Andrew J. Plantinga, and Robert N. Stavins, "What Drives Land Use Change in the United States? A National Analysis of Landowner Decisions," *Land Economics* 84, no. 4 (2008): 529–50.

26. Roger Claassen et al., "Grassland to Cropland Conversation in the Northern Plains: The Role of Crop Insurance, Commodity, and Disaster Programs," US Department of Agriculture, Economic Research Service, June 2011; and Roger Claassen, Joseph C. Cooper, and Fernando Carriazo, "Crop Insurance, Disaster Payments, and Land Use Change: The Effect of Sodsaver on Incentives for Grassland Conversion," *Journal of Agricultural and Applied Economics* 43, no. 2 (2011): 195–211.

27. Ruiqing Miao, David A. Hennessy, and Hongli Feng, "Sodbusting, Crop Insurance, and Sunk Conversion Costs," *Land Economics* (2014): 601–22.

28. Miao, Hennessy, and Feng, "Sodbusting, Crop Insurance, and Sunk Conversion Costs."

29. Ethan Ligon, "Supply and Effects of Specialty Crop Insurance," in *The Intended and Unintended Effects of US Agricultural and Biotechnology Policies*, eds. Joshua S. Graff Zivin and Jeffrey M. Perloff (Chicago: University of Chicago Press, 2012), 113–42.

30. Vincent H. Smith and Barry K. Goodwin, "The Environmental Consequences

of Subsidized Risk Management and Disaster Assistance Programs," *Annual Review of Resource Economics* 5 (2013): 35–60.

31. Goodwin, Vandeveer, and Deal, "An Empirical Analysis of Acreage Effects of Participation in the Federal Crop Insurance Program."

32. Glauber, "The Growth of the Federal Crop Insurance Program, 1990–2011."

33. Cory G. Walters et al., "Crop Insurance, Land Allocation, and the Environment," *Journal of Agricultural and Resource Economics* 32, no. 2 (2012): 301–20; Roger Claassen, Christian Langpap, and JunJie Wu, "Impacts of Federal Crop Insurance on Land Use and Environmental Quality" (selected paper, Agricultural & Applied Economics Association, San Francisco, 2015).

34. Jisang Yu, Aaron Smith, and Daniel A. Sumner, "Effects of Crop Insurance Premium Subsidies on Crop Acreage," *American Journal of Agricultural Economics* 100, no. 1 (January 2018): 91–114, https://academic.oup.com/ajae/article/100/1/91/4443107.

35. Glauber, "The Growth of the Federal Crop Insurance Program, 1990–2011."

36. Under the US program, revenue products are mostly available for crops, for which there are viable futures markets for price discovery purposes (for example, corn, wheat, and cotton).

37. Vincent H. Smith and Barry K. Goodwin, "Crop Insurance, Moral Hazard, and Agricultural Chemical Use," *American Journal of Agricultural Economics* 78, no. 2 (1996): 428–38.

38. US Department of Agriculture, Economic Research Service, "Estimation of Prevented Planting Payment Rates by Crop and Region," December 11, 1996.

39. Kramer, "Federal Crop Insurance: 1938–82."

40. Congressional Budget Office, "CBO's January 2017 Baseline for Farm Programs."

41. The GAO was called the General Accounting Office before 1994. See, for example, US Government Accountability Office, "Crop Insurance: FCIC Needs to Improve Its Oversight of Reinsured Companies," 1988; US Government Accountability Office, "Crop Insurance: Private Company Loss Adjustment Improving, but Overpayments Still High," 1988; US Government Accountability Office "Crop Insurance: Program Has Not Fostered Significant Risk-Sharing by Insurance Companies," 1992; and US Government Accountability Office, "Crop Insurance: USDA Needs to Improve Oversight of Insurance Companies and Develop a Policy to Address Any Future Insolvencies," 2004.

42. Olivier Mahul and Charles J. Stutley, "Government Support to Agricultural Insurance: Challenges and Opportunities for Developing Countries," World Bank, 2010, https://openknowledge.worldbank.org/bitstream/handle/10986/2432/538810PUB0Gove101Official0Use0Only1.pdf.

43. Vincent H. Smith, "The US Federal Crop Insurance Program: A Case Study in Rent-Seeking," Mercatus Center, September 20, 2017, https://www.mercatus.org/publications/US-federal-crop-insurance-rent-seeking.

44. Bruce Babcock, "Cutting the Fat: It Won't Kill Crop Insurance," Environmental Working Group, December 3, 2015, http://www.ewg.org/research/cutting-the-fat#.WYtL_4Tyu00.

45. Vincent H. Smith, Joseph W. Glauber, and Robert Dismukes, "Rent Dispersion in the US Agricultural Insurance Industry," International Food Policy Research Institute, May 2016, http://www.ifpri.org/publication/rent-dispersion-us-agricultural-insuranceindustry.

46. Eric J. Belasco and Vincent H. Smith, "The Budget Deal and Crop Insurance: The Sky Is Not Falling," American Enterprise Institute, October 28, 2015, http://www.aei.org/publication/the-budget-deal-and-crop-insurance-the-sky-is-not-falling/.

47. Glauber, "The Growth of the Federal Crop Insurance Program, 1990–2011."

48. Glauber, "Crop Insurance and Private Sector Delivery."

49. Glauber, "Crop Insurance and Private Sector Delivery."

50. Under Annex 2 of the Uruguay Round Agreement on Agriculture, domestic support measures that have no, or at most minimal, trade-distorting effects or effects on production are excluded from reduction commitments. Paragraph 7 of Annex 2 includes criteria that identify qualifying income insurance and income safety-net programs, while paragraph 8 includes criteria that identify qualifying natural disaster assistance programs, including crop insurance. The United States, like many other developed countries, has chosen to notify crop insurance as amber box because the program fails to meet the criteria laid out in paragraphs 7 and 8. See Smith and Glauber, "Agricultural Insurance in Developed Countries"; Joseph W. Glauber, "Agricultural Insurance and the World Trade Organization," International Food Policy Research Institute, 2015, http://www.ifpri.org/publication/agricultural-insurance-and-world-trade-organization; and Glauber, "Crop Insurance and Private Sector Delivery."

51. From 1995 to 2011, the US notified crop insurance subsidies as non-product-specific support. Since 2012, the US has notified premium subsidies on a crop-specific basis and have submitted revised notifications for crop insurance subsidies dating back to the 2008 reporting year.

52. Christian Tau, Simon Schropp, and Daniel A. Sumner, "The Economic Effects on the World Market for Cotton of US Cotton Subsidies Under the 2014 US Farm Bill," International Centre for Trade and Sustainable Development, September 2015.

53. US Government Accountability Office, "Crop Insurance: Reducing Subsidies for Highest Income Participants Could Save Federal Dollars with Minimal Effect on the Program," March 2015, http://www.gao.gov/assets/670/669062.pdf.

54. Anton Bekkerman, Erik J. Belasco, and Vincent H. Smith, "The Distribution of Farm Studies" (working paper, Montana State University).

55. Smith and Goodwin, "The Environmental Consequences of Subsidized Risk Management and Disaster Assistance Programs."

56. Vincent H. Smith, "Premium Payments: Why Crop Insurance Costs Too Much," American Enterprise Institute, July 12, 2011, https://www.aei.org/wp-content/uploads/2011/11/-premium-payments-why-crop-insurance-costs-too-much_152221377467.pdf; and Smith and Goodwin, "The Environmental Consequences of Subsidized Risk Management and Disaster Assistance Programs."

57. Vincent H. Smith and Myles Watts, "Index Based Agricultural Insurance in Developing Countries: Feasibility, Scalability and Sustainability," Bill & Melinda Gates Foundation, November 2009.

58. Congressional Budget Office, "An Analysis of the President's 2018 Budget," July 2017.

59. Congressional Budget Office, "CBO's January 2017 Baseline for Farm Programs."

60. Babcock, "Cutting the Fat."

61. Vincent H. Smith, "Limiting Premium Subsidies for Crop Insurance," R Street Institute, April 2016, https://www.rstreet.org/wp-content/uploads/2016/04/61.pdf.

62. Babcock, "Cutting the Fat."
63. Glauber, "Crop Insurance and Private Sector Delivery."

4

Title I of the US Farm Bill:
An Overview of the Commodity Title

BARRY K. GOODWIN

Over most of its history, the US farm bill has conveyed most of its direct support to farmers through programs now contained in Title I—also frequently called the "commodity title." The prominence of Title I as a vehicle for transferring economic welfare from US taxpayers to farmers has diminished somewhat with the increasing prominence of crop insurance and conservation programs (Titles XI and II, respectively). However, the commodity programs legislated in Title I still convey significant subsidies to the agricultural sector. In particular, according to cost estimates of the 2014 Farm Bill made by the Congressional Budget Office (CBO), Title I programs were projected to cost over $28 billion and account for 4.8 percent of total farm bill outlays on major programs, including nutritional assistance (typically about 70 percent of the total costs), over 2014–18.[1] Today, at about $7 billion, Title I program subsidies amount to about 35 percent of the $20 billion in subsidies paid directly to farmers each year. In the 1980s and 1990s, however, the share of all federal funds flowing to farmers via Title I programs would have been much higher. Figure 1 illustrates the history of spending on the major US farm bill programs and highlights the increasing importance of crop insurance and conservation spending relative to commodity program spending.

Most current Title I commodity programs are simply slightly revised and renamed versions of earlier subsidy programs. The two major commodity programs, which are the primary focus of this chapter, are Agricultural Risk Coverage (ARC) and Price Loss Coverage (PLC). Other Title I initiatives include dairy programs and the US sugar program, which are covered extensively elsewhere in these volumes. Title I of the 2014 Farm Bill also

Figure 1. Farm Bill Spending by Major Mandatory Programs

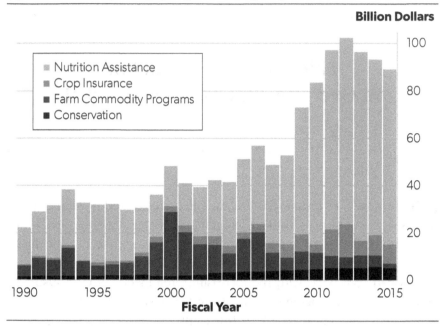

Source: Renée Johnson and Jim Monke, "What Is the Farm Bill?," Congressional Research Service, April 26, 2018, 6.

reauthorized four disaster relief programs targeted specifically to livestock and tree commodities. Title I contains several specific commodity payment provisions, including rhetorical (but generally not binding) limits on payments and eligibility constraints tied to a household's total adjusted gross income (AGI).

Title I also contains the coupled price support provisions that function through marketing loans and loan deficiency payments and are tied to actual crop production. These programs were historically important in establishing minimum price guarantees through nonrecourse marketing loans made at legislated loan rates. In recent years, market prices have been far above loan rates for most commodities, and thus these traditional price support programs have not resulted in significant payments to growers. The structure of ARC and PLC highlights another central feature of Title I programs—the importance of base acreage and yields. Program base acreage and yields were cost control measures introduced in the 1980s. PLC and ARC payments are made on a production base determined by historical acreage and yields for each crop rather than on actual production—a feature that results in many puzzling issues and some unintended consequences. The base owner is generally entitled to the payment, and the payment is not tied to current production, or any production for that matter. An exception arises when a tenant farmer cash leases base land, in which case landowners are free to set lease terms in a manner that allows capture of the subsidies. Crop-share lease arrangements generally require a division of subsidies in a manner consistent with the share terms of the lease agreement.[2]

A Brief Overview of the History of Title I Programs

Most farm programs can be traced to the 1933 Agricultural Adjustment Act—the first farm bill.[3] A part of the New Deal legislation, the 1933 act was intended to raise farm prices and farm household incomes, which were much lower than the incomes of nonfarm households. An important feature of the first farm bill was the establishment of a list of "basic commodities," which led to a list (with significant modifications) of "program commodities" that are typically protected through Title I.[4] The initial list of basic commodities included corn, cotton, hogs, milk, rice, tobacco, and wheat. Subsequent legislation added barley, grain, flax, rye, peanuts, and sorghum. An interesting omission from this list is soybeans, which were a minor crop at the time. The US Supreme Court found the initial farm bill's production control provisions unconstitutional in the *Hoosac Mills* decision of 1933. Marketing agreements and orders were implemented in the 1937 Agricultural Marketing Agreement Act and 1938 Agricultural Adjustment Act to address these judicial concerns, and the resulting farm legislation continued these Title I provisions through the 1980s with many modifications but the same fundamental principles.

In the early- to mid-1980s, crop-specific acreage and yield bases were established for program crops. Deficiency payments, defined by the difference in market prices and loan rates, were restricted to acreage allotments by the 1973 Farm Bill. The 1977 and 1981 Farm Bills limited the payments to a base defined as a proportion of total planted acreage. The base defined how much land would be eligible for deficiency payments and how much must be idled to receive the payments. The 1985 Farm Bill established an acreage base for each farm that was defined as the average plantings for each crop over the preceding five years. Base yields were defined as the average yield between 1981 and 1985, with high and low years excluded. This base has continued to shape Title I payments since 1986 and remains a relevant determinant of each individual's payments under the 2014 act.

A major change in US farm policy, at least by appearances, occurred with the 1996 Farm Bill. The legislation introduced a system of fixed payments that were to be made on each farm's production base for each eligible crop. Base was determined by the acreage and yields that had been established in the 1980s. These fixed payments were set to decline every year until the act expired in 2002. This seemed to signal to many observers, who in retrospect were naive regarding congressional intentions, that the fixed payments would serve as a buyout of base as a part of a transition to the free market. The intriguing characteristic of the fixed payments (also known as the Agricultural Market Transition Act and production flexibility contract payments) was that a farm business had to do nothing to receive the payments. Landowners with base acres and lessees of such land did not have to produce (anything) and would receive payments as long as they did not plant fruits and vegetables or take the land out of "good agricultural use," a requirement with loose restrictions.[5]

The restriction on planting fruits and vegetables on base was first established in the 1990 Farm Bill. Many fruit and vegetable producers favored the restriction because it served as a barrier to competition. Landowners with a history of growing fruits and vegetables were not allowed to update or switch base with other crops, although the legislation allowed some exceptions. In a World Trade Organization (WTO) dispute settlement case brought by Brazil against US cotton subsidies, the WTO panel found that this restriction distorted production decisions and that US direct payments tied to base were deemed to be subject to restrictions on domestic support.[6] Fixed direct payments were considered exempt from such disciplines before this ruling and, despite the WTO finding, continued to be notified to the WTO as exempt under Annex 2 (green box) of the 1994 WTO Agricultural Agreement through the 2013 crop year. The issue became moot when the 2014 Farm Bill eliminated fixed direct payments.

Alas, legislators' intentions quickly became clear when Congress stepped away from the supposed transition to the market and provided significant ad hoc payments on base that were known as market loss assistance (MLA).[7] The fixed direct payments that the 1996 act authorized totaled about $5 billion per year as the bill expired in 2002. MLA payments were determined using the same base parameters as the fixed payments and were even termed "double-AMTA payments." Payments on crops totaled $2.8 billion in 1998, $5.6 billion in 1999 and 2000, and $4.6 billion in 2001. Over $1 billion in payments were also made to producers of dairy, tobacco, and other commodities.

One of the many notable issues associated with MLA is that it signaled Congress' hasty retreat from promises to move agricultural policy toward less government support. An examination of the agricultural economy also highlights the factors underlying the MLA program. In 1996, farm prices were strong, and it was politically convenient to promise reductions in government spending through direct (decoupled) payments. However, when prices fell in 1998, the free-market concept advocated by so many policymakers suddenly became a bad idea. These events demonstrated that things had not really changed in terms of congressional commitment to subsidies for farmers. It also demonstrated a key principle that has guided farm policy both before and since then. Congress is unable or unwilling to refrain from providing these welfare transfers. If it cannot do it through the farm bill or crop insurance (now part of the farm bill), it will do it through ad hoc disaster assistance. Rhetorical arguments favoring a "transition to the market" have proved to be vacuous, and policymakers quickly abandon any such ideals when market prices moderate.

MLA payments demonstrated another important fact about US agricultural policy. Policymakers moved quickly to formalize and codify these ad hoc payments as a fixture of the 2002 Farm Bill. MLA payments were transformed into the Countercyclical Payment Program (CCP) and embedded in the commodity title. This action at least brought the payments into the policy debate as a component of the omnibus farm legislation. As I discuss in greater detail below, the MLA payments that became CCP payments subsequently became PLC payments in the 2014 Farm Bill.

The 2002 Farm Bill brought about significant changes in programs having base acreage. A major change was the option to add soybeans to a farm's base acreage. Farmers could add the average acreage and yield over the 1998–2001 period. Alternatively, base acres in other crops could be traded for soybean base. Farmers could also choose not to update their base, and for farmers with the more valuable corn base, this was typically the preferred option. Various base yield updating options were available to farmers and landowners. As is the case with most program modifications in the farm bill, the suite of options allowed farmers to pick the option they most favored. According to Jim Monke, 78 percent of farms updated their base, with 37 percent updating acreage and 41 percent adding oilseed acreage to their base.[8] Of the 37 percent that updated their base acreage, 28 percent of the total also updated their base yields.

A second important development in Title I commodity programs that shaped current agricultural policy arose in the 2008 Farm Bill. In 2008, Ohio State University Professor Carl Zulauf proposed a conceptual framework for an alternative safety-net program. The new program quickly garnered support from Ohio and Illinois corn growers and, eventually, the National Corn Growers Association. It was known as the Average Crop Revenue Election (ACRE) program and was introduced by Sens. Sherrod Brown (D-OH) and Richard Durbin (D-IL). The ACRE program provided a revenue guarantee based on state-level revenues and farm-level revenues in a double-trigger type of scheme. ACRE was the first revenue-based Title I program and was offered as an alternative to CCPs. Producers who enrolled in ACRE gave up eligibility for CCPs and agreed to accept both a 20 percent reduction in direct payments and a 30 percent reduction in marketing loan rates.

For most base owners, surrendering CCP and a portion of fixed payments for a gamble on ACRE revenue payments was an unattractive option. However, ACRE subsequently proved to provide generous subsidies for those who did enroll. This was particularly the case given the near-historically high prices that characterized markets for most commodities in 2008–09. However, these high prices and strong incomes illustrate two features of ACRE that are especially troubling from a safety-net perspective. First, revenue guarantees were based on annually updated historical yields and prices, which necessarily means that the revenue guarantee the program provided is ratcheted up as prices and yields increase. The higher your income, the higher your guarantee. Second, ACRE payments were recoupled to production because they were made on planted acres rather than base, with the proviso that acres eligible for such payments could not exceed a farm's total base area for all crops. Of course, knowing with certainty whether the ACRE

Figure 2. 2009 Base Acreage Enrolled in the ACRE Program

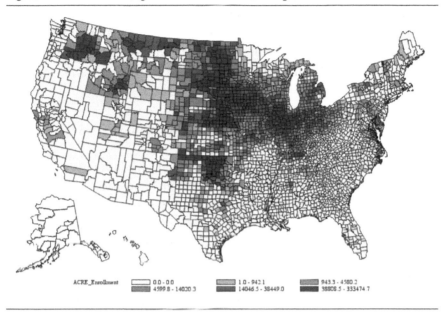

Source: US Department of Agriculture, Economic Research Service; and US Department of Agriculture, Farm Service Agency.

Figure 3. Proportion of 2009 Base Acreage Enrolled in ACRE Program

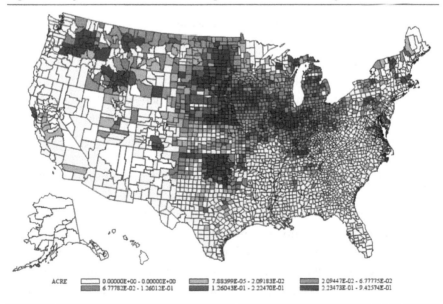

Source: US Department of Agriculture, Economic Research Service; and US Department of Agriculture, Farm Service Agency.

program should be preferred to the alternative required perfect foresight about future prices. In the end, about 8 percent of farms and 13 percent of eligible acres were enrolled in the ACRE program.[9] Figures 2 and 3 illustrate patterns of enrollment in the ACRE program. Notably, enrollment was highly concentrated in the Corn Belt.

Title I in the 2014 Farm Bill

The 2014 Farm Bill defined the policy provisions that currently apply to US agriculture. The 2014 legislation brought about some sweeping changes in subsidy programs. As has been discussed by Vincent Smith et al. (Chapter 1, Volume I), the farm economy was enjoying record-high incomes before the legislation. The provision of decoupled payments amounting to many thousands of dollars directly to landowners or farmers, who generally are a wealthy and high-income group, became untenable even for the most generous members of the Agriculture Committees. Many government policymakers and individuals in the nonfarm economy pay little attention to the farm bill. Although the bill itself may be scored at nearly a trillion dollars (over a 10-year period), the farm subsidy costs are modest and account for about only $200 billion of that amount. Thus, they may seem modest when compared to some other programs, but they are certainly not trivial to the relatively small group of subsidy recipients. However, work undertaken by groups such as the Environmental Working Group brought a refreshing transparency to farm policy. Individual payment totals by program were made available, and, as a result, many in the press and nonfarming public could see that the farm bill often resulted in large sums of taxpayer money being paid to wealthy individuals.[10]

The 2014 legislation eliminated the decoupled, direct payments that had been made every year since 1996. The aforementioned policy transparency and "subsidies to millionaires" recognition led to a situation in which Agriculture Committee members could no longer argue that these payments were appropriate. Crop insurance had become the major policy instrument for subsidies, and calls to eliminate the "shallow loss" of insurance deductibles became an important part of the discussion. Debate over the 2014 legislation did raise several important issues, including proposed cuts to nutritional assistance and divorcing farm subsidies from this nutritional assistance. In the end, the nutrition programs were kept in the farm bill, and reductions in Supplemental Nutrition Assistance Program (SNAP) benefits (which largely reflected improvements in the macro economy) were touted as cuts to the farm bill.

The 2014 legislation maintained direct payments in a slightly revised form. That is, payments determined by base acreage and production were maintained with the provision that the payments would be triggered by declines in prices or revenues. The quantity of base production eligible for payments was fixed, but the amounts of the payments were determined by the extent of the shortfall in prices or revenues. Again, payments were made on a fixed base and required no current production of the base crop. Farmers were presented with two options that really represented modest modifications of the CCP program and the ACRE program. A new version of the CCP program was introduced in the form of the PLC, and the new version of ACRE was called ARC.

An important aspect of PLC as compared to CCP is that the reference prices that trigger payments were increased substantially. The program maintained the marketing loan provisions of previous farm bills with some modest changes in loan rates. Figure 4 illustrates the new loan rates and PLC reference prices for each commodity. Table A1 presents market year average prices, loan rates, and reference prices, and Figures 5 and 6 present market year average prices and reference prices for selected crops.

The ARC program was offered as an alternative to the PLC program in the 2014 Farm Bill. There were two versions of ARC. The first, and the only one that really proved to be relevant, based a revenue guarantee for each crop on the five-year Olympic averages of market prices and county-level yields. The county-level ARC provides coverage on a crop-by-crop basis. An alternative provides individual farm coverage but on a whole farm revenue basis. The individual version of ARC uses an Olympic average of the product of farm-level yields and average price estimates of crop revenues. In the end, few producers chose the individual version of ARC. The ARC program provides coverage based on 86 percent of the alternative moving average estimates of crop revenues. Yields below 70 percent of the average were capped at that level before calculating the revenue guarantee. ARC payments were limited to 10 percent of the ARC revenue guarantee, which

Figure 4. Loan Rates and PLC Reference Prices as a Percentage of Market Average Farm Price

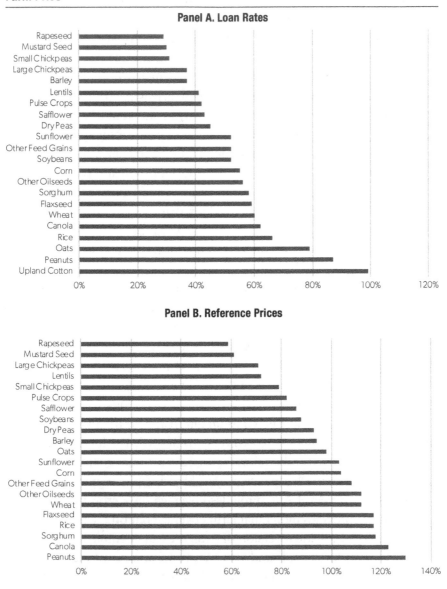

Note: Note average weekly price used for cotton and rice. Other feed grain includes sorghum, barley, and oats, and other oilseeds include sunflower, flaxseed, canola, rapeseed, mustard, safflower, crambe, and sesame.

Source: Randy Schnepf, "Farm Safety-Net Payments Under the 2014 Farm Bill: Comparison by Program Crop," Congressional Research Service, August 11, 2017, 20.

Figure 5. Market Year Price and PLC Reference Prices (Dollar per Unit)

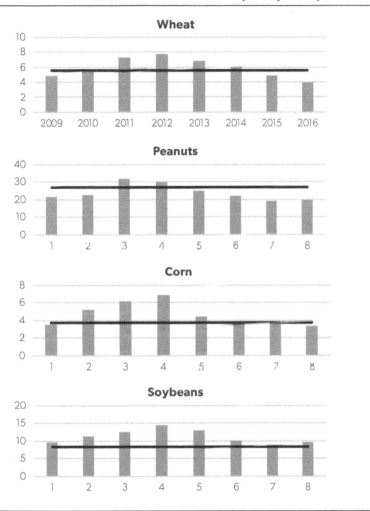

Source: Author's calculations.

effectively provides the so-called shallow loss protection between 86 percent and 76 percent of the guarantee. Significantly, ARC differed from the ACRE program in that payments were made on base rather than actual area. Effective base was limited to 85 percent, meaning that the payments were made on only 85 percent of a farm's base production—a limitation that also had been a feature of earlier legislation.

Figure 6. Commodity Credit Corporation and Crop Insurance Outlays as a Percentage of the Value of Output

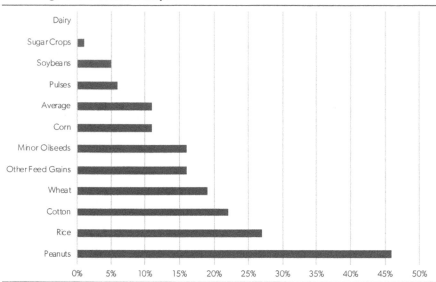

Source: Renée Johnson and Jim Monke, "What Is the Farm Bill?," Congressional Research Service, April 26, 2018, 6.

Farmers could choose either PLC or ARC on a crop-by-crop basis (except for farms enrolled in the individual ARC program), and their choice was binding for the entire period covered by the 2014 Farm Bill. Not surprisingly, farm business choices largely reflected the relationship between PLC reference prices and market prices. For commodities that had enjoyed high prices in the preceding years, the ARC guarantee was advantageous as the high prices locked in a high guarantee. In contrast, for commodities that realized a large difference in the PLC reference price over market prices, farmers preferred the PLC program. Tables A2 and A3 present aggregate, crop-specific choices. Corn and soybean growers were almost unanimous in selecting ARC. In contrast, nearly all rice and peanut growers selected PLC.

Along with the choice of a Title I program, producers could keep their current base or update their base acreage and yields using 90 percent of their average yields from 2008 to 2012. ARC payments are based on county yields for nearly all growers, and thus updating yields does not affect ARC

Figure 7. Total Base Acreage for All Crops in 2015

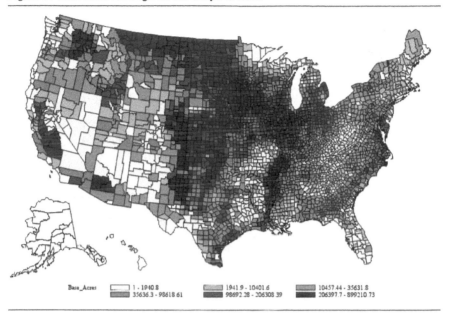

Base_Acres | 1 - 1940.8 | 1941.9 - 10401.6 | 10457.44 - 35631.8
35636.3 - 98618.61 | 98692.28 - 206308.39 | 206397.7 - 899210.73

Source: Farm Service Agency data.

payments (although the use of recent county yields necessarily updated the realized guarantee relative to the former CCP production base). Table A4 presents statistics summarizing the base-updating decisions following the 2014 legislation. Considerable increases in base yields are apparent for most commodities. Figure 7 presents the current base situation across all crops, as established by changes made in response to the 2014 Farm Bill.

One major development in the 2014 Farm Bill was eliminating the cotton program in response to Brazil's challenges under the WTO. Cotton base was redefined as "generic base," and landowners could claim subsidies based on how the land on their farm was allocated to production. For example, a former cotton producer could plant peanuts on his or her generic base and realize the benefits of the high peanut reference price in the PLC program. Indeed, such a reallocation of land toward peanuts was observed and is documented elsewhere in this volume. Figure 8 illustrates generic base and peanut base following the 2014 legislation and highlights that the former cotton base, now generic, closely follows patterns of

Figure 8. Generic Base and Peanut Base Acreage in 2015

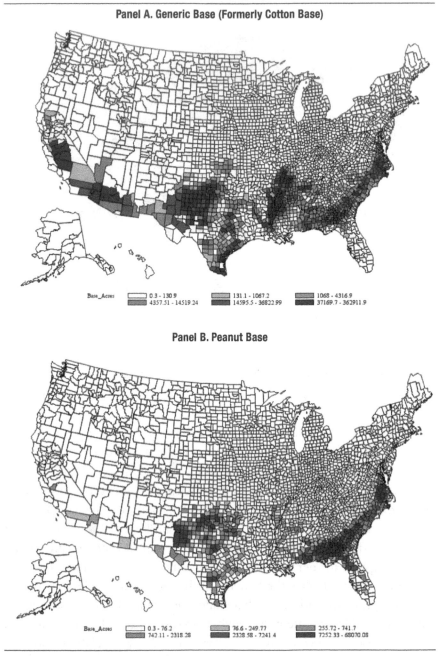

Panel A. Generic Base (Formerly Cotton Base)

Panel B. Peanut Base

Source: US Department of Agriculture, Farm Service Agency.

Figure 9. Total PLC and ARC Payments Made in 2016

Panel A. PLC

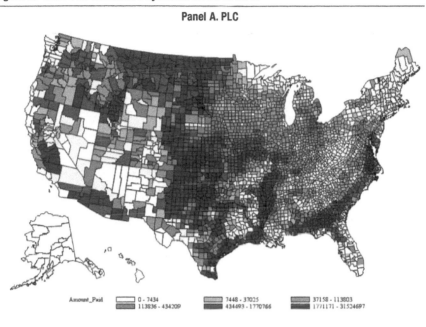

Amount_Paid
0 - 7434
113836 - 434209
7448 - 37025
434493 - 1770766
37158 - 113803
1771171 - 31524697

Panel B. ARC

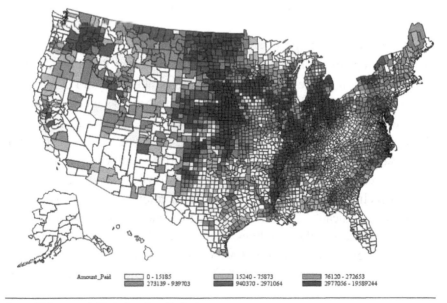

Amount_Paid
0 - 15185
273139 - 939703
15240 - 75873
940370 - 2971064
76120 - 272653
2977056 - 19589244

Source: US Department of Agriculture, Farm Service Agency.

Figure 10. CBO Project Reallocation of Base Acreage

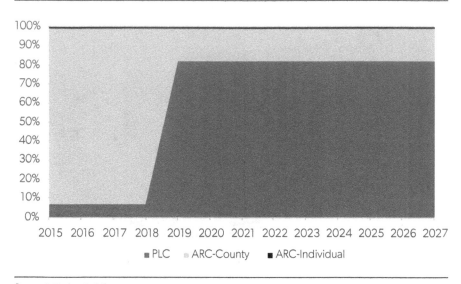

Source: Author's calculations.

peanut base. Table A5 illustrates the allocation of generic base to alternative commodities.

At the time of writing this chapter, all indications are that ARC and PLC will likely remain an important part of the 2018 Farm Bill. Figure 9 presents information on the amount and geographic allocation of PLC and ARC payments in 2015 and 2016. Not surprisingly, these payments are mainly concentrated in the Midwest Corn Belt states and the Great Plains (from Texas through Kansas to North Dakota and Montana). The recent history of market prices relative to PLC reference prices and ARC averages again becomes relevant to the choice, if indeed landowners are given the choice again, which seems quite likely. The CBO used long-run price predictions to derive an indication of how producers may choose to allocate their base. Figure 10 illustrates their findings. It is no surprise that most base is likely to be allocated to PLC because of recent and current lower prices for crops such as corn and wheat (see Table A1) and hence lower revenue guarantees of ARC.

Payment Limits and Means Testing

Payment limits and means testing have been important issues in recent farm bill deliberations. Payment limits, typically not binding, have been a component of every farm bill since the 1933 act. Before the 2008 Farm Bill, individuals were limited to $40,000 in direct payments, $65,000 for CCPs, and $75,000 for marketing loan gains. However, long-standing legislation had permitted the "three-entity rule," which allowed three entities to collect the limits on a single farm. The first entity was limited to 100 percent, and the others were limited to 50 percent of the total. This essentially doubled the payment limit to total $360,000. However, marketing loan gains and loan deficiency payments paid in commodity certificates, which could be exchanged for commodities and then sold, were not subject to limits.

The 2014 Farm Bill made significant changes that limited PLC, ARC, and marketing loan gains to $125,000 per individual, which could be doubled in the case of a couple or joint entity. An interesting aside was that peanuts, which had been afforded a generous buyout, had their own separate payment limit.

Disqualifying individuals from being eligible for payments on the base of an AGI limit has also been a feature of recent policy debates. The 2002 Farm Bill established an AGI limit of $2.5 million, meaning households with a three-year average AGI exceeding this amount would not be eligible for payments. The 2008 Farm Bill split the total AGI limit to $750,000 for farm income and $500,000 for nonfarm income. The 2014 Farm Bill revised this to a single limit of $900,000 (double for married couples filing separate federal returns), beyond which a landowner would become ineligible for PLC or ARC payments, as well as marketing loan gains.

Recent debate over a new 2018 Farm Bill again addressed payment limits and means testing. The House version of the new farm bill, passed on June 21, 2018, contained some ironic if not startling changes to both payment limits and nutritional assistance. Heated rhetoric among conservatives and, notably, the Freedom Caucus vowed that SNAP recipients become subject to tighter work requirements to be eligible for benefits. An unpublished (but widely reported) CBO analysis estimated that the work requirements would force 400,000 households with one million people out of the SNAP program.

At the same time, the CBO estimated that the House version would increase spending on Title I programs by $154 million. For the House Committee on Agriculture, it appears that charity begins (and only stays) at home (i.e., with the agricultural state constituencies).

Even more impressive were the proposed changes to payment limits and means testing that were contained in the House bill. The feeble payment limits would be modified to allow a wide range of farm household members (first cousins, nieces, and nephews), as well as exempting most corporate farms (limited liability companies and subchapter S corporations) from being subject to a single payment limit. Instead, limits would apply to an unlimited number of pass-through entities. The AGI restriction would be set at $900,000, with entities making more than this being ineligible for commodity or conservation payments. Further, the corporate entities noted above would not be subject to any AGI limits, making way for unlimited payments to the wealthiest of the wealthy among farm operators and landowners.

Concluding Remarks

Over the past 45 years since *World Agriculture in Disarray* was published, significant changes have been made to how the government supports farmers. First, support has largely moved away from commodity price support toward income support. When D. Gale Johnson wrote his seminal work, nonrecourse loans were the primary form of support in the United States. They led to market price distortions, production distortion, high government stocks, and costly disposal programs that distorted world markets. Domestic consumers were big losers, and the programs were characterized by substantial levels of deadweight economic welfare losses. The move to direct payments in the form of loan deficiency payments arguably lowered deadweight losses (in the sense consumers benefited from lower market prices), but government outlays and production distortions remained high as loan rates were high relative to market prices. With few changes in the levels of loan rates since the mid-1990s, and the appreciation of commodity prices over the past 15 years, marketing loan rates for most crops are now low relative to current market prices, except for cotton. For the first three years of the 2014 Farm Bill, the federal government continued to make marketing loan payments in the hundreds of millions of dollars, and most of those payments were targeted to one or two crops.

Second, the one lasting legacy of the Freedom to Farm Act is that it eliminated the annual acreage reduction programs and concomitant base planting provisions that had so restricted planting decisions. The 1985 act had severe penalties for overplanting (and underplanting) base acres. In the late 1980s, the soybean to corn price ratio was over three, yet little changed in the soybean area. The introduction of flex acres in the 1990 Farm Bill really allowed the soybean area to respond to prices and started the trend of movement out of wheat and small grains to soybeans, in that farmers still could not overplant corn until Freedom to Farm came along. Freedom to Farm really did allow producers to respond to changes in prices even if planting flexibility remained limited. So arguably acreage decisions are now much more responsive to market prices.

Nevertheless, ARC and PLC payments are still large and, according to recent empirical work, may affect production decisions. Marketing loan rates for most crops remain "out of the money"; that is, loan rates are lower than market prices, and the program is not generating any subsidy payments. However, if prices for commodities such as wheat and corn drop sharply, as in the late 1990s, marketing loans could still result in substantial payments (and distort production). Further, base-updating expectations (a feature of almost every farm bill since 1996) still may have some distortionary effects if producers think it is best to build base even when market prices suggest planting another crop. Thus, Title I programs can still create incentives for production distortions, generate economic inefficiencies, and contribute to trade disputes in which US agricultural policy is the subject of complaints by other countries. They remain a genuine contributor to the policy disarray reflected by the structure of current US agricultural policy.

Appendix A

Table A1. Loan Rate, PLC Reference Prices, and Marketing Year Average Prices

Commodity	2009–10 Price	2010–11 Price	2011–12 Price	2012–13 Price	2013–14 Price	2014–15 Price	2015–16 Price	2016–17 Price	Reference Price	National Loan Rate
Wheat	**$4.870**	$5.700	$7.240	$7.770	$6.870	$5.990	**$4.890**	**$3.890**	$5.500	$2.940
Barley	**$4.660**	**$3.860**	$5.350	$6.430	$6.060	$5.300	$5.520	$4.960	$4.950	$1.950
Oats	**$2.020**	$2.520	$3.490	$3.890	$3.750	$3.210	**$2.120**	**$2.060**	$2.400	$1.390
Peanuts	**$0.217**	**$0.225**	$0.318	$0.301	**$0.249**	**$0.220**	**$0.193**	**$0.197**	$0.268	$0.178
Corn	**$3.550**	$5.180	$6.220	$6.890	$4.460	$3.700	**$3.610**	**$3.360**	$3.700	$1.950
Grain Sorghum	**$3.220**	$5.020	$5.990	$6.330	$4.280	$4.030	**$3.310**	**$2.790**	$3.950	$1.950
Soybeans	$9.590	$11.300	$12.500	$14.400	$13.000	$10.100	$8.950	$9.470	$8.400	$5.000
Dry Peas	**$0.090**	**$0.098**	$0.153	$0.157	$0.146	$0.120	$0.128	$0.110	$0.110	$0.054
Lentils	$0.268	$0.257	$0.250	$0.207	**$0.198**	$0.244	$0.310	$0.285	$0.200	$0.113
Large Chickpeas	$0.291	$0.305	$0.421	$0.379	$0.309	$0.286	$0.306	$0.321	$0.215	$0.113
Small Chickpeas	$0.203	$0.208	$0.215	$0.274	$0.227	$0.208	$0.251	$0.249	$0.190	$0.074
Sunflower Seed	**$0.151**	$0.233	$0.291	$0.254	$0.214	$0.217	**$0.196**	**$0.174**	$0.202	$0.101
Canola	**$0.162**	**$0.193**	$0.240	$0.265	$0.206	**$0.169**	**$0.156**	**$0.166**	$0.202	$0.101
Flaxseed	**$8.150**	$12.200	$13.900	$13.800	$13.800	$11.800	**$8.950**	**$8.000**	$11.284	$5.650
Mustard Seed	$0.304	$0.259	$0.336	$0.358	$0.372	$0.348	$0.318	$0.327	$0.202	$0.101
Rapeseed	$0.263	$0.234	$0.270	$0.261	$0.251	$0.349	$0.432	$0.252	$0.202	$0.101
Safflower	**$0.171**	**$0.172**	$0.244	$0.276	$0.279	$0.250	$0.245	$0.207	$0.202	$0.101
Crambe	$0.368	$0.328	$0.378	$0.365	$0.351	$0.419	$0.518	$0.305	$0.202	$0.101
Sesame Seed	$0.280	$0.306	$0.350	$0.320	$0.440	$0.460	$0.390	$0.320	$0.202	$0.101
Rice (Long Grain)	**$0.129**	**$0.110**	**$0.134**	$0.145	$0.154	**$0.119**	**$0.111**	**$0.096**	$0.140	$0.065

Note: Bold values indicate positive PLC payments.
Source: Unpublished data from the US Department of Agriculture, Farm Service Agency.

Table A2. Farm Counts and Base Acres on Farms That Made an ARC or PLC Election (National by Crop)

Covered Commodity	PLC		ARC-County Option		ARC-Individual Option		Total ARC and PLC Programs	
	Farm Count	Base Acres	Farm Count	Base Acres	Farm Count	Base Acres	Farm Count	Base Acres
Barley	63,507	3,876,590	46,420	1,127,214	1,350	181,913	111,277	5,185,717
Canola	16,155	1,436,766	1,134	31,814	131	7,736	17,420	1,476,317
Corn	121,968	6,388,066	1,238,481	90,057,276	2,393	323,106	1,363,342	96,768,447
Crambe	69	1,698	46	889	1	16	116	2,603
Dry Peas	3,325	196,636	4,058	219,471	252	25,783	7,635	441,890
Flaxseed	3,261	145,584	2,212	82,871	33	1,837	5,506	230,292
Grain Sorghum	123,691	5,965,661	106,410	2,998,211	281	15,557	230,382	8,979,430
Lentils	1,836	151,080	1,583	116,798	171	19,185	3,590	287,063
Large Chickpeas	402	19,412	744	56,636	100	9,587	1,246	85,634
Long-Grain Rice	29,123	4,007,809	155	6,912	–	–	29,278	4,014,721
Medium-Grain Rice	13,241	167,293	856	6,532	–	–	14,097	173,824
Mustard	325	13,845	258	9,431	26	1,439	609	24,715
Oats	46,354	671,385	150,788	1,410,063	628	13,778	197,770	2,095,226
Peanuts	49,026	2,013,443	329	6,781	1	18	49,356	2,020,243
Rapeseed	54	1,100	58	1,335	3	45	115	2,481
Safflower	1,124	62,521	794	33,401	45	3,145	1,963	99,068
Sesame	145	4,378	46	828	–	–	191	5,206
Small Chickpeas	120	5,004	271	15,006	45	2,057	436	22,067
Soybeans	42,295	1,688,365	1,017,775	52,635,553	2,072	191,053	1,062,142	54,514,972
Sunflowers	13,697	920,546	14,048	710,724	264	19,683	28,009	1,650,954
Temperate Japonica Rice	1,386	355,082	639	197,020	46	23,092	2,041	575,194
Wheat	271,445	27,045,581	527,343	35,394,613	3,694	1,258,950	802,482	63,699,144
Generic	–	–	–	–	97	8,294	194,224	17,582,910
US Total		55,137,844.79		185,119,381	5,560	2,106,275	1,760,345	242,355,206

Source: Unpublished data from the US Department of Agriculture, Farm Service Agency.

Table A3. Allocation of Farms and Base Acreage Among PLC and ARC

	Percentage of Farms Electing			Percentage of Bases Electing		
	PLC	ARC-County	ARC-Individual	PLC	ARC-County	ARC-Individual
Barley	57%	42%	1%	75%	22%	4%
Canola	93%	7%	1%	97%	2%	1%
Corn	9%	91%	0%	7%	93%	0%
Crambe	59%	40%	1%	65%	34%	1%
Dry Peas	44%	53%	3%	44%	50%	6%
Flaxseed	59%	40%	1%	63%	36%	1%
Grain Sorghum	54%	46%	0%	66%	33%	0%
Lentils	51%	44%	5%	53%	41%	7%
Large Chickpeas	32%	60%	8%	23%	66%	11%
Long-Grain Rice	99%	1%	0%	100%	0%	0%
Medium-Grain Rice (Southern)	94%	6%	0%	96%	4%	0%
Mustard	53%	42%	4%	56%	38%	6%
Oats	23%	76%	0%	32%	67%	1%
Peanuts	99%	1%	0%	100%	0%	0%
Rapeseed	47%	50%	3%	44%	54%	2%
Safflower	57%	40%	2%	63%	34%	3%
Sesame	76%	24%	0%	84%	16%	0%
Small Chickpeas	28%	62%	10%	23%	68%	9%
Soybeans	4%	96%	0%	3%	97%	0%
Sunflowers	49%	50%	1%	56%	43%	1%
Temperate Japonica Rice	68%	30%	2%	62%	34%	4%
Wheat	34%	66%	0%	42%	56%	2%
US Total	—	—	—	23%	76%	1%

Source: Unpublished data from the US Department of Agriculture, Farm Service Agency.

Table A4. Base Yield Updating with 2014 Farm Bill

Covered Commodity	Number of Farms Electing PLC	Number of Farms Electing PLC and Updating Yields	Base on Farms Electing PLC and Updating Yields	CCP Yield on Farms Electing PLC and Updating Yield	Updated Yield	Percentage Change in Yield	Number of Farms Electing ARC-CO	Number of Farms Electing ARC-CO and Updating Yields 2	Base on Farms Electing ARC-CO and Updating Yields	CCP Yield on Farms Electing ARC-CO and Updating Yield	Updated Yield
Barley	63,507	14,195	1,435,167	50.0	71.3	42.4%	46,420	3,648	236,870	49.4	64.6
Canola	16,155	6,383	866,331	1,101.5	1,622.7	47.3%	1,134	109	6,773	940.0	1,417.7
Corn	121,968	37,506	3,068,446	102.9	132.0	28.3%	1,238,481	676,359	64,715,977	114.2	145.5
Crambe	69	0	—	—	—	—	46	1	8	853.0	1,355.0
Dry Peas	3,325	399	24,344	1,321.5	1,878.0	42.1%	4,058	689	53,208	1,386.2	1,930.8
Flaxseed	3,261	1,004	52,729	12.1	19.4	60.4%	2,212	519	23,663	12.1	18.0
Grain Sorghum	123,691	17,716	1,399,899	51.1	67.6	32.3%	106,410	16,024	953,581	54.4	72.9
Lentils	1,836	313	25,130	707.5	1,174.6	66.0%	1,583	506	42,308	774.4	1,190.6
Large Chickpeas	402	36	1,923	955.4	1,579.6	65.3%	744	122	11,228	941.0	1,393.6
Long-Grain Rice	29,123	15,160	2,854,457	4,814.2	6,409.3	33.1%	155	19	2,885	4,144.1	5,898.5
Medium-Grain Rice	13,241	2,405	79,312	5,087.2	6,402.6	25.9%	856	135	2,042	5,005.8	6,571.0
Mustard	325	17	683	622.4	753.6	21.1%	258	34	1,615	601.5	864.1
Oats	46,354	1,846	57,804	44.2	65.6	48.4%	150,788	8,194	193,221	47.5	64.5
Peanuts	49,026	10,268	737,430	3,024.8	3,793.4	25.4%	329	9	647	3,099.2	3,419.2
Rapeseed	54	0	—	—	—	—	58	1	0	1,340.0	1,670.0
Safflower	1,124	162	12,387	952.0	1,051.8	10.5%	794	92	4,889	823.5	1,102.2
Sesame	145	2	156	434.9	697.7	60.4%	46	1	14	234.0	475.0
Small Chickpeas	120	5	143	1,132.1	1,761.6	55.6%	271	15	954	1,182.4	1,372.9
Soybeans	42,295	19,206	1,014,246	28.4	37.4	31.5%	1,017,775	612,542	35,588,621	32.9	40.8
Sunflowers	13,697	4,476	455,473	1,152.9	1,500.4	30.9%	14,048	3,207	299,515	1,178.3	1,505.6
Temperate Japonica Rice	1,386	825	256,442	7,021.2	7,943.8	13.1%	609	283	122,663	7,055.5	7,861.0
Wheat	271,445	74,047	10,211,064	34.3	45.3	31.9%	527,343	166,037	17,727,571	34.6	46.2

Source: Unpublished data from the US Department of Agriculture, Farm Service Agency.

Table A5. Plantings Attributed to Generic Base (Thousands of Acres)

Covered Commodity	PLC		ARC-County		ARC-Individual	Total
	Covered Commodity Contract Base Acres	Plantings Attributed to Generic Base Acres	Covered Commodity Contract Base Acres	Plantings Attributed to Generic Base Acres	Covered Commodity Contract Base Acres	
Wheat	25,262.5	2,015.3	34,181.7	586.9	1,233	63,279.4
Oats	607.9	31.7	1,293.6	22.6	13.4	1,969.2
Long-Grain Rice	3,973.5	151	5	0.1	0	4,129.6
Medium-Grain Rice	473.6	11.9	162	1	20.1	668.6
Flaxseed	144.2	0	81.5	0	1.8	227.5
Corn	6,318.6	446.5	88,000.5	1,515	321.4	96,602
Small Chickpeas	4.8	0.3	14.7	0	2	21.8
Large Chickpeas	14.9	5.2	55.5	1.4	9.5	86.5
Grain Sorghum	5,620.5	1,174.9	2,792.5	128.8	14.3	9,731
Dry Peas	190.8	0	215.1	0	25.6	431.5
Peanuts	1,963.4	706.6	5.9	1	0	2,676.9
Sunflowers	911.4	48.6	696.1	5.4	19.4	1,680.9
Safflower	46.2	5.2	29.5	0.8	2.8	84.5
Soybeans	1,765.7	130.8	51,580.4	3,095.4	190.1	56,762.4
Barley	3,288.8	39.4	1,049.1	2.4	176.2	4,555.9
Rapeseed	1	0.1	1.3	1.4	0	3.8
Mustard	13.8	0.1	9.3	0	1.4	24.6
Sesame	4.2	16	0.8	5.2	0	26.2
Lentils	146.7	0	113.9	0	19.2	279.8
Canola	1,425.6	14.7	30	5.3	7.6	1,483.2
Crambe	1.6	0	0.9	0	0	2.5
Total	52,179.7	4,798.3	18,0319.3	5,372.7	2,057.8	244,727.8

Source: Unpublished data from the US Department of Agriculture, Farm Service Agency.

Notes

1. See Renée Johnson and Jim Monke, "What Is the Farm Bill?," Congressional Research Service, April 26, 2018.

2. Eligibility for direct subsidy payments generally requires a landowner to assume a share of the risk, as in a share agreement.

3. An excellent overview of the history of early farm bills is contained in US Department of Agriculture, Economic Research Service, "History of Agricultural Price-Support and Adjustment Programs, 1933–1984," *Agricultural Information Bulletin*, no. 485 (1984).

4. Title I has covered various commodities over the history of the farm bill, and commodities currently covered in Title I were addressed in other titles in earlier farm bills.

5. Notable agricultural uses included either leaving land fallow, as a horse's pasture or a game animal hunting habitat, or planting stands of timber for eventual harvest. A 2006 news article noted the use of program base to establish 10-acre "cowboy starter kits" that had both farm subsidy payments and room for a horse in the backyard. Dan Morgan, Gilbert M. Gaul, and Sarah Cohen, "Farm Program Pays $1.3 Billion to People Who Don't Farm," *Washington Post*, July 2, 2006.

6. In the question of serious prejudice, the panel failed to find evidence that cotton direct payments contributed to price suppression in world cotton markets. The US used this finding to argue that direct payments were consistent with Annex 2 (green box) criteria that payments be minimally trade distorting.

7. Sen. Paul Wellstone (D-MN) famously termed the "freedom to farm" provisions of the 1996 act as "freedom to fail." The implication was (and is) that farm businesses should not have the freedom to fail.

8. Jim Monke, "Farm Commodity Programs: Base Acreage and Planting Flexibility," Congressional Research Service, September 14, 2005.

9. ACRE statistics were taken from Farm Service Agency sources. Additional details are available in Andrea Woolverton and Edwin Young, "Factors Influencing ACRE Program Enrollment," US Department of Agriculture, Economic Research Service, December 2009.

10. A number of stories highlighted this issue. See, for example, Ron Nixon, "Billionaires Received Farm Subsidies, Report Finds," *New York Times*, November 7, 2013. The phenomenon is not unique to the US. Sir James Dyson, the vacuum cleaner mogul, is the largest private recipient of EU farm subsidies, receiving £1.6 million.

5

US Farm Policy and Trade:
The Inconsistency Continues

JOSEPH W. GLAUBER AND DANIEL A. SUMNER

> *The propensity to truck, barter, and exchange one thing for*
> *another is common to all men.*
> —Adam Smith, *The Wealth of Nations*[1]

Trade is natural. Humans (and other species) trade with other individuals and groups trade with other groups because the natural gains from trade are so compelling. International trade is simply the result of trades that cross national boundaries.[2] There is nothing special about international trade except that national governments seem to be more attune to taxing and regulating such trade—and nowhere more than in agriculture.

As longtime students of agricultural and trade policy may have noticed, our title refers back to D. Gale Johnson's famous 1950 study of the inconsistencies between agricultural and trade policy. In this chapter we show that, while specifics have changed in the past 70 years, US farm policy remains inconsistent with the sort of open international markets that Johnson envisioned and that would most benefit US and world agriculture and the economy more broadly.

In 2016, US agricultural exports totaled $130 billion, and US agricultural imports totaled about $113 billion (Figure 1). The United States Department of Agriculture (USDA) estimates that the share of agricultural production value that was exported rose from 13 percent in 1990 to 20 percent in 2013.[3] For field crops such as cotton, rice, soybeans, and wheat and for many horticultural, fruit, and nut crops, the percentage exported is higher still.

For example, more than 70 percent of upland cotton and two-thirds of all almond production is exported. In the US, agricultural productivity is growing faster than domestic demand for farm commodities. At the same time, global demand growth is accelerating due to the increase in global population, income growth, and rapid urbanization. Thus, US exports are expected to expand and account for a larger share of future domestic production.

A large portion of the $113 billion of agricultural imports are products not produced commercially in the United States due to seasonality, climate, and other natural conditions. Some products are imported for further processing because the United States has natural advantages at that stage of production. For example, the United States imports feeder pigs from Canada and feeder cattle from Mexico because of the availability of low-cost animal feed and efficient meat processing facilities in the United States.

Since the earliest days of the Republic (and even during the colonial period before that), policies have attempted to augment agricultural exports or impede imports. For example, in 1789, duties were imposed on imported sugar in part to raise government revenues.[4] In more recent times, tariffs have been used mostly to protect domestic producers from import competition. While today US agricultural tariffs are some of the lowest in the world, high tariffs and other import impediments remain for many commodities, including sugar, orange juice, fresh tomatoes, and selected dairy products.

US policies have also encouraged agricultural exports to raise prices for domestic producers. Such policies have directly subsidized exports, provided subsidized credit (or credit insurance) for foreign importers, or dumped surplus US production into foreign markets in the guise of food aid. In some cases, all three policies have been used to shift products out of US domestic markets.

In addition to explicit trade subsidies and barriers, the United States has long subsidized domestic production of tradable products through price and income support policies and input subsidies such as crop insurance. To the degree that such policies increase production of favored commodities, they also encourage exports and suppress imports. The form and function of today's policies affect production patterns less than before. Nonetheless, the support provided to farm output, and especially to some politically favored commodities, is currently about $15 billion a year.

Since passage of the Uruguay Round Agreements Act (URAA) in 1994, US agricultural policies have been subject to disciplines under the World

Trade Organization (WTO) and its rules-based negotiated agreements. The URAA's Agreement on Agriculture (AoA), for example, specifies quantitative limits on production-distorting domestic support policies. US domestic support levels have remained below WTO bindings since reporting began in 1995. Apart from cases Canada and Brazil brought against the US in 2007 (later suspended), no one has challenged whether US subsidies (or those of any other major agricultural trading partner) have exceeded the URAA limits. This may be a sign that such limits were designed to be loose enough that no realistic policy options have been precluded.

The URAA also placed limits on export subsidy programs, bound nontariff barriers, and reduced allowable tariffs on agricultural products. These policies have directly affected trade of specific commodities and have occasioned challenges that refined their interpretations and emphasized the binding nature of the restrictions.

Importantly, the URAA also brought agricultural trade under the general WTO rules and disciplines that apply to other trade in goods. Under these provisions, US agricultural policies have been challenged several times, and the United States, as with other members, has attempted to defend its policies under WTO dispute settlement procedures.

For example, Brazil successfully challenged US cotton subsidies by claiming that those policies stimulated US production, thereby causing substantial price depression or suppression in world markets. In that case, Brazil also successfully argued that the US export credit subsidy programs for other commodities and cotton were export subsidies subject to disciplines. More recently, Mexico and Canada successfully challenged—under provisions related to technical barriers to trade—specific features of the US government's implementation of country-of-origin labeling laws that required retailers to provide certain country-of-origin labels for muscle cuts of beef and pork.

Here, we examine the international trade implications of US farm policy and how international trade agreements affect trade and consequences of trade policy. The analysis follows in the intellectual tradition of D. Gale Johnson's seminal research, *Trade and Agriculture: A Study of Inconsistent Policies* and *World Agriculture in Disarray*,[5] which identify how agricultural policies distort both domestic and international markets, as well as numerous American Enterprise Institute studies, several by Johnson, which examine

Figure 1. US Agricultural Trade Since 1935 (Million USD 2009)

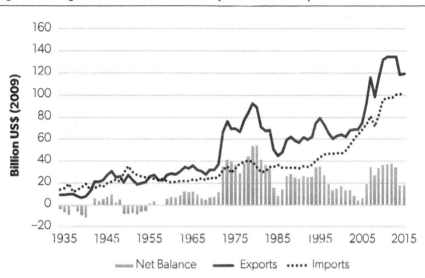

Source: US Department of Agriculture, Foreign Agricultural Service, "Global Agricultural Trade System," https://www.fas.usda.gov/data.

the topic. Since then, several of the specific policy concerns these studies highlighted have been partially remedied, in part because of the intellectual efforts of Johnson and others.

Trends in US Agricultural Trade Since the 1930s

Trade has always been important for US agriculture, but over the past 50 years, US producers and consumers have become increasingly tied to global markets. Figure 1 shows US agricultural imports and exports since 1935, adjusted for inflation. After rising slowly and steadily before 1970, the value of US agricultural exports jumped sharply with the commodity price spikes of the early 1970s. That increase accompanied large grain purchases by the former Soviet Union, jumps in nonfarm commodity prices, and a change in monetary policy that allowed the dollar to float against major currencies. Exports continued strong throughout the 1970s, but in the early 1980s, with tightening monetary policy and domestic support prices above marketing clearing world prices, exports fell sharply, especially for US commodities with price supports.

The 1985 Farm Bill lowered support prices. These reductions in support and a weakening dollar against major currencies allowed exports to rise from 1985 to 1996. The Asian financial crisis in the late 1990s and successive record global grain harvests contributed to a fall in world prices and a decline in exports in the latter half of the 1990s.

From 2004 to 2014, the value of agricultural exports doubled, even after adjusting for general inflation. The sharp growth was due to a strong global demand for agricultural commodities, particularly in emerging economies; a weaker dollar, which enhanced US competitiveness; and higher agricultural prices driven in part by strong demand for energy products, including biofuels.

Exports reached a record $137.8 billion (2009 dollars) in 2014. A stronger dollar and lower commodity prices pushed export values lower in 2015 through 2017. Exports totaled almost $121 billion in 2016, down $17 billion from 2014 levels but more than 60 percent higher than 10 years earlier.

Imports since 1935 have exhibited less variability than exports, but their growth has been equally impressive. From 1996 to 2015, adjusting for inflation, annual imports grew by 4.4 percent. Imports in 2016 were near record levels at $103 billion.

The United States has had a positive trade balance in agriculture since 1960. In 2016, the agricultural trade balance was $18 billion, adjusted for inflation. While down almost 50 percent from 2014 levels, the trade balance was higher than in 2015 and above the average trade balance during the previous decade (2000–09).

The United States is a large net exporter of bulk commodities, particularly soybeans, corn, wheat, and cotton. Cotton is complex because the United States exports raw cotton and imports processed cotton products in the form of textiles and apparel. The United States is a major exporter of tree nuts, processed tomato products, and other storable and bulk horticultural products, but it is generally a net importer for consumer-oriented agricultural goods such as wine and beer, fresh fruits and vegetables, and snack foods (Figure 2).

The US is both a large exporter and large importer of intermediate agricultural goods that are used in food processing. For example, Mexico imports

Figure 2. Composition of US Agricultural Trade, 2014–16 Average

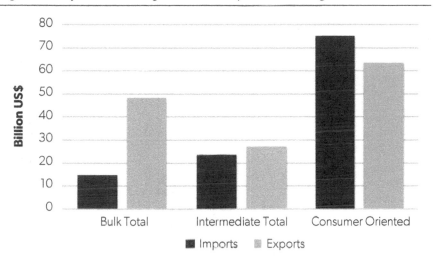

Source: US Department of Agriculture, Foreign Agricultural Service, "Global Agricultural Trade System," https://www.fas. usda.gov/data.

malting barley and hops from the United States for beer production (some of which is exported to the United States). The US imports cattle and pigs from Canada, brings them to slaughter weight, and then processes them into meat products (some of which are sold back to Canada). The US is a net exporter of beef and pork products.

Detailed Export Trends. The top five markets for US exports are China, Canada, Mexico, Japan, and the European Union. Those five markets account for about 60 percent of US agricultural exports. Figure 3 shows the growth of exports to the top export destination and how the top export market has changed since 1970.

For most of the 1970s and 1980s, Europe was the top destination for US agricultural exports. With the growth of subsidies, increases in external barriers, and trade diversion caused by their Common Agricultural Program in the late 1970s and early 1980s, as a bloc, the EU member countries became more insular for many commodities, so US exports to Europe fell. Japan eclipsed the EU as the major importer of US agricultural products starting

Figure 3. Top Destinations for US Agricultural Exports

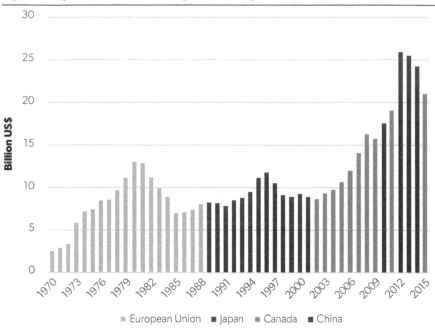

Source: US Department of Agriculture, Foreign Agricultural Service, "Global Agricultural Trade System," https://www.fas. usda.gov/data.

in the late 1980s. Negotiated trade agreements such as the 1984 US-Japan beef-citrus understanding and the 1988 Japanese Beef Market Access Agreement[6] helped partially open the Japanese market to these commodities, augmenting an already-strong market for US soybeans and other products.

The Canada–United States Free Trade Agreement (CUSFTA) in 1987 eliminated tariffs for all but a few notable agricultural products (e.g., dairy, sugar, and poultry). The North American Free Trade Agreement (NAFTA), completed in 1992, saw the phaseout of all agricultural tariffs between the US and Mexico by 2008. By 2003, Canada and Mexico were respectively the number one and two destinations for US agricultural exports.

Since 2010, China has been the top destination for US exports in all but one year (2015), when it was a close second to Canada. In the past, China was a sporadic customer for US grain and oilseeds, largely importing when yields were affected by drought or other adverse weather (e.g., in 1980,

1989, and 1995). After accession to the WTO in 2001 and with growing meat, dairy, and poultry sectors driven by an emerging middle class, China began importing large quantities of soybeans and later feed grains and other feedstuffs.

Textile, shoe, and apparel production stimulated demand for cotton and other inputs such as hides and skins. The US has become a major supplier for those raw materials, and China is now the largest import market for those export commodities, although export volumes to China for individual crops are often constrained by tariff-rate quotas. China is also a major market for horticultural products such as tree nuts, oranges, grapes, raisins, and wine. Table 1 documents that field crop exports are a significant percentage of production exported for corn, cotton, soybeans, rice, and wheat and have been important for a long time. Over most of the period since 1960, about half of rice and wheat production is typically exported. The share of soybean and cotton production that is exported has increased, particularly since 2000. For cotton, the increase is largely due to the collapse of the domestic cotton milling industry in the late 1990s when many domestic mills closed and cotton was diverted to markets in Mexico, Latin America, and Asia. From about two-thirds of cotton being milled in the US in the 1960s, currently about one-quarter of cotton production is milled in the United States.

The growth of soybean exports reflects the growth of animal feeding in China. China imports more than 60 percent of the world soybean exports. For the US, this means about one in every four acres planted to soybeans is exported to China. Corn exports typically accounted for 20–25 percent of domestic production until 2000 when biofuel production began to grow.

In 2000–01, corn use for ethanol accounted for about 6 percent of domestic production. Corn exports that year totaled 1.94 billion bushels and accounted for 19 percent of production. By 2014–15, 5.2 billion bushels of corn were used for ethanol—about 35 percent of corn production that year—while corn exports accounted for about the same quantity as in 2000–01, but only 13 percent of production.

Table 1 also represents the US share of world trade for selected commodities since 1960. For all crops but cotton, US market share has declined. Market shares for corn, wheat, and rice are about half of what the US share was in the 1970s. The market share for soybeans has declined from more than

Table 1. Average Share of US Production Exported for Selected Crops and Share of World Exports, by Decade, Since 1960

Decade	Corn	Cotton	Soybeans	Rice	Wheat
			Percentage of Production		
1960–69	12.2%	34.1%	30.0%	56.7%	53.9%
1970–79	24.6%	43.9%	38.0%	57.7%	57.6%
1980–89	26.3%	47.8%	38.8%	52.7%	58.9%
1990–99	20.8%	40.2%	33.9%	46.5%	48.7%
2000–09	17.9%	68.5%	37.9%	49.2%	48.5%
2010–17f	13.0%	75.4%	46.6%	49.9%	48.2%
			Percentage of Production		
1960–69	52.8%	26.3%	91.4%	18.9%	37.5%
1970–79	73.0%	19.7%	90.4%	22.0%	43.0%
1980–89	73.8%	20.9%	74.0%	20.4%	37.9%
1990–99	70.0%	25.6%	63.8%	13.7%	29.9%
2000–09	59.7%	37.4%	45.0%	11.3%	23.9%
2010–17f	35.9%	30.3%	39.8%	8.2%	17.6%

Source: US Department of Agriculture, "Production, Supply and Distribution Online (PS&D)," https://www.fas.usda.gov/databases/production-supply-and-distribution-online-psd.

90 percent in the 1960s and 1970s to less than 40 percent since 2010. US cotton exports as a share of world trade have increased since 2000, reflecting the decline of the domestic milling industry discussed above, but that market share has fallen back to 30 percent since 2010.

Recent media reports[7] have raised concerns that declining world market shares indicate that US field crops have become less competitive in world markets. But evidence points to the contrary. First, the US continues to export a large share of production. If the US were truly uncompetitive, exports would fall both in absolute and relative terms (that is, as a share of production). Second, for crops such as corn, exports as a share of production have fallen but only because alternative domestic uses such as for biofuel production have been more profitable.

With growth of corn use for ethanol projected to stop over the next 10 years, the USDA projects that corn exports will grow both in absolute volume and relative to production, which is also projected to keep growing.[8]

Figure 4. Change in Planted Acres Since 1990

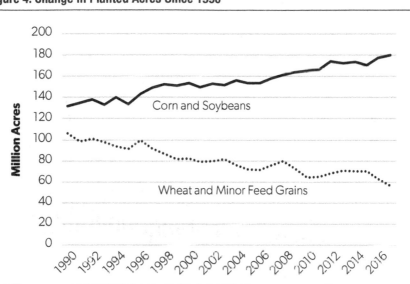

Source: US Department of Agriculture, National Agricultural Statistics Service, "Quick Stats," https://quickstats.nass.usda. gov/.

One factor that could change that would be expanded exports of pork or poultry meat, which would allow more corn to be fed here, while that corn would be implicitly exported as meat.

One of the major reasons why US export share has fallen for many commodities is limits on US production and slower productivity growth in the United States relative to other places. To meet growing global consumption (and to maintain its share of the global market), US planted area must increase, yields must rise, or production must be diverted from other domestic uses to exports (or a combination of these factors).

Cropland in the US is limited, but higher prices led to large shifts in the crop mix after 1990. Figure 4 shows that wheat and minor feed grains acreage declined by about 43.5 million planted acres from 1990 to 2016, which was almost completely offset by an increase of 45.5 million acres planted to corn and soybeans.

Part of the shift in area reflects changes that occurred in the 1990 and 1996 Farm Bills.[9] Before 1990, producers faced steep penalties if they under- or overplanted their crop-specific acreage base. With planting

Figure 5. US Imports by Source

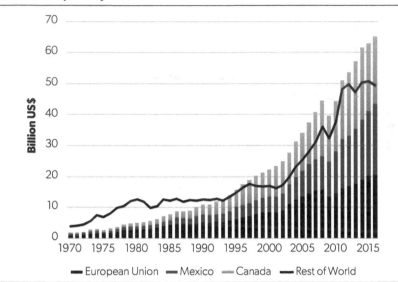

Source: US Department of Agriculture, Foreign Agricultural Service, "Global Agricultural Trade System," https://www.fas.usda.gov/data.

flexibility, producers made cropping decisions largely based on market prices (and per-unit subsidies), which favored corn and soybeans over wheat and minor feed grains. Thus, US wheat became less competitive with corn and soybeans than wheat in other countries.

Outside the United States, much additional field cropland has been brought into production worldwide over the past 30 years. Harvested area in the rest of the world increased by more than 100 million hectares.[10] For wheat, much of the growth in exports has come out of the Black Sea, where countries of the former Soviet Union now account for about 30 percent of world wheat trade.

Russia and Ukraine produce substantial quantities of corn as well. In Brazil, soybean production, and to a lesser extent corn production, has expanded as yields have increased and more land has been brought into production. Thus, while US field crop production remains competitive in world markets, the US share of exports has fallen partly because of expanded domestic demand (ethanol) and partly because of land capacity limit and relatively slow productivity growth.

Detailed Import Trends. Mexico, Canada, and the European Union are the top three import suppliers to the US market, accounting for about 55 percent of total US agricultural imports in 2016 (Figure 4). The growth of Canada and Mexico largely parallels the export picture. In the mid-1980s, they accounted for about 20 percent of US exports. With the passage of CUSFTA and then NAFTA, imports increased to the extent that their combined share of the US market has almost doubled.

The United States generally imports consumer-oriented products such as fresh fruits and vegetables, processed dairy products, meats, snack foods, and beer and wine. Of total imports from Mexico, Canada, and the EU, almost 72 percent were consumer oriented (Figure 5). Another 23 percent of imports were intermediate products used in further food processing in the United States, such as live animals, sugars and sweeteners, essential oils, and cocoa paste. About 5 percent of imports were bulk commodities, largely small quantities of grain from Canada, raw cane sugar and coffee from Mexico, and coffee and tea from the EU.

To summarize, few of the raw agricultural commodity imports directly compete with US production either because of seasonality or because the US produces little of the product (bananas and coffee). Other products are processed and are often branded products that give consumers access to variety. Wine is an example in which the United States is both a major importer and a significant exporter. Wine brands from the United States are found in markets around the world, while wine from many nations compete for consumers in the United States. Other imports include largely raw materials to be processed in the United States.

This classification does leave a few imported commodities, such as orange juice, sugar, and fresh market tomatoes, that do compete directly with US production, and in those cases the United States has attempted to put restrictions in place and tariffs on other imports.

Effects of US Agricultural Policies on Trade

Many US agricultural policies may affect trade. Those policies include border measures such as tariffs that raise consumer prices and insulate producers from global competition, export subsidies that divert production to foreign markets at the expense of domestic consumers and foreign producers, and domestic support policies that distort production decisions and insulate producers from market signals.[11]

Policies That Restrict Imports. Although tariffs on agricultural imports date back to the early years of the United States, today, because of unilateral and multilateral rounds of liberalization, US agricultural tariffs have fallen substantially and are among the lowest in the world. The current average trade-weighted bound tariff is 3.8 percent, and the average simple (unweighted) bound tariff is 4.8 percent.[12] Of course, trade-weighted averages give a misleading picture when tariffs themselves may dramatically reduce the imports for products with high tariffs.

Further, there are important exceptions. Tariffs are relatively high for sugar, peanuts, orange juice, and selected dairy products, which limit imports and insulate domestic prices from lower world prices. The tariff picture is also complicated when considering imports of raw materials because much of the processed product is subsequently exported. In this case, a duty drawback means the effective tariff is much lower (as in the case of tobacco and wine). Table 2 shows the pattern of average and maximum tariffs across product categories.

The United States also makes use of domestic trade remedy laws such as antidumping measures and countervailing duties to protect selected agricultural products against imports from countries. Countervailing duties apply on a handful of products, including raw and roasted in-shell pistachios from Iran, fresh garlic from China, pasta from Italy and Turkey, honey from China, and numerous fresh fish and seafood products from China, Vietnam, India, Thailand, and Brazil.[13]

The United States has also used safeguard provisions under the URAA that allow countries to impose temporary tariffs on imports in the event of domestic price declines or import surges.[14] While in recent years their use has declined, under the URAA, the United States has the right to impose safeguards on 189 narrowly defined agricultural and food products (mostly covering dairy and sugar tariff lines). The United States' most recent use of safeguard provisions was in October 2015, when it imposed prohibitive tariffs on butter and sour cream imports for the rest of the 2015 calendar year.[15]

Table 2. Average and Maximum US-Bound Tariff Levels for Selected Product Groups (Ad Valorem)

Product Group	Average Tariff	Maximum Tariff
Animal Products	2.3%	26%
Dairy Products	16.8%	188%
Fruit, Vegetables, and Plants	4.9%	132%
Coffee and Tea	3.3%	44%
Cereals and Preparations	3.5%	44%
Oilseeds, Fats, and Oils	4.4%	164%
Sugars and Confectionery	12.3%	55%
Beverages and Tobacco	14.8%	350%
Cotton	4.8%	18%
Other Agricultural Products	1.1%	52%
Fish and Fish Products	1.0%	35%

Source: World Trade Organization, "Merchandise Trade Statistics," accessed May 22, 2017, https://www.wto.org/english/res_e/statis_e/merch_trade_stat_e.htm.

Nontariff barriers such as country-of-origin labeling requirements, quality standards, and sanitary and phytosanitary standards can also create effective barriers to imports and raise domestic food and sometimes farm prices. Although such barriers are often intended to deal with concerns such as food safety or plant health, their effect on import flows and prices can bring challenges under the WTO. The United States has often pressed importing countries to relax such barriers that limit US farm and food exports.

Countries that wish to ship products to the United States similarly complain that our measures are sometimes used for protection from competition rather than from some legitimate safety or other public good. For example, in 2015, under threat of retaliation from Canada and Mexico, the United States announced an end to mandatory country-of-origin labeling for certain muscle cuts of beef and pork after the WTO found such regulations violated agreements to avoid undue trade barriers related to agreements on technical barriers to trade.[16]

Policies That Promote Exports. The United States has a long history of using export enhancement tools to augment exports, including direct export subsidies, subsidized credit for buyers who import US farm products, food aid, and subsidized promotion of US farm products in export markets. In the 1950s, support prices that exceeded world market prices stimulated production and reduced domestic use, causing government-held surpluses that were disposed of in world markets as direct food aid or concessional sales.[17]

Subsidized export credit guarantees encouraged importers to purchase US commodities. By the early 1990s, almost all wheat exports were shipped abroad either as food aid or marketed with export subsidies, including export credit guarantees. Export subsidies rose and fell inversely with global prices and totaled as much as $1.3 billion for wheat in 1993.[18]

Under the URAA, the United States agreed to discipline its use of export subsidies. By 1995, US export subsidies, except those for dairy, were largely discontinued. After years of disuse, the Export Enhancement Program was eliminated by the 2008 Farm Bill, and the parallel Dairy Export Incentives Program was terminated by the 2014 Farm Bill. The recently concluded Nairobi Declaration under the WTO prohibits using export subsidies by developed countries by 2020 and limits the tenor on subsidized export credit guarantees to 18 months.[19] The United States had already agreed to tenor limits of 24 months as part of the settlement with Brazil in the United States–Upland Cotton dispute.[20]

US foreign food aid under Public Law 480 (also known as the Food for Peace program) has moved from primarily long-term commodity procurement for distribution as development aid (Title I) to primarily emergency and disaster food assistance and developmental programs to improve food security (Title II). Average spending on US international food aid programs during fiscal years 2006–13 was about $2.5 billion annually, with Title II activities averaging nearly $1.9 billion (76 percent) of annual outlays.[21] Food aid issues are treated in greater detail in Chapter 3 of Volume II.[22]

The United States also provides about $200 million annually for promoting US commodities overseas under the Market Access Program and several smaller related programs. Similar to generic advertising (checkoff) programs, the extent of increased demand for US products overseas because of these programs is limited.[23] USDA-sponsored studies often find positive impacts on exports, but even a positive impact on exports of promoted products does not demonstrate a positive national return on the investment of taxpayer funds.

Domestic Support Programs. Market price support policies and associated land set aside to reduce production were the primary vehicle for supporting US producers from the early days of New Deal legislation through the early 1970s. Nonrecourse loans were originally the vehicle for market price support for grains, sugar, cotton, and oilseed producers. These loans have been redesigned for most commodities to provide direct income support to producers when prices fall below government-set minimums. Market price support is generally considered a highly distorting form of commodity support because it encourages production and maintains prices at artificially high prices for consumers. Of course, a need to limit output or deal with the surplus production is a natural consequence of price supports.

Cash payments, to farmers from the government, supplement producer revenue directly rather than through higher market prices. Currently, the United States provides two types of direct payments: (1) nonrecourse loans with marketing assistance loan provisions paid on actual production and (2) the Agricultural Risk Coverage (ARC) and Price Loss Coverage (PLC) programs with payments paid on historical production. Marketing loans support the effective price received by producers at the loan rate while allowing market prices to fall to market-clearing levels. Marketing loans have not provided income support for more than a decade because loan rates are low relative to prices in the marketplace.

Price-based PLC payments and revenue-based ARC payments are the main subsidies the 2014 Farm Bill introduced and are the field crop subsidy programs currently under consideration for continuation in the next farm bill. These programs link payments to historical production of specific program crops and tie payments to annual realized prices or crop revenues.[24]

While payments are not tied directly to crop plantings, they encourage planting the "program" crops eligible for PLC and ARC payments, as they provide direct safety-net benefits only to the extent that the payment recipient produces the crop covered by the program for which payments are received. The degree of production stimulus has not been estimated for these programs specifically, but that stimulus is likely in the range of earlier programs that tied payments to historical production.[25]

As discussed below, cotton is a special case among the field crops in that it is not eligible for PLC and ARC payments. Cotton continues to participate in the crop insurance program and is eligible for a "shallow loss" area-based revenue insurance program that has not attracted much participation despite an 80 percent premium subsidy.

Crop Insurance. The US crop insurance program has witnessed dramatic growth over the past 25 years.[26] With an annual premium volume of more than $9 billion, it is the largest agricultural insurance program in the world. For major row crops such as corn, wheat, soybeans, and cotton, participation is particularly high; producers typically insure more than 85 percent of eligible acreage and generally at high coverage levels. Participation is also extensive for many additional crops, ranging from dry beans and peas to several fruits and processed vegetable crops.

The program has also involved developing a myriad of products, including revenue products that insure against both price and yield declines, area-based products, and more recently, margin products that insure against declines in revenue or increases in input costs. The 2014 Farm Bill also authorized supplemental coverage options that augment existing subsidized insurance coverage for some producers. With an annual estimated cost to taxpayers of about $8.5 billion, the US crop insurance program is the largest domestic support program in the United States.[27]

Insurance is delivered by private companies, but the USDA approves the insurance products offered, sets premiums, offers substantial premiums subsidies (more than 50 percent of the actuarially fair premium for the most popular products), pays administrative and operations costs for insurance companies, and covers substantial reinsurance costs. In addition to products with subsidized farmer-paid premiums, catastrophic loss policies are offered, for which taxpayers cover the full premium.

When crop insurance is available and priced so that farms acquire coverage, farms produce more. But the pure subsidy impact also matters. Recent papers by Bruce Babcock[28] and Xiaodong Du, Hongli Feng, and David Hennessy[29] point out that if producers are participating in the crop insurance program primarily to "harvest" subsidies, farms do not seem to buy enough insurance. However, over time, producers have tended to sign up for higher coverage levels in which the per-unit subsidies tend to be higher. Joseph Glauber[30] shows that the average coverage levels for most row crops have grown significantly and continuously since the late 1990s, when subsidies were increased for higher coverage levels.

Empirical evidence shows that the US crop insurance program has increased planted area of the covered crops. Barry Goodwin, Monte Vandeveer, and John Deal[31] examined midwestern corn and soybean producers and wheat and barley producers in the Northern Plains and found that a 30 percent decrease in premium costs was likely to increase barley acreage by about 1.1 percent and corn acreage by about 0.5 percent. Soybean and wheat acreage showed no statistically significant impact.

Goodwin and Vincent Smith point out that earlier studies used data before significant subsidy increases and expansion of coverage with new products.[32] More recently, Jisang Yu, Aaron Smith, and Daniel Sumner find that increased crop insurance subsidy rates have had significantly positive impacts on production of major field crops. They find the acreage elasticity to crop insurance subsidies to be about 1.2, much larger than the equivalent area elasticity to market price.[33]

Nonetheless, they showed that the magnitude of the impact on overall acreage of each of the field crops is likely small. For example, their estimates imply that a 20 percent increase in crop insurance subsidies for corn caused an increase in corn acreage of about 0.8 percent. Given the large increase in crop insurance subsidies and expansion coverage in the past, this suggests that the impacts are moderate but not negligible.

Crop insurance subsidies have likely had small impacts on production for crops and in areas where insurance is broadly available across crops. Crop insurance likely has larger impacts on crop choice when insured crops compete against uninsured crops, or when crops in which revenue insurance is available compete against crops in which only yield insurance is available.[34]

Dairy Subsidy Policy. The 2014 Farm Bill suspended long-standing price support programs for milk and a direct payment program tied to milk prices. The replacement, a payment tied to the national average margin between milk price and an index of feed prices, has not attracted much farmer participation at the coverage levels that require farmer-paid premiums. Although milk prices have been low by historical standards, low feed prices have limited the anticipated (and actual) payouts from the program. The impact on milk production remains positive because the long-term expected value of the subsidy is positive. However, the magnitude of the effect is subject to much debate because it depends on the accuracy of long-term forecasts

Figure 6. Trends in US Domestic Support

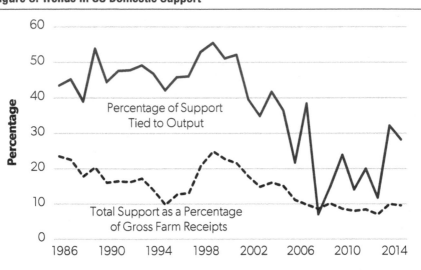

Source: Organisation for Economic Co-operation and Development, "Producer and Consumer Support Estimates Database," accessed May 22, 2017, http://www.oecd.org/tad/agricultural-policies/producerandconsumersupportestimates database.htm.

about milk and feed prices, given that premiums, which were thought to have had substantial subsidy, were written into the farm bill.

Milk marketing orders could also affect trade. These policies, operated by the federal government and also by a few states (including California, which produces almost 20 percent of US milk), raise the price of beverage milk and other products that are mostly not traded internationally (price discrimination) and use that revenue to raise the average revenue per unit of milk produced (price pooling). The result is more production of traded products such as dry milk power, butter, cheese, and whey. Hence, marketing orders have the potential to stimulate US dairy exports and suppress imports. The policy parameters and impacts are regional, and no recent national estimates of the quantitative impacts on trade are available.

In summary, US domestic support, as measured by the Organisation for Economic Co-operation and Development's Producer Support Estimate, has declined by more than 50 percent since 1986 (Figure 6). However, since many of the US domestic support programs are tied to price or revenues, they vary substantially from year to year. For example, US support levels declined to about 10 percent of gross farm receipts in the mid-1990s, but as world prices fell in the late 1990s, support levels more than doubled by the early 2000s. The percentage of support tied to production has also fallen since 1986, but the degree to which subsidies are tied to production rose with the passage of the 2014 Farm Bill.

US Farm Policy and the WTO

Agricultural subsidies have long been criticized for their distortionary impacts in world markets.[35] During the 1950s and 1960s, US price supports resulted in large inventories of grains and cotton. Those surpluses were often dumped on world markets as concessional food aid[36] or through direct export subsidies.[37] Food aid recipients may have gained through lower food prices and increased food availability, but foreign producers were hurt through lower prices, and in many instances, commercial exports were displaced by subsidized sales. High price supports also insulated US producers from market signals, which distorted production decisions and depressed world prices.[38]

As US agricultural supports have evolved away from direct price support based on actual plantings to income support programs decoupled from production, the distortionary effects are less clear. However, Goodwin and Ashok Mishra[39] and Nathan Hendricks and Daniel Sumner[40] have questioned whether payments are truly decoupled from production, even if the effects are less commodity specific than payments tied to planted acreage.

Since 1995, the United States has been obligated to report agricultural subsidies to the WTO under the URAA. Domestic support disciplines under the URAA distinguish among programs that are viewed as minimally trade distorting and those that are not. Green box subsidies are judged to have only minimal trade-distorting effects and are exempt from reduction under the URAA. To be included in the green box, programs must not be tied to current production or current market prices and must meet specific policy criteria spelled out in Annex 2 of the URAA.[41]

Amber box subsidies are classified as having more than minimal trade-distorting effects and are capped under the terms of the AoA. Amber box support includes payments to producers that are tied to current

Table 3. Classification of Selected US Domestic Support Policies for WTO Reporting Purposes

Type of Support	Examples	Classification for WTO Reporting Purposes
Conservation Acreage Set Asides	Conservation Reserve Program	Green
Conservation Cost-Share Programs	Conservation Stewardship Program; Environmental Quality Incentives Program	Green
Nutrition Programs	Supplemental Nutrition Assistance Program; National School Lunch Program; Women, Infants, and Children Program	Green
Market Price Support	Sugar Loan Program	Product-Specific Amber
Output-Based Income Support	Marketing Assistance Loan Program	Product-Specific Amber
Crop Insurance Premium Subsidies	Federal Crop Insurance Program	Product-Specific Amber
Decoupled Price-Linked Countercyclical Program	Price Loss Coverage	Non-Product-Specific Amber
Decoupled Revenue-Linked Countercyclical Program	Agricultural Risk Coverage	Non-Product-Specific Amber
Margin Insurance	Dairy Margin Protection Plan	Product-Specific Amber
Biofuel Program	Biomass Crop Assistance Program	Non-Product-Specific Amber

Source: World Trade Organization, "Agriculture Management Information System," accessed May 22, 2017, http://agims. wto.org/Pages/SearchNotifCirculated.aspx?ReportId=1201&Reset=true&ReportType=12.

production levels, market price support programs, and other policies that make payments based on current output and current market prices such as crop insurance programs. These subsidies are converted into an Aggregate Measurement of Support (AMS) using a set of predetermined and prescribed accounting rules. Under the AoA, each country commits to maintain its total current AMS below an agreed level. For the United States, the AMS cap on amber box program subsidies is $19.1 billion.

Figure 7. US Total Trade-Distorting Support

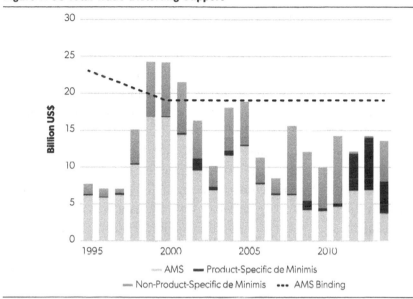

Source: World Trade Organization, "Agricultural Information Management System," http://agims.wto.org/.

Amber box subsidies are further classified into two groups—product-specific and non-product-specific support—and both categories are subject to de minimis tests that exempt support below a specific share of the value of production from the reported AMS. For developed countries such as the United States, if the estimated level of support is less than 5 percent of the value of current production, support is considered de minimis and excluded from calculations of the total current AMS.

Table 3 reflects how the United States has self-notified selected agricultural domestic support programs to the WTO. Most of the programs that provide price or income support to producers are reported as amber unless they meet criteria to qualify for Annex 2 (green box) designation. Environmental programs such as the Conservation Reserve Program and Conservation Stewardship Program are reported as green box as were fixed historical payments under the 1996–2008 Farm Bills.

US domestic support levels, as measured by the reported AMS, have remained below WTO bindings since reporting began in 1995 (Figure 7). If de minimis support were included, the total AMS would have exceeded limits in 1999–2001. Because of the countercyclical nature of many US farm programs, outlays and AMS levels can fluctuate year to year based on prices, which has raised concerns that new programs could breach AMS bindings if prices for major commodities were to fall to low levels.[42] Since 2002, farm bills have included authority for the US secretary of agriculture to cut agricultural spending if it appeared that WTO limits would be breached; however, as this situation has never arisen, it is unclear how such remedies would be imposed.

Moreover, countries have raised concerns with how the United States has classified domestic support. In 2007, Canada and Brazil brought separate cases to the WTO Dispute Settlement Body arguing that the United States had misclassified several programs such as crop insurance and countercyclical payments as non-product-specific support. Had the programs been notified as product-specific amber support, they argued, the US AMS would have exceeded US bindings. The cases were ultimately suspended (likely since support levels had fallen considerably by 2008 due to then-record-high commodity prices). Presumably, such cases could be renewed or new cases could be brought to the WTO that would raise similar concerns if support levels were to rise again and seem likely to remain above the limits for an extended period.

Implications of WTO Dispute Settlement Cases for Agricultural Policy

Since 1995, more than 500 disputes have been brought to the WTO, and more than 350 rulings have been issued.[43] As of May 2017, the US has brought 114 cases against other countries, of which 26 were for alleged violations of the AoA. The US has been the respondent in 129 cases, of which 10 were for alleged violations of the AoA. Many of the cases brought by the United States have involved agricultural products, although in some cases the claim did not involve violations of the AoA.

For example, in 1999, the United States challenged the European Union over using geographic indications (EC–Trademarks and Geographical Indications) under the Trade-Related Aspects of Intellectual Property Rights Agreement. In fact, complainants in WTO disputes will often cite violations in several agreements, so even if a measure is challenged under the AoA, challenges under other agreements may be more relevant and important. Several WTO cases involving US policies have influenced WTO precedent and US laws and regulation affecting agricultural commodities.

The Brazil cotton case (US–Upland Cotton) is probably the most prominent agricultural subsidy dispute to be settled at the WTO. In 2003, Brazil claimed that a wide range of US cotton programs were stimulating additional US cotton production and exports, causing serious prejudice to Brazil cotton producer interests by suppressing and depressing world cotton prices. In addition, Brazil charged that both the US export credit programs (for cotton and other commodities) and the cotton Step 2 program, which paid exporters a competitiveness payment, constituted prohibited export subsidies and should be withdrawn.

The serious prejudice charge was brought not under the AoA, but under the Subsidies and Countervailing Measures (SCM) Agreement. Under the SCM Agreement, the relevant question for the dispute settlement panel was whether, without US cotton subsidies, US cotton production would have been lower and therefore world market prices substantially higher.[44]

In September 2004, a WTO dispute settlement panel ruled that (1) certain US agricultural support payments for cotton suppressed and depressed cotton prices enough to cause serious prejudice and should be either withdrawn or modified to end the serious prejudice, and (2) US Step 2 payments and agricultural export credit guarantees for cotton and other unscheduled commodities were prohibited subsidies under WTO rules and should be withdrawn.[45] Brazil won several additional rounds of appeal and was finally awarded the right to retaliate by withdrawing trade concessions that benefited the United States.

After a few hundred million dollars in payments from the US government to the Brazilian cotton industry, in 2014 Brazil agreed to suspend the WTO retaliation in return for changes made to the cotton program as part of the 2014 Farm Bill. However, dissatisfaction with the resultant program (known informally as the Stacked Income Protection Program), a revenue insurance program that replaced the direct and countercyclical programs, prompted the cotton industry to successfully lobby for a new countercyclical payment program for seed cotton, which Congress passed in early 2018. Such a program could trigger a WTO challenge by Brazil and perhaps other cotton market participants.

Table 4. Support Levels as a Percentage of Revenue and US Share of Global Exports, Before and After the 2014 Farm Bill

Crop	Domestic Support as a Percentage of Production Value		US Exports as a Percentage of World Exports	
	2013	2015*	2011–13	2014–17
Corn	4.9	12.8	31.0	34.9
Cotton	9.2	17.6	26.4	33.7
Peanuts	3.5	48.6	14.5	16.6
Rice	1.4	24.2	7.8	8.1
Soybeans	3.5	6.8	38.6	39.3
Wheat	9.0	20.6	19.1	14.4

Note: *2015 support levels include payments for ARC and PLC but do not include crop insurance subsidy.
Source: US Department of Agriculture, "Production, Supply and Distribution Online (PS&D)," https://www.fas.usda.gov/databases/production-supply-and-distribution-online-psd; World Trade Organization, "Agriculture Management Information System," accessed May 22, 2017, http://agims.wto.org/Pages/SearchNotifCirculated.aspx?ReportId=1201&Reset=true&ReportType=12; and US Department of Agriculture, Foreign Agriculture Service, "PSD Online," accessed May 22, 2017, https://apps.fas.usda.gov/psdonline/app/index.html#/app/home.

The US–Upland Cotton dispute dealt with specific policies and market issues and may not provide a template for challenges to other crop programs as some have argued.[46] Indeed, no other major case has followed this path, although some proposed cases with similar elements have been settled at the early stages. Table 4 shows how US farm subsidies have changed between the 2013 reporting year (the 2008 Farm Bill and market conditions during that period) and the 2015 reporting year (2014 Farm Bill and 2015 market conditions). ARC and PLC payments are included in support levels for 2015.[47] Each of the selected crops shows an increase in domestic support measured as a percentage of that crop's production value.

Furthermore, crop insurance subsidies are not included in these calculations. Table 4 also shows that export market shares have increased for all crops shown except wheat since the passage of the 2014 Farm Bill. While a successful challenge under the SCM Agreement would require far more rigorous analysis, the Brazil cotton dispute resolution suggests that US programs are likely vulnerable to challenge, and it should send a cautionary note to advocates of higher subsidies.

Conclusions

US agricultural trade has grown significantly over the past 25 years. That trend is anticipated to continue as larger shares of projected US productivity gains are expected to be exported, and import growth is likely to continue reflecting global trends toward more diverse diets. While the United States will continue as a major exporter of food and fiber, its share of world trade will likely diminish as production growth slows relative to that in other places.

The symptoms of disarray in world agriculture that Johnson addressed in the early 1970s have been mitigated somewhat. Policy reforms stimulated in part by trade agreements and formation of the WTO have reduced production and export subsidies and have lowered tariffs to facilitate market-driven trade. Moreover, income gains, in part because of such liberalization, have fueled demand growth, which has further stimulated trade.

Despite progress, distortions remain. After more than 80 years, New Deal farm programs remain fixtures in domestic and global agricultural markets. Farm programs may have been viewed in the 1930s as temporary emergency measures, but they have so far proved impervious to attempts to eliminate them and the market distortions they create. And while program specifics have been altered, they continue to transfer billions of dollars from taxpayers and consumers to favored industries, thereby modifying production patterns and affecting market prices. The policies continue to have serious consequences for not only world markets and international relationships but also domestic consumers and taxpayers.

Notes

1. Adam Smith, *The Wealth of Nations* (Chicago: University of Chicago Press, 1976).

2. We emphasize the compelling nature of trade at the outset to help clarify that when governments attempt to impede trade, such policy takes substantial effort. International trade conventionally means trade between individuals or other entities located in different nation-states. International trade seldom refers to trade between nations. It may even refer to shipments from one division of a company to another, as when a company ships raw materials for further processing across a border. Here we will use conventional shorthand and sometimes use trade between the United States and some other country to refer to shipments that are from some person or company located in the United States to

some individual or company located in some other country. For example, we will use the term "US exports" to mean shipments to buyers located outside the United States.

3. US Department of Agriculture, Economic Research Service, "US Agricultural Trade," accessed May 22, 2017, https://www.ers.usda.gov/topics/international-markets-trade/us-agricultural-trade/.

4. Murray R. Benedict, *Farm Policies of the United States, 1790–1950* (New York: Twentieth Century Fund, 1953); and Frank William Taussig, *The Tariff History of the United States* (New York: J. P. Putnam's Sons, 1910).

5. D. Gale Johnson, *Trade and Agriculture: A Study of Inconsistent Policies* (New York: John Wiley and Sons, 1950); and D. Gale Johnson, *World Agriculture in Disarray* (New York: St. Martin's Press and New Viewpoints, 1973).

6. William D. Gorman, Hiroshi Mori, and Biing-Hwan Lin, "Beef in Japan: The Challenge for United States Exports," *Journal of Food Distribution Research* (February 1990): 17–30, http://ageconsearch.umn.edu/record/26965/files/21010017.pdf.

7. Jesse Newman and Patrick McGroarty, "Plowed Under: The Next American Farm Bust Is upon Us," *Wall Street Journal*, February 8, 2017, https://www.wsj.com/articles/the-next-american-farm-bust-is-upon-us-1486572488?tesla=y; and Alan Bjerga, Cindy Hoffman, and Blacki Migliozzi, "How US Farmers Are Winning—and Losing—with Exports," Bloomberg News, March 13, 2017, https://www.bloomberg.com/graphics/2017-commodity-exports/.

8. US Department of Agriculture, Economic Research Service, "International Baseline Data," accessed May 22, 2017, https://www.ers.usda.gov/data-products/international-baseline-data/.

9. Planting flexibility applied to row crops only; restrictions remained on fruit and vegetable production on base acres. Those restrictions were partially relaxed in the 2014 Farm Bill.

10. US Department of Agriculture, Foreign Agriculture Service, "PSD Online," accessed May 22, 2017, https://apps.fas.usda.gov/psdonline/app/index.html#/app/home.

11. This section draws heavily on two reports: Joseph W. Glauber and Anne Effland, "US Agricultural Policy: Its Evolution and Impact," International Food Policy Research Institute, July 2016, http://www.ifpri.org/publication/united-states-agricultural-policy-its-evolution-and-impact; and Joseph W. Glauber, Daniel A. Sumner, and Parke E. Wilde, *Poverty, Hunger, and US Agricultural Policy: Do Farm Programs Affect the Nutrition of Poor Americans?*, American Enterprise Institute, January 9, 2017, http://www.aei.org/publication/poverty-hunger-and-us-agricultural-policy-do-farm-programs-affect-the-nutrition-of-poor-americans/.

12. The bound tariff rate is the most-favored-nation tariff rate resulting from negotiations under the General Agreement on Tariffs and Trade and incorporated as an integral component of a country's schedule of concessions or commitments to other World Trade Organization members. World Trade Organization, "Merchandise Trade Statistics," accessed May 22, 2017, https://www.wto.org/english/res_e/statis_e/merch_trade_stat_e.htm.

13. US International Trade Commission, "Antidumping and Countervailing Duty Actions," accessed May 22, 2017, https://usitc.gov/sites/default/files/trade_remedy/documents/orders.xls.

14. Qualifying products are restricted to those products for which nontariff barriers

were converted to tariffs as a part of the Uruguay Round WTO agreement.

15. World Trade Organization, "Agriculture Management Information System," accessed May 22, 2017, http://agims.wto.org/Pages/SearchNotifCirculated.aspx?ReportId=1201&Reset=true&ReportType=12.

16. US Department of Agriculture, Agricultural Marketing Service, "Removal of Mandatory Country of Origin Labeling Requirements for Beef and Pork Muscle Cuts, Ground Beef, and Ground Pork," February 2016, https://www.ams.usda.gov/rules-regulations/removal-mandatory-country-origin-labeling-requirements-beef-and-pork-muscle-cuts.

17. Christopher B. Barrett and Daniel G. Maxwell, *Food Aid After Fifty Years: Recasting Its Role* (London: Routledge, 2005).

18. Bruce L. Gardner, "The Political Economy of U.S. Export Subsidies for Wheat," in *The Political Economy of American Trade Policy*, ed. Anne O. Krueger (Chicago: University of Chicago Press, 1994), 291–334, http://www.nber.org/papers/w4747.

19. The tenor is the length of time until the loan is due.

20. Randy Schnepf, "Status of the WTO Brazil-US Cotton Case," Congressional Research Service, October 1, 2014, http://nationalaglawcenter.org/wp-content/uploads/assets/crs/R43336.pdf.

21. Randy Schnepf, "US International Food Aid Programs: Background and Issues," Congressional Research Service, September 14, 2016, https://fas.org/sgp/crs/misc/R41072.pdf.

22. Erin C. Lentz, Stephanie Mercier, and Christopher B. Barrett, *International Food Aid and Food Assistance Programs and the Next Farm Bill*, American Enterprise Institute, October 19, 2017, http://www.aei.org/publication/international-food-aid-and-food-assistance-programs-and-the-next-farm-bill/.

23. Gary W. Williams and Oral Capps Jr., "Measuring the Effectiveness of Checkoff Programs," *Choices* 21, no. 2 (2006): 73–78, http://www.choicesmagazine.org/2006-2/checkoff/2006-2-05.htm; and Michael K. Wohlgenant, "Retail-to-Farm Transmission of Generic Advertising Effects," *Choices* 21, no. 2 (2006): 67–72, http://www.choicesmagazine.org/2006-2/checkoff/2006-2-04.htm.

24. Eligible crops include wheat, oats, barley, corn, grain sorghum, rice, soybeans, sunflower seed, rapeseed, canola, safflower, flaxseed, mustard seed, crambe and sesame seed, dry peas, lentils, small chickpeas, large chickpeas, and peanuts.

25. Jesús Anton and Chantal Le Mouël, "Do Counter-Cyclical Payments in the 2002 US Farm Act Create Incentives to Produce?," *Agricultural Economics* 31, no. 2–3 (December 2004): 277–84, http://www.sciencedirect.com/science/article/pii/S0169515004001033; Erik J. O'Donoghue and James B. Whitaker, "Do Direct Payments Distort Producers' Decisions? An Examination of the Farm Security and Rural Investment Act of 2002," *Applied Economic Perspectives and Policy* 32, no. 1 (2010): 170–193, https://academic.oup.com/aepp/article/32/1/170/7984/Do-Direct-Payments-Distort-Producers-Decisions-An; and Arathi Bhaskar and John C. Beghin, "How Coupled Are Decoupled Farm Payments? A Review of the Evidence," *Journal of Agricultural and Resource Economics* 34, no. 1 (2009): 130–53, https://www.jstor.org/stable/41548405?seq=1#page_scan_tab_contents.

26. Joseph W. Glauber, "Crop Insurance Reconsidered," *American Journal of Agricultural Economics* 86, no. 5 (2004): 1179–95; and Joseph Glauber, "The Growth of the Federal Crop Insurance Program, 1990–2011," *American Journal of Agricultural Economics*

95, no. 2 (2012): 482–88.

27. Congressional Budget Office, "Baseline Projections for Selected Programs," accessed August 22, 2017, https://www.cbo.gov/about/products/baseline-projections-selected-programs#25.

28. Bruce A. Babcock, "Using Cumulative Prospect Theory to Explain Anomalous Crop Insurance Coverage Choice," *American Journal of Agricultural Economics* 97, no. 5 (2015): 1317–84.

29. Xiaodong Du, Hongli Feng, and David A. Hennessy, "Rationality of Choices in Subsidized Crop Insurance Markets," *American Journal of Agricultural Economics* 99, no. 3 (2017): 732–56.

30. Glauber, "The Growth of the Federal Crop Insurance Program, 1990–2011."

31. Barry K. Goodwin, Monte L. Vandeveer, and John L. Deal, "An Empirical Analysis of Acreage Effects of Participation in the Federal Crop Insurance Program," *American Journal of Agricultural Economics* 86, no. 4 (2004): 1058–77.

32. Barry Goodwin and Vincent H. Smith, "What Harm Is Done in Subsidizing Insurance?," *American Journal of Agricultural Economics* 95, no. 2 (2012): 489–97.

33. Jisang Yu, Aaron Smith, and Daniel A. Sumner, "Effects of Crop Insurance Premium Subsidies on Crop Insurance Premium," *American Journal of Agricultural Economics* 100, no. 1 (2017).

34. JunJie J. Wu and Richard M. Adams, "Production Risk, Acreage Decisions and Implications for Revenue Insurance Programs," *Canadian Journal of Agricultural Economics* 49, no. 1 (2001): 19–35.

35. Johnson, *World Agriculture in Disarray*; and Organisation for Economic Co-operation and Development, "National Policies and Agricultural Trade," 1987.

36. Barrett and Maxwell, *Food Aid After Fifty Years.*

37. Gardner, "The Political Economy of U.S. Export Subsidies for Wheat"; and Daniel A. Sumner, *Agricultural Trade Policy: Letting Markets Work* (Washington, DC: AEI Press, 1995), http://www.aei.org/publication/agricultural-trade-policy/.

38. Johnson, *World Agriculture in Disarray.*

39. Barry K. Goodwin and Ashok K. Mishra, "Another Look at Decoupling: Additional Evidence of the Production Effects of Direct Payments," *American Journal of Agricultural Economics* 87, no. 5 (2005): 1200–10; and Barry K. Goodwin and Ashok K. Mishra, "Are 'Decoupled' Farm Program Payments Really Decoupled?," *American Journal of Agricultural Economics* 88, no. 1 (2006): 73–89.

40. Nathan P. Hendricks and Daniel A. Sumner, "The Effects of Policy Expectations on Crop Supply, with an Application to Base Updating," *American Journal of Agricultural Economics* 96, no. 3 (2014): 903–23.

41. A third category of trade-distorting support, called blue box support, is addressed in Article 6.5 of the URAA. Any subsidies and other forms of income transfers that would normally be included in the amber box are placed in the blue box if the program under which those income transfers occur also requires farmers to limit production. Under the URAA, blue box expenditures are not capped and, therefore, not subject to any WTO disciplines. The United States notified its deficiency payment program as blue box in 1995, but that program was eliminated in the 1996 Farm Bill.

42. Joseph W. Glauber and Patrick Westhoff, "WTO Compliance Under the 2014

Farm Bill," in *The Economic Welfare and Trade Relations Implication of the 2014 Farm Bill*, ed. Vincent H. Smith (Bingley, UK: Emerald Group Publishing, 2016): 59–74.

43. World Trade Organization, "Agriculture Management Information System."

44. That analysis is materially different from many of the studies previously discussed that consider the effects of removing all agricultural subsidies (i.e., from all crops). Here, the analysis examines removing cotton subsides only (i.e., subsidies for other crops were assumed unaffected).

45. Schnepf, "Status of the WTO Brazil-US Cotton Case."

46. Scott D. Andersen and Meredith Taylor, "Brazil's Challenge to US Cotton Subsidies: The Road to Effective Disciplines of Agricultural Subsidies," *Business Law Brief* 6, no. 1 (2009).

Section III

Commodity-Specific Programs

6

Analysis of the US Sugar Program

JOHN C. BEGHIN AND AMANI ELOBEID

The US sugar program is a protectionist scheme destined to transfer income to sugar growers and processors at the cost of sugar users and consumers. The program's nature has changed little over time, and it works by reducing the flow of sugar imports to the United States. Its existence had been threatened under the North American Free Trade Agreement (NAFTA) because of increasing imports from Mexico, but a recent bilateral US-Mexico agreement has removed this threat. The entrenched US sugar lobby has been effective at blocking any meaningful reform and removing threats from preferential agreements with other sugar-producing nations. Sugar interests are concentrated, whereas losses born by most consumers and users are more diffuse and small at the individual level. Yet collectively, the losses to consumers and users are large in aggregate for the country, in the order of $2.4–$4 billion. The US sugar program should be repealed.

In the following sections, we provide some background and review of the US sugar program's history; its key features; its impact on producers, consumers, and users; its cost to society; and its impact on trade and world prices. We also devote some attention to recent market and policy developments under NAFTA. Policy implications are drawn.

Background

The United States is one of the largest sugar producers in the world, surpassed by only Brazil, China, the European Union, India, and Thailand. In 2014–15, the United States produced almost 7.9 million metric tons raw value (mtrv) of sugar and is estimated to produce 8.2 million mtrv in

2015–16.[1] This accounted for 4.4 percent of world sugar production in 2015 and 4.9 percent in 2016.

Sugar producers and processors in the United States benefit from government support in the form of price support loans, domestic marketing allotments, tariff-rate quotas (TRQs),[2] and the diversion of excess sugar to ethanol production. The sugar policy is part of the US farm bill and is administered by the US Department of Agriculture (USDA) ideally at no budgetary cost to the federal government, when possible, by avoiding loan forfeitures.[3] Through the sugar program, sugar producers and sugar processors have enjoyed domestic raw sugar prices well above the world sugar prices, varying from 238 percent over the world price in 1999 to 17 percent over the world price in 2013 (Table 1).

Brief History of the US Sugar Policy

The US sugar industry has enjoyed trade protections since 1789 when the first import tariff against foreign-produced sugar was imposed to generate government revenue. In 1842, protection was expanded to promote domestic sugar production and restrict trade. Since then, the US government has continued to provide support and protection for the domestic sugar industry. Under the Sugar Act of 1934, which as amended remained in force until 1974, sugar beets and sugarcane were considered basic commodities, and import quotas and marketing allotments were imposed to protect mostly sugar beet producers from declining sugar prices.[4] Marketing allotments limited how much domestically produced sugar could be sold by sugar processors during any given year. In addition, sugar beet and sugarcane farmers received a direct subsidy for the sugar they produced. The Food and Agriculture Act of 1977 also offered support to sugar beet and sugarcane producers through government loan rates for sugar beet and sugarcane. (The loan rate is the price per pound of sugar at which processors can take out loans.)

The current sugar program was established in the Agriculture and Food Act of 1981 (1981 Farm Bill) and, with some modifications, has been renewed in subsequent farm bills. The program continued to support domestic prices of sugar beet and sugarcane. The secretary of agriculture

Table 1. Comparison of the World and US Raw and Refined Sugar Price (Cents per Pound)

Marketing Year	World Raw Price	US Raw Price	Difference Between US and World Price	World Refined Price	US Refined Price	Difference Between US and World Price
1999	6.5	22.1	238%	9.8	27.0	175%
2000	7.3	18.4	153%	9.1	21.9	141%
2001	9.0	21.1	133%	11.4	22.1	95%
2002	6.4	20.6	225%	10.6	25.5	141%
2003	7.3	21.8	199%	10.1	27.0	169%
2004	6.5	20.5	216%	10.3	23.7	131%
2005	9.1	20.9	131%	12.5	25.6	106%
2006	14.8	22.6	52%	18.4	36.0	96%
2007	10.3	20.9	103%	14.9	25.7	73%
2008	11.7	21.3	81%	15.6	29.9	92%
2009	14.9	22.1	48%	18.9	35.9	90%
2010	21.0	34.2	63%	26.5	50.3	90%
2011	28.4	38.5	35%	32.6	55.8	71%
2012	22.9	32.5	42%	27.8	49.3	77%
2013	18.0	21.0	17%	22.8	28.8	26%
2014	16.8	23.1	37%	20.7	30.7	48%
2015	13.4	24.7	84%	17.1	34.9	104%

Note: World raw sugar price is the Intercontinental Exchange (ICE) Contract no. 11 nearby futures price, and the US raw sugar price is the ICE Contract no. 14–16 nearby futures price, duty fee paid, New York. World refined sugar price is the ICE Contract no. 407 (also referred to as no. 5) London daily price, free on board Europe, spot, through June 2006 and the average of nearest futures after June 2006.
Source: US Department of Agriculture, Economic Research Service, "Sugar and Sweetener Yearbook Tables: World Production, Supply, and Distribution, Centrifugal Sugar," 2016, Tables 3b and 4, https://www.ers.usda.gov/data-products/sugar-and-sweeteners-yearbook-tables/.

was authorized to support sugarcane through purchasing processed sugar to attain a raw sugar price of 16.75 cents per pound and guarantee a sugar beet price that would be deemed fair and reasonable relative to the support level of sugarcane. Price support would be ensured through the provision of nonrecourse loans, which were to increase from 17 cents per pound for raw sugar for the 1982 crop to 18 cents per pound for the 1985 crop. Sugar beet prices were also supported through nonrecourse loans at levels deemed fair and reasonable in relation to sugarcane.[5]

One major addition to the 1977 Farm Bill's provisions was the Refined Sugar Re-Export Program, established in 1983. The program allowed sugarcane processors to purchase raw sugar at world prices (duty free) and export a similar amount in 90 days.[6] The sugar program was expected to operate at no cost to the federal government by avoiding forfeitures of sugar under the loan program. This was to be accomplished by sufficiently restricting imports of sugar through import quotas to maintain domestic prices above the loan rates for cane and beet processed sugar. Import quotas were retained in the 1990 Farm Bill (Food, Agriculture, Conservation, and Trade Act of 1990), which also directed the USDA to establish marketing allotments on domestically produced sugar beet and sugarcane that would raise sugar imports if the amount of imported sugar was less than 1.25 million short tons raw value (strv). The secretary of agriculture had the authority to allocate marketing allotments between sugar derived from sugar beets and sugarcane and adjust or suspend those allotments depending on market conditions.[7]

Nonrecourse loans and import restrictions (TRQs) continued under the 2002 Farm Bill (Farm Security and Rural Investment Act of 2002). Marketing allotments, which had not been used between 1996 and 2002, were to be imposed when imports were projected to be below 1.531 million short tons. An inventory management authority allowed the secretary of agriculture to establish marketing allotments to balance markets, avoid forfeitures, and comply with World Trade Organization (WTO) and NAFTA import commitments.

In addition, a sugar payment-in-kind program permitted sugar beet and sugarcane producers and processors to reduce crop production in exchange for sugar in the USDA's Commodity Credit Corporation (CCC) inventory. Under the program, producers could offer bids for the amount of sugar the CCC held that producers would obtain in exchange for a given reduction in harvesting planted acres. Further, under the 2002 Farm Bill, marketing assessments on all processed sugar and forfeiture penalties on sugar beet and sugarcane processors were terminated, and the interest rate on CCC sugar loans was reduced.[8]

The Food, Conservation, and Energy Act of 2008[9] required the USDA to manage the US domestic supply of sugar and sugar imports to keep market prices above the loan rates for cane and beet sugar. The bill also introduced a sugar-for-ethanol program, which authorizes the USDA to purchase excess US sugar resulting from increased imports coming in from Mexico through NAFTA and other countries through free trade agreements. The surplus sugar is then sold to US bioenergy producers to process into ethanol.

Minimum guaranteed prices for raw sugar and refined beet sugar were also increased in 2008. The program also mandated that the overall allotment quantity (OAQ) be set at no less than 85 percent of estimated US human sugar consumption for food.[10] However, this provision has not always been met, with the OAQ falling below 85 percent in many years. An additional provision allowed the USDA to increase WTO quotas for sugar beyond the minimum level if there is a shortage of sugar because of adverse weather or war.

Key Elements of the Current Sugar Program

The Agricultural Act of 2014, the current farm bill,[11] retains most of the 2008 Farm Bill's provisions relating to the protection of US sugar through mechanisms that guarantee minimum domestic prices for sugarcane and sugar beet producers and processors. In terms of price support, during the 2014–18 fiscal years, domestic sugarcane and sugar beet processors can obtain non-recourse loans at set loan rate levels using sugar as collateral, which can be repaid with interest after the processors sell the sugar. The loans are available at the beginning of each fiscal year (October). The processors must repay the nine-month loan by the end of the fiscal year (September 30 of the following calendar year). To obtain the loan, the sugar must come from domestically grown sugar beets or sugarcane, grown in compliance with "cross compliance" highly erodible land and wetlands regulations.

Processors must pay sugarcane and sugar beet farmers an amount proportional to the loan received by the processors. The processors can sell the sugar and repay the loan if market prices exceed the loan rate. Alternatively, a processor has the choice of forfeiting the sugar under loan to the USDA's CCC. The CCC is then responsible for disposing the forfeited sugar, which counts against the processor's marketing allotments made in the year of the loan. The loan rate for raw cane sugar is 18.75 cents per pound, and the loan rate for refined beet sugar is 24.09 cents per pound.[12]

For each marketing year, the USDA determines the amount of domestically produced sugar from sugar beets and sugarcane that each processor is allowed to sell through sugar marketing allotments, which are adjusted based on harvest conditions. However, the production and processing of sugarcane and sugar beet are not restricted. The OAQ is set with the goal of avoiding forfeitures of sugar to the CCC by restricting total supply so that the volume of domestic plus imported sugar does not reduce prices below the loan forfeiture levels for both raw cane sugar and refined beet sugar. The OAQ is split between cane sugar and beet sugar, with the cane sugar allotment fulfilling 45.65 percent and the beet sugar allotment fulfilling 54.35 percent of the OAQ. The program also allocates the allotment among states and among processors in each state.

As in the 2008 Farm Bill, the OAQ is set at 85 percent of projected US human sugar consumption for food. A deficit resulting from a processor being unable to meet its allotment can be offset by reassigning the OAQ to other processors in that state, to other states by using CCC inventories, or through imports.[13] Sugar produced in excess of a processor's allotment must be stored at the processor's expense until it is given permission to sell the sugar in the future. Excess sugar can also be exported or used by another processor to meet its allocation.[14]

The USDA also administers the Feedstock Flexibility Program, known as the sugar-to-ethanol program, through which the CCC sells excess sugar to ethanol producers to avoid accumulating stocks associated with sugar loan forfeitures. The CCC sugar is processed into fuel-grade ethanol and other biofuels. Forfeited sugar can also be sold for human food use in the event of an emergency sugar shortage.[15] In a continued effort to limit sugar supplies and keep domestic prices high, the USDA is authorized to take bids from refiners and sugar brokers for surplus sugar purchased by the USDA under loan forfeitures in return for surrendering import rights.[16]

The sugar program also includes trade protection in the form of TRQs that limit the amount of sugar imported into the United States. Imports under the TRQs have low or zero duty and must meet US WTO quota commitments.[17] The USDA establishes the volume of the raw cane sugar TRQs, which is then allocated among sugar-exporting countries (currently 40 countries) by the US trade representative. The TRQs are based on each country's export share during the period 1975–81 when trade was relatively unrestricted. Annual TRQs may be increased if a shortage is expected. Any imports that exceed a country's quota are subject to high over-quota tariffs.

The in-quota tariff for sugar is 0.625 cents per pound, and the out-of-quota tariffs are 15.36 cents per pound for raw sugar and 16.21 cents per pound for refined sugar. Imported sugar also enters the US domestic market under various trade agreements, including the Dominican Republic–Central American Free Trade Agreement (DR-CAFTA) and free trade bilateral agreements with Colombia, Panama, and Peru.[18] Additionally, until December 2014, sugar imports from Mexico were allowed unrestricted, duty-free access into the United States under NAFTA. However, in December 2014, the US and Mexican governments agreed to limit the quantity of sugar from Mexico and fix the price received for the Mexican sugar imported into the United States. (See below for more details on Mexico and NAFTA.)[19]

Welfare, Trade, and Price Effects of the Sugar Program

The US sugar program has been analyzed and reviewed numerous times, especially in the context of the American Enterprise Institute's initiatives on US farm bills.[20] The typical way to assess the sugar program's cost is to look at the welfare consequences and gains from removing the program.[21] The removal includes opening trade to sugar imports and removing impediments, price support, and interventions in domestic supply.

The sugar program has been costly to consumers and users of sugar. Table 2 summarizes estimates of the welfare effects of the sugar program from several investigations of the program. Fully removing the program would dramatically reduce domestic prices of sugar and induce substantial gains to sugar users (consumers and food processors) in the order of $2.4–$4 billion (2009 dollars).[22] The lion's share of these gains comes from ending transfers to the US sugar industry and subsequent gains in efficiency from the reduced misallocation of resources the sugar program imposes on consumers and food processors. Net welfare gains would be smaller, in the order of $1.2 billion (ranging between $0.437 and $2.565 billion), as transfers to the US sugar industry are an important part of the consumer loss.

Some moderate net employment effects (an increase of 17,000 to 20,000 jobs) would ensue in US food-processing sectors that are sugar

Table 2. Welfare Effects of the Sugar Program (All in 2009 Billion Dollars)

Study	Gains to Users	Losses to Producers	Net Welfare Gains
Beghin and Elobeid (2015)*	$3.13 to $4.036	−$2.637 to −$3.512*	$0.437 to $0.642*
US Government Accountability Office (2000) and Beghin et al. (2003)**	$2.562	−$1.383	$1.179
Gwo-Jiun Leu, Andrew Schmitz, and Ronald Knutson (1987)***	$3.810	−$1.245	$2.565
Michael Wohlgenant (2011)****	$2.441	−$1.433	$1.008

Note: *Original figures updated to 2009 dollars. Sugar producer welfare changes are in terms of gross margin changes. They overstate the loss of profit of the sugar industry and understate net welfare gains. **Original numbers in 1999 dollars updated to 2009 dollars. ***Updated figures to 2009 dollars. ****Computation of losses and gains does not account for loss in tariff revenues.

Source: John C. Beghin and Amani Elobeid, "The Impact of the U.S. Sugar Program Redux," *Applied Economic Perspectives and Policy* 37, no. 1 (March 2015): 1–33, https://academic.oup.com/aepp/article-abstract/37/1/1/2731967/The-Impact-of-the-U-S-Sugar-Program-Redux1?redirectedFrom=fulltext; US Government Accountability Office, "Sugar Program: Supporting Sugar Prices Has Increased Users' Cost While Benefiting Producers," June 9, 2000, http://www.gao.gov/products/RCED-00-126; John C. Beghin et al., "The Cost of the U.S. Sugar Program Revisited," *Contemporary Economic Policy* 21 (2003): 106–16; Gwo-Jiun M. Leu, Andrew Schmitz, and Ronald D. Knutson, "Gains and Losses of Sugar Program Policy Options," *American Journal of Agricultural Economics* 69 (August 1987): 591–602; and Michael K. Wohlgenant, *Sweets for the Sweet: The Costly Benefits of the US Sugar Program*, American Enterprise Institute, July 12, 2011, http://www.aei.org/publication/sweets-for-the-sweet-the-costly-benefits-of-the-us-sugar-program/.

intensive. Some moderate adverse employment effects occur in the sugar-crop and sugar-processing industries. These are much smaller than the increase in employment in food-processing sectors. The net employment gains would occur because imports of sugar-containing products would decline substantially if free trade in sugar itself were permitted. Such processed product imports would no longer compete with domestically produced sugar-intensive processed foods. Hence the sugar program distorts trade in sugar-intensive imports, which increase to abate the high cost of sugar at home. Imports of raw sugar would expand, resulting in a modest increase in world prices of raw and refined sugar.

The sugar program has substantially affected international trade of sugar. Recent estimates indicate that US imports of sugar would increase by a range of 1.6–2.7 million metric tons (mmt).[23] The US sugar program is also estimated to have depressed world sugar prices by constraining imports of raw and refined sugar through the complex TRQ system. This effect has penalized sugar (cane) exporters and lowered the cost of imports for other net importers of sugar. However, estimated effects on world prices have been relatively moderate in the order of 1–2 cents per pound (c/lb).[24]

Alternative Sugar Program Reforms

Short of full termination of the sugar program, less extensive reforms have been proposed over time.[25] These proposals evaluate the potential welfare impacts of transforming the sugar program into a conventional commodity program, similar to those provided for commodities such as corn and wheat. This change would be costly for taxpayers, and welfare gains to consumers are moderate.

The study by David Abler et al.[26] replaces the existing US sugar program with what the authors describe as a "standard" program similar to the program already in place for other US crops. The new program would reduce the loan rates for sugar beet and sugarcane and include a fixed direct payment paid to producers (paid at the time). It is important to note that fixed payments are no longer available to farmers for any commodity under the current farm bill. The authors look at two scenarios, one with low (moderate) imports from Mexico and the other with significantly higher imports from Mexico. Under both scenarios domestic US prices fall and US sugar production increases because of the direct payments, which are assumed not to be fully decoupled in production decisions in the Abler et al. analysis.[27] US sugar consumption increases in response to the lower prices. Direct payments, which average $463 million, increase the total cost of the sugar program under the low-import scenario.[28] In addition to direct payments, small loan deficiency payments and countercyclical payments are a negligible addition to the cost under the high-import scenario.

More recently in the current farm bill debate, a proposal called the Sugar Policy Modernization Act has received much attention as it attempts to lower loan rates for sugar, remove supply constraints implied by allotments, and increase supplies to avoid bottleneck in domestic markets by being less restrictive in the administration of import quotas. These policy changes, short of repealing the program, would move the sugar program in the "right" direction by lowering the cost of sugar to users in the US.

In terms of welfare implications, deadweight losses are small.[29] Crop producers and sweetener users gain while sweetener processors and taxpayers lose. The surplus of beet and cane growers increases by $158 million and $122 million, respectively, while beet-refining and cane-processing profits decline by $106 million and $28 million, respectively, in the low-import scenario compared to the baseline.[30] High fructose corn syrup (HFCS) processors also lose. The added cost to taxpayers of the change to a regular program totals $471 million in the low-import scenario (from a baseline cost of $229 million) and $362 million in the high-import scenario relative to the baseline cost of $408 million. The analysis also concludes that a "standard" program would allow for easier accommodations of trade liberalization either to meet WTO commitments or through bilateral or multilateral trade agreements.

The cost of a buyout for sugar beet and cane growers and processors, as estimated by David Orden,[31] is relatively expensive as compared to the other two buyouts for tobacco and peanuts. Orden provides estimates in the range of $2–$3 billion annually for a 10-year period and corresponding to 25 years of lost protection of $1.1–$1.7 billion. Even partial buyouts to retire the most inefficient segments of the US sugar industry, as estimated by Stephen Haley, Owen Wagner, and Orden, are quite expensive.[32]

The Mexico-NAFTA Interface with the Sugar Program

Although the protectionist nature of the sugar program has remained unchanged, changes in its environment have led to new and interesting developments. In particular, NAFTA and sweetener trade with Mexico have been controversial and somewhat disruptive to the US sugar industry despite the slow and progressive nature of the reforms in these sectors. This section devotes special attention to NAFTA and its implications for the US sugar industry.

NAFTA was implemented in January 1994. The implementation of the NAFTA sugar provisions was gradual and allowed for a 14-year adjustment period before sugar imports from Mexico would be free of tariffs and quantitative restrictions. After 2008, imports from Mexico increased quite rapidly in part because of ample Mexican sugar supplies, high prices in the US market following a worldwide short crop, and a progressive substitution of HFCS for sugar in Mexican food processing, which reduced domestic use of sugar.[33] These conditions led to forfeitures in the US market in the 2012–13 crop year and led to the US sugar industry petitioning the US Trade Commission and US Department of Commerce to investigate alleged dumping by Mexico.[34]

The impact on the US sugar industry of free trade in sugar under NAFTA has been analyzed by Abler et al.; Gary Brester; Haley, Wagner, and Orden; Knutson, Westhoff, and Pablo Sherwell; and more recently, in an ex post fashion, after full implementation by Karen Lewis and Troy Schmitz and Lewis.[35] The analyses of Brester; Haley, Wagner, and Orden; and Schmitz and Lewis identify the pro-competitive effects of NAFTA on the US sugar market.[36] Knutson, Westhoff, and Sherwell did not consider this issue.[37]

Brester[38] examines the pro-competitive effects of NAFTA on the US sugar market and how these effects have compromised the sugar program before the recent US-Mexico agreements to manage sugar trade. The impacts occur through increasing supply in the US market and depressing prices below sugar loan rates, especially when world prices are low (lower than loan rates), inducing higher TRQ fill rates because the US market appears attractive relative to other export markets.

The provision of "no cost" to taxpayers is compromised when forfeitures take place in this situation. The USDA has to sell forfeited sugar at a loss to ethanol plants. Brester concludes that the US sugar industry will have to reduce output by 5–10 percent to remain within its import commitments and meet the no-cost provision.[39] Brester did not consider the consequences of the two suspension agreements (discussed in the next section) that were being negotiated at the time and eventually were adopted.[40]

Since 2013, NAFTA has had important effects on the US domestic sugar market and domestic sugar prices, as Schmitz and Lewis show.[41] According to the authors, under NAFTA, sugar imports from Mexico undermine the sugar program in its current form by driving sugar prices below their loan rates and leading to loan forfeitures by sugar processors. As a result, in FY2014, the USDA had to sell sugar to ethanol processors at a net loss to the federal government. Net government outlays for the sugar program reached $259 million.[42] Schmitz and Lewis' assessment abstracts from the effects of the recent agreements between the United States and Mexico to limit Mexico's exports of sugar to the United States, under the United States' threat to implement countervailing (CVD) and antidumping (AD) punitive duties if ever the suspension agreements are removed.[43] Welfare gains arising from the full implementation of the NAFTA sugar agreement in sugar markets are potentially substantial.

Schmitz and Lewis argue that sugar users benefit substantially from NAFTA based on a counterfactual in which the TRQ constraining Mexican sugar exports is binding at 250,000 mtrv—that is, its pre-2008 constrained maximum level.[44] US consumers and sugar users gain $1.7 billion (2008–13 average of consumer surplus[45] gains) under price-inelastic (less responsiveness of demand to price) market assumptions and $0.6 billion under the assumption that the demand for sugar by US consumers is more responsive to price. Net welfare gains are $362 million, on average, for the same period (price-inelastic case) and $168 million (higher price response case). Over the same period, annual producer losses are estimated to average $1.338 billion (if demand is price insensitive) and $474 million (if demand is more price responsive).

However, trade diversion[46] is substantially in favor of Mexican exporters and at the cost of lower-cost exporters. Mexican sugar exports have benefited from the bilateral trade opening even though they are relatively high cost. The Mexican sugar industry is also distorted and subsidized but to a lesser extent than its US counterpart.[47] The Organisation for Economic Co-operation and Development reports a 2011–15 average protection ratio of 1.60 and 1.19 for US and Mexican sugar, respectively. A ratio of one indicates no distortion. The US and Mexican ratios indicate implicit tariff equivalents of 60 percent and 19 percent in the two countries, respectively. The trade diversion in sugar under NAFTA has been at the cost of low-cost sugar exporters such as Brazil and Thailand. The latter countries are constrained by historical allocations of TRQs (export volume).

Beyond diverting trade from lower- to higher-cost sources of imports, there is a key difference between the pro-competitive effects of NAFTA on the US sugar market and those obtained under full liberalization. US-Mexico bilateral trade is subject to more shocks than US trade with the rest of the world. The latter is deeper and less volatile. As shown in Schmitz and Lewis,[48] NAFTA's pro-competitive effects are highly variable from one year to the next because they depend on US and Mexican local market conditions and world market conditions.

Other preferential trade agreements (US-Australia, DR-CAFTA, and the US-Colombia Trade Promotion Agreement, among others) would have the potential to be comparably disruptive but were mollified by the effective US sugar lobby and have not had the negative effects that NAFTA has had on the US sugar market. These other preferential trade agreements included limited expansions of US sugar imports under tight TRQs. Similarly, the Trans-Pacific Partnership negotiations have mostly spared the US sugar industry from further competitive pressures.[49] The stalled Transatlantic Trade and Investment Partnership (TTIP) negotiations would, if successful, lead to further pressure on the US sugar industry. TTIP has the potential to compromise the US sugar industry as the EU sugar industry has emerged from a deep restructuration with renewed productivity and lower-cost structure than its US counterpart.[50] The stalled negotiations have muted this potential disruption for now.

Suspension Agreements. Mexican sugar exports to the United States have been so extensive that the US sugar lobby pushed for and obtained trade restriction on sugar imports sourced from Mexico. They did so via two agreements signed in December 2014 (the Countervailing Duty Suspension Agreement and the Antidumping Investigation Suspension Agreement). These agreements put in place a policy program equivalent to an export restraint program combined with a minimum export price floor to minimize the displacement of US sugar production by Mexican imports. These constraints on sugar exports from Mexico to the United States compromise the rationalization effects of NAFTA and prevent the lowering of the cost of sugar for US sweetener users. These two agreements induce welfare losses in the United States for sugar users compared to the 2008–14 period.

The Key Elements of the CVD and AD Suspension Agreements. The provisions of the sugar program remain in place (allotments, trade barriers, TRQs, and nonrecourse loan deficiency payments). The agreements suspend CVD and AD duties that the US government would have imposed on Mexican sugar exports entering the US market.

Following legal challenges to the suspension agreements by the US raw sugar refiners, a CVD and AD investigation was completed. The final determinations concluded that the US industry had been materially injured, and large CVD and AD duties were established. The CVD and AD duties would be imposed without the suspension agreement, and their values would match these implicit dumping and subsidy rates. Hence, they would be nearly prohibitive or at least would have substantial adverse effects on Mexican exports to the United States (i.e., no or almost no sugar imports would be sourced from Mexico). The CVD and AD duties are explained below.

The CVD agreement is a comprehensive export restraint agreement[51] with an annual export limit based on an estimate of US sugar needs that the USDA determines. The maximum export level is set equal to 100 percent of US annual needs as estimated by the USDA and takes into account expected use, production, and imports under existing TRQs. The formula is:

Maximum Export Level = (Total Use x 1.135) – Beginning Stocks – Production – TRQ Imports – Other Program Imports – ("Other High Tier" + "Other")

The CVD agreement as amended in June 2017 also spreads these exports to the United States over the year and precludes concentration at specific times of the year. It also limits the quantity of refined sugar sourced from Mexico, which can enter the US market at 30 percent of the total exports from Mexico. The maximum purity standard for raw sugar is lowered to reduce the flow of high-quality raw sugar going directly into food processing. Note that historically the USDA has a mixed track record managing the flow of sugar imports and allegedly has induced unnecessary price increases by restricting imports to ensure that no sugar forfeitures take place under the loan deficiency payment program.[52]

The AD agreement sets a minimum price level to prevent Mexican exports from landing "too cheaply" in the US market. The minimum prices are set at 28 c/lb for refined sugar, the dry weight (as amended from 26 c/lb in June 2017), and 23 c/lb for other sugars (as amended from 22.25 c/lb in June 2017). These prices are well above world prices and transfer surplus from sugar buyers to the exporters and US sugar producers by reducing the competition they would face without these two agreements

Table 3. CVD and AD Duties

Margins in Preliminary and Final Determinations in AD and CVD Cases Concerning Sugar Imports from Mexico

	CVD		AD	
Producer/Exporter	Preliminary	Final	Preliminary	Final
	Percentage			
FEESA	17.01%	43.93%	39.54%	40.48%
Grupo GAM	2.99%	5.78%	47.26%	42.14%
All Others	14.87%	38.11%	40.76%	40.74%

Source: US Department of Agriculture, Economic Research Service.

and without punitive CVD and AD taxes. The reference prices constitute a new price floor in US sugar markets.

According to the US Department of Commerce and US International Trade Commission (USITC) findings, dumping margins are: Fondo de Empresas Expropiadas del Sector Azucarero (FEESA), 40.48 percent; Ingenio Tala S.A. de C.V. and certain affiliated companies of Grupo Azucarero Mexico S.A. de C.V. (collectively, the GAM Group), 42.14 percent; and all others, 40.74 percent. The USITC determined countervailing subsidy rates as follows: FEESA, 43.93 percent; Ingenio Tala S.A. de C.V. and certain other cross-owned companies of Grupo Azucarero Mexico S.A. de C.V. (collectively, the GAM Group), 5.78 percent; and all others, 38.11 percent. These final values are shown with their preliminary values in Table 3.

Not surprisingly, sugar users find that the suspension agreements are second-best outcomes and preferable to moving into a world of CVD and AD duties. The latter would increase sugar prices even more by restricting imports from Mexico. The Sweetener Users Association is advocating a reform of the suspension agreements to allow for larger imports of raw sugar from Mexico and alleviating the shortage of raw sugar for coastal sugar refiners.[53]

The impact of the suspension agreement has been analyzed by Jarret Whistance, Andrick Payen, and Wyatt Thompson[54] using the FAPRI-MU models[55] and by Wilson Sinclair and Amanda Countryman.[56] The former authors consider the impact of the agreements relative to two baselines, one without preliminary CVD and AD duties and an alternative baseline with these punitive duties in place. In their baseline, prices are maintained above the minimum sugar prices of 26 c/lb. Hence, the price floor under the suspension agreement will not be binding in this environment. Under the suspension agreement, Mexican exports fall sharply and further increase US prices. Effects are small when the baseline does not contain the CVD and AD duties. Using alternative assumptions, Sinclair and Countryman[57] estimate that the agreements increase US sugar prices, translating to an average annual increase in producer surplus of approximately $620 million and decrease in consumer surplus of $1.48 billion.

Alternatively, the effects of the suspension agreement relative to a baseline with punitive duties are quite large. Sugar exports from Mexico to the United States fall, and US prices increase. In Mexico, the restriction on exports to the United States reduces Mexican prices and increases domestic use. The authors also investigate the implications of noncompetitive behavior in the Mexican sugar industry and price discrimination between the price-inelastic domestic Mexican market and the more price-responsive US export market. Exports are larger in that context.

With price discrimination, the impact of the suspension agreement is also more pronounced since the export restraint is substantially binding in this environment. US prices fall below the loan rate, and forfeitures occur in the early years of the projections (relative to a baseline without CVD and AD duties). Price discrimination incentives offset some of the duties' trade-restricting impact when the suspension agreements are removed.

Still, according to these authors, the suspension agreements increase prices in the US market by about 1.6 c/lb for raw sugar and 2.2 c/lb for refined sugar (averaged over 10 years) above baseline levels. One can derive a back-of-the-envelope estimate of consumers' loss from the suspension agreements—change in price x (deliveries plus change in deliveries divided by 2)— implied by their investigation, which is about $400 million for the scenario assuming no suspension, no CVD or AD tariffs, and strategic pricing by the Mexican sugar industry. The Mexican export expansion under this alternative scenario is about 700,000 strv, from a baseline level of 1.8 million strv. Their scenario provides an upper-bound value of the trade effect of the suspension scenarios. The analysis does not explain where the extra sugar goes. (The change in imports exceeds the change in deliveries, and there is no change in production or stocks.)

Steven Zahniser, Getachew Nigatu, and Michael McConnell[58] also provide some back-of-the-envelope estimates of the impact of suspension agreements' quantitative restriction by using the voluntary export restraint formula specified in the agreements. They show that, under recent market conditions (FY2016), the quantitative restrictions have constrained the flow of imports during some periods of the year and are lower than they were before the agreement (not a strict comparison as in Whistance, Payen, and Thompson).[59] They also show that the minimum reference prices established by the suspension agreements are likely to be binding, especially for raw sugar. They do so by comparing historical import unit values and the reference prices.

The December 2016 World Agricultural Supply and Demand Estimates forecast is that US imports of Mexican sugar will reach 0.972 million strv in 2016–17 under the suspension agreement. Hence, imports in the baseline of Whistance, Payen, and Thompson,[60] inclusive of the suspension agreements, appear high relative to the recent historical import levels (1.532 million strv in 2014–15 and 1.309 million strv in 2015–16). The same remark holds for the latest USDA forecast figures (0.972 million strv). In any case, these levels are much higher than pre-2008 levels when Mexican sugar exports to the United States were constrained by TRQs. In 2007, Mexican exports to the United States were set below 0.250 million mtrv and actually fell short of that amount.

NAFTA has expanded US sugar imports, lowered US domestic prices, and provided some integration of Mexican and US markets. The minimum reference prices that the suspension agreements set compromise gains in efficiency and establish price floors above US loan rates (28 ¢/lb and 23 ¢/lb minimum prices for refined beet sugar and raw cane sugar, respectively, in the suspension agreements, versus 24.09 ¢/lb and 18.75 ¢/lb for loan rates of refined beet sugar and raw cane sugar, respectively). The policy developments under the CVD and AD investigations and the suspension agreements are dismaying.

The New Suspension Agreement of June 2017. In practice, the two suspension agreements have led to an increased direct use of unrefined sugar in food processing, a relative shortage of raw sugar for refiners, and elevated prices for sugar users. The quality of raw sugar imported from Mexico has been refined enough to be used directly for human consumption, when it is delivered in liquid form.

A significant share of raw sugar imports under the suspension agreements has been of high quality and was used directly in US food processing in liquid form. These raw sugar imports have been bypassing US refiners but did not violate the suspension agreements. US cane refiners had been in a more competitive market environment with reduced availabilities of raw sugar to refine and with a close substitute for their output in the form of the liquid raw sugar coming from Mexico. These refiners were behind the recent push and successful renegotiation of the suspension agreements.[61] Note that the refined-raw spread in minimum prices increased to 5 c/lb under the amended suspension agreements.

Policy Recommendations

The major recommendation, as in recent previous AEI assessments of the US sugar program,[62] is the total removal of the sugar program's main components (TRQs, allotments, and sugar loan rates). This major reform would induce gains to sugar users (consumers and food processors) in the order of $2.4–$4 billion (2009 dollars). The lion's share of these gains would come from ending transfers to the US sugar industry. Net welfare gains would be smaller, in the order of $1 billion ($0.437–$2.565 billion), as transfers from sugar users to the US sugar industry are the largest part of the consumer loss associated with the current program.

Some moderate positive employment effects (an increase of 17,000 to 20,000 jobs) would ensue in US food-processing sectors, which are sugar intensive. The latter would occur once imports of sugar-containing products contract drastically. These imports would no longer be needed to abate the high cost of domestic sugar under the sugar program.

NAFTA has provided some welfare gains to US sugar users by integrating sweetener markets between Mexico and the United States, but at the cost of substantial trade diversion. Mexican sugar exports have benefited from the bilateral trade opening, although they are relatively high cost. The trade diversion under NAFTA has been at the expense of low-cost exporters (e.g., Brazil and Thailand), which are constrained by historical allocations of TRQs.

The suspension agreements have partially compromised the welfare gains achieved under the NAFTA sweetener market integration by limiting pro-competitive effects of Mexican exports of sugar to the United States. The suspension agreements and the AD and CVD duties should be removed to further pressure a reform of the US sugar program.

Short of a full removal of the sugar program, milder reforms of the program have been proposed.[63] These policies consider the transformation of the sugar program into a conventional commodity program. This potential transformation is quite costly to taxpayers but lowers the cost to sugar users.

The cost of a hypothetical buyout is expensive—in the range of $2–$3 billion annually for a 10-year period and corresponding to 25 years of lost protection of $1.1–$1.7 billion. Even partial buyouts to retire the most inefficient segments of the US sugar industry are expensive.

The most recent agreement with Mexico reached in June 2017 is an adverse development. It compromises the pro-competitive effect of NAFTA in the US sugar market by limiting the flow of sugar exports from Mexico. In addition, this agreement could serve as an example of successful "managed trade" for other sensitive products with Mexico and other countries and further undermine market integration and interdependence of countries based on respective comparative advantages.

Notes

1. US Department of Agriculture, Economic Research Service, "Sugar and Sweetener Yearbook Tables: World Production, Supply, and Distribution, Centrifugal Sugar," 2016, Tables 3b and 4, https://www.ers.usda.gov/data-products/sugar-and-sweeteners-yearbooktables/.

2. A TRQ is a two-tier tariff system. For imports below the designated quota, imports are taxed at a low tariff, called the in-quota tariff. For imports beyond the quota level, a much higher tariff rate, called the out-of-quota tariff, is imposed, often precluding

imports beyond the quota level.

3. Mark A. McMinimy, "Revisiting U.S.-Mexico Sugar Agreements," CRS Insight, August 12, 2016, https://fas.org/sgp/crs/row/IN10552.pdf.

4. Donald Mitchell, "Sugar Policies: Opportunity for Change," in *Global Agricultural Trade and Developing Countries,* eds. M. Ataman Aksoy and John C. Beghin (Washington, DC: World Bank Publications, 2006), 141–59; and Coalition for Sugar Reform, "History of the Sugar Program: America & Sugar: A Salty Tale," http://sugarreform.org/why-reform/history-of-the-sugar-program/.

5. James Johnson et al., "Provisions of the Agricultural and Food Act of 1981," US Department of Agriculture, Economic Research Service, January 1982, https://www.ers.usda.gov/publications/pub-details/?pubid=41763; and National Agricultural Law Center, "Farm Bills: Agricultural and Food Act of 1981: Pub. L. No. 97-98, 95 Stat. 1213," accessed January 25, 2017, http://nationalaglawcenter.org/wp-content/uploads/assets/farmbills/1981-1.pdf.

6. Mitchell, "Sugar Policies," 141–59.

7. Mitchell, "Sugar Policies," 141–59.

8. Mitchell, "Sugar Policies," 141–59; and Brandon Willis and Doug O'Brien, "Summary and Evolution of U.S. Farm Bill Commodity Titles—Expanded Discussions," National Agricultural Law Center, http://nationalaglawcenter.org/farmbills/commodity/expanded-discussion/#sugar-90.

9. The Food, Conservation, and Energy Act of 2008, Pub. L. No. 110-246.

10. Remy Jurenas, *Sugar Policy and the 2008 Farm Bill,* Congressional Research Service, January 30, 2009, http://nationalaglawcenter.org/wp-content/uploads/assets/crs/RL34103.pdf; and McMinimy, "Revisiting U.S.-Mexico Sugar Agreements."

11. The Agricultural Act of 2014, Pub. L. No. 113-79.

12. The Agricultural Act of 2014, Pub. L. No. 113-79.

13. Cane sugar allotments can be filled only with sugar processed from sugarcane and beet sugar allotments only from sugar processed from sugar beet grown in the state covered by the allotment for each crop.

14. Jurenas, *Sugar Policy and the 2008 Farm Bill.*

15. Renée Johnson and Jim Monke, *What Is the Farm Bill?,* Congressional Research Service Report, November 2016, https://fas.org/sgp/crs/misc/RS22131.pdf.

16. McMinimy, "Revisiting U.S.-Mexico Sugar Agreements."

17. This is currently 1.139 million mtrv and 22,000 tons of refined sugar.

18. The TRQ under CAFTA totaled 140,580 mtrv in 2016 and 53,000 metric tons, 7,325 metric tons, and 2,000 metric tons for Colombia, Panama, and Peru, respectively.

19. McMinimy, "Revisiting U.S.-Mexico Sugar Agreements."

20. John Beghin, "U.S. Sugar Policy: Analysis and Options," in *The 2007 Farm Bill and Beyond,* eds. Bruce L. Gardner and Daniel A. Sumner (Washington, DC: AEI Press, 2007), 47–51; Michael K. Wohlgenant, *Sweets for the Sweet: The Costly Benefits of the US Sugar Program,* American Enterprise Institute, July 12, 2011, http://www.aei.org/publication/sweets-for-the-sweet-the-costly-benefits-of-theus-sugar-program/; and Mark A. McMinimy, *U.S. Sugar Program Fundamentals,* Congressional Research Service, April 6, 2016, https://fas.org/sgp/crs/misc/R43998.pdf.

21. Welfare effects of a policy pertain to the efficiency in the allocation of resources under the policy and its distributional effects (winners and losers). Policies reducing exchanges in markets presumably distort the allocation of resources and reduce welfare by inducing an inefficient allocation of resources.

22. Variations in results across studies estimating the sugar programs' impacts derive mainly from variations in the difference between world and US sugar prices over time (as shown in Table 1). The growing size of the US sugar market with its increasing population is another element. Modeling assumptions and different ways of measuring producer and consumer welfare also play a role in the different estimates of the program's welfare effects. However, the direction and magnitudes of the estimates of the welfare effects and costs of the sugar program remain remarkably consistent across studies and over time.

23. Wohlgenant estimates an increase from 2.1 mmt to 3.9 mmt of sugar after the removal of the program. Michael K. Wohlgenant, *Sweets for the Sweet: The Costly Benefits of the US Sugar Program*, American Enterprise Institute, July 12, 2011, http://www.aei.org/publication/sweets-for-the-sweet-the-costly-benefits-of-the-us-sugar-program/. The results presented by Beghin et al. indicate an increase in imports from 1.7 mmt to 3.3 mmt after reform. John C. Beghin et al., "The Cost of the U.S. Sugar Program Revisited," *Contemporary Economic Policy* 21 (2003): 106–16. Beghin and Elobeid estimate that ending the sugar programs increases sugar imports from 52 percent to 84 percent over the projected years of their analysis from a baseline level of imports of 3.5 million short tons of raw sugar equivalent. John C. Beghin and Amani Elobeid, "The Impact of the U.S. Sugar Program Redux," *Applied Economic Perspectives and Policy* 37, no. 1 (March 2015): 1–33, https://academic.oup.com/aepp/article-abstract/37/1/1/2731967/The-Impact-of-the-U-S-Sugar-Program-Redux1?redirectedFrom=fulltext

24. Beghin et al. find that world prices would have increased by 1 to 2 c/lb in 1996 and 1998 (from a base of 10 to 12 c/lb), or by roughly 10 percent to 13 percent. Beghin et al., "The Cost of the U.S. Sugar Program Revisited." Wohlgenant estimates an 8.5 percent price increase from an unknown base. Wohlgenant, *Sweets for the Sweet.* Beghin and Elobeid estimate a world price effect of about 1 c/lb for world raw sugar price, or a 2–5 percent increase. Beghin and Elobeid, "The Impact of the U.S. Sugar Program Redux." As a reference, simulations of global trade liberalization in sugar markets give estimates of price effects of 3–5 c/lb. Amani Elobeid and John Beghin, "Multilateral Trade and Agricultural Policy Reforms in Sugar Markets," *Journal of Agricultural Economics* 57, no. 1 (2006): 23–48.

25. David J. Abler et al., "Changing the U.S. Sugar Program into a Standard Crop Program: Consequences Under the North American Free Trade Agreement and Doha," *Applied Economic Perspectives and Policy* 30, no. 1 (Spring 2008): 82–102, https://www.jstor.org/stable/30224835; and Stephen Haley, Owen Wagner, and David Orden, "The U.S. Sugar Program: Reform Pressures and Options," in *The Future of Global Sugar Markets,* ed. David Orden (Washington, DC: International Food Policy Research Institute, 2008): 41.

26. Abler et al., "Changing the U.S. Sugar Program into a Standard Crop Program"; and Haley, Wagner, and Orden, "The U.S. Sugar Program."

27. Decoupling refers to not having an incentive effect on production decisions.

28. Payment limits would reduce expenditures on direct payments from $463 million to $224 million.

29. Deadweight losses refer to the net welfare losses associated with a market intervention. It is computed by comparing estimated gains by winners and losses by losers to obtain the net welfare cost to society from the distortion (i.e., policy).

30. Results for the high-import scenario are as follows: Beet and cane producer surpluses increase by $215 million and $147 million, respectively, and beet refiners and cane processors' profits decline by $86 million and $40 million, respectively, relative to the baseline.

31. David Orden, "Feasibility of Farm Program Buyouts," Louisiana State University, January 23, 2007, http://farmpolicy.typepad.com/farmpolicy/files/orden_buyouts.pdf.

32. Stephen Haley, Owen Wagner, and David Orden, "The U.S. Sugar Program: Reform Pressures and Options," in *The Future of Global Sugar Markets*, ed. David Orden (Washington, DC: International Food Policy Research Institute, 2008): 41.

33. Gary W. Brester, *20 Years in, NAFTA Finally Sours the U.S. Sugar Program*, American Enterprise Institute, September 4, 2014, http://www.aei.org/publication/20-years-in-nafta-finally-sours-the-us-sugar-program/.

34. Steven Zahniser, Getachew Nigatu, and Michael McConnell, "A New Outlook for the U.S.-Mexico Sugar and Sweetener Market," US Department of Agriculture, August 2016, https://www.ers.usda.gov/publications/pub-details/?pubid=74634.

35. Abler et al., "Changing the U.S. Sugar Program into a Standard Crop Program"; Haley, Wagner, and Orden, "The U.S. Sugar Program"; Ronald D. Knutson, Patrick Westhoff, and Pablo Sherwell, "Trade Liberalizing Impacts of NAFTA in Sugar: Global Implications," *International Food and Agribusiness Management Review* 13, no. 4 (2010): 16, https://ageconsearch.umn.edu/bitstream/96338/2/20100014_Formatted.pdf; Karen Elizabeth Lewis, "Analysis of the United States' Sugar Industry," Arizona State University, May 2014, https://repository.asu.edu/attachments/134812/content/Lewis_asu_0010E_13593.pdf; and Troy G. Schmitz and Karen Elizabeth Lewis, "Impact of NAFTA on U.S. and Mexican Sugar Markets," *Journal of Agricultural and Resource Economics* 40, no. 3 (2015): 387–404, http://www.waeaonline.org/UserFiles/file/JARESeptember20153Schmitzpp387-404.pdf.

36. Brester, *20 Years in, NAFTA Finally Sours the U.S. Sugar Program*; Haley, Wagner, and Orden, "The U.S. Sugar Program"; and Schmitz and Lewis, "Impact of NAFTA on U.S. and Mexican Sugar Markets."

37. Knutson, Westhoff, and Sherwell, "Trade Liberalizing Impacts of NAFTA in Sugar."

38. Brester, *20 Years in, NAFTA Finally Sours the U.S. Sugar Program*.

39. Brester, *20 Years in, NAFTA Finally Sours the U.S. Sugar Program*.

40. Brester, *20 Years in, NAFTA Finally Sours the U.S. Sugar Program*.

41. Schmitz and Lewis, "Impact of NAFTA on U.S. and Mexican Sugar Markets."

42. McMinimy, "Revisiting U.S.-Mexico Sugar Agreements."

43. Schmitz and Lewis, "Impact of NAFTA on U.S. and Mexican Sugar Markets."

44. Schmitz and Lewis, "Impact of NAFTA on U.S. and Mexican Sugar Markets."

45. Consumer surplus refers to monetary valuation of the well-being of consumers derived from consuming a good.

46. Trade diversion occurs when a country sources its imports from an exporter, which is not the lowest-cost source of exports, because of policy distortions creating incentives to do so.

47. Organisation for Economic Co-operation and Development, "Producer and Consumer Support Estimates Database," 2016, http://www.oecd.org/tad/agricultural-policies/producerandconsumersupportestimatesdatabase.htm; and Zahniser, Nigatu, and McConnell, "A New Outlook for the U.S.-Mexico Sugar and Sweetener Market."

48. Schmitz and Lewis, "Impact of NAFTA on U.S. and Mexican Sugar Markets."

49. Thomas Earley, "Oral Statement by Thomas Earley on Behalf of the Sweetener Users Association to the U.S. International Trade Commission," January 14, 2016, https://www.usitc.gov/press_room/documents/testimony/105_001_004d2.pdf.

50. John C. Beghin, Jean-Christophe Bureau, and Alexandre Gohin, "The Impact of a U.S.-EU Free Trade Agreement on Biofuel and Feedstock Markets," *Journal of Agricultural Economics* 68, no. 2 (2014): 321–44, http://www.card.iastate.edu/products/publications/synopsis/?p=1231.

51. A voluntary export restraint scheme operates when exporters agree to limit their exports in exchange for receiving higher prices than would prevail under competitive markets. Consumers bear the cost of such a scheme by facing higher prices and consuming fewer units.

52. Beghin and Elobeid, "The Impact of the U.S. Sugar Program Redux."

53. Sweetener Users Association to Commerce Secretary Penny Pritzker, September 19, 2016, Washington, DC, http://d31hzlhk6di2h5.cloudfront.net/20160920/e8/ba/95/7a/5d3f6h099cf944a79f0b2238/SUA_Ltr_to_Secretary_Pritzker__U.S.-Mexico_Sugar_Suspension_Agreements__9-19-2016.pdf.

54. Jarret Whistance, Andrick Payen, and Wyatt Thompson, "Suspension Agreements and Antidumping/Countervailing Duties: U.S.-Mexico Sugar Markets and the Effects of Alternative Trade Policies," Agricultural & Applied Economics Association and Western Agricultural Economics Association, July 2015, http://ageconsearch.umn.edu/record/205550/files/SuspensionAgreementEffects_AAEA_2015.pdf.

55. FAPRI-MU is the Food and Agricultural Policy Research Institute at University of Missouri–Columbia.

56. Wilson Sinclair and Amanda Countryman, "Not So Sweet: Economic Implications of Restricting U.S. Sugar Imports from Mexico," Colorado State University, 2017.

57. Sinclair and Countryman, "Not So Sweet."

58. Zahniser, Nigatu, and McConnell, "A New Outlook for the U.S.-Mexico Sugar and Sweetener Market."

59. Whistance, Payen, and Thompson, "Suspension Agreements and Antidumping/Countervailing Duties."

60. Whistance, Payen, and Thompson, "Suspension Agreements and Antidumping/Countervailing Duties."

61. McMinimy, "Revisiting U.S.-Mexico Sugar Agreements"; and US Department of Commerce, "Draft Amendments to the Mexican Sugar Suspension Agreements," press release, June 6, 2017, https://www.commerce.gov/news/fact-sheets/2017/06/draft-amendmentsmexican-sugar-suspension-agreements.

62. Beghin, "U.S. Sugar Policy"; and Wohlgenant, *Sweets for the Sweet.*

63. Abler et al., "Changing the U.S. Sugar Program into a Standard Crop Program"; and Haley, Wagner, and Orden, "The U.S. Sugar Program."

7

Dairy Policy Progress:
Completing the Move to Markets?

DANIEL A. SUMNER

The US dairy industry, which has long been an important and central part of American agriculture, has made remarkable gains over the past 30 years. Productivity has risen rapidly, and competitiveness has improved for both dairy farms and processing firms, many of which continue to be farmer-owned cooperatives. These gains have facilitated a shift from milk markets that were dominated by government regulations and subsidies to a much more self-reliant and resilient dairy industry.

In the 1980s, milk policy used high tariff walls and import quotas to keep milk products from the rest of the world out of the United States while using export subsidies to dump domestically produced milk products into world markets. The government policies dominated in domestic milk markets as well, with high congressionally mandated minimum prices implemented by the US Department of Agriculture's (USDA) purchase and storage of processed dairy products. When purchase and storage became excessively expensive, the USDA initiated a program to buy whole dairy herds and kill the cows while banning the dairy producer from producing milk.

In subsequent years, improved dairy farm and processor productivity and competitiveness, along with a recognition that federal dairy policy had failed to create or maintain an economically healthy industry, facilitated the shift away from many, but not yet all, of these policies.

This chapter summarizes the economics of the US dairy industry and recent US dairy policy. These summaries provide the background needed to evaluate current dairy policies and assess the likely implications of a new and more market-based US dairy policy. AEI has had a long tradition of evaluating dairy policy as a part of its broader program of work on agricultural policy effort.[1]

189

The current dairy farm policy in the United States revolves around two major programs. The long-standing (around since the 1930s) Federal Milk Marketing Order (FMMO) program covers most regions and regulates minimum prices buyers must pay based on the "end use" of the milk. Under the FMMOs, buyers must pay a higher or lower price for milk depending on whether they are using raw milk to make cheese, yogurt, or fresh beverages, among myriad other products. Farmers receive regionally determined and regulated weighted averages of these buyer-paid prices. California, the state that produces the most milk, has its own similar program, but it may soon join the FMMO system.[2]

The second major component of current US dairy policy is the Margin Protection Program (MPP), which only began with the Agricultural Act of 2014 and was revised in the Bipartisan Budget Act of 2018.[3] The MPP is government-subsidized (net) revenue insurance that covers shortfalls in the difference between a national average price of milk and a USDA-calculated average cost of feed used to produce milk. The MPP has been operating for only a few years, has not satisfied its producer advocates, and has not been widely used by dairy farms.[4]

In addition to these two major programs, US dairy policy relies on several old and new measures, including some residual trade barriers. Import barriers used to be central to US dairy policy, but, as discussed below, they are now mainly an annoyance. US dairy farms continue to use agricultural policies such as laws and regulations that (1) benefit farmer-owned cooperatives, (2) facilitate and subsidize domestic and international market promotion, and (3) subsidize milk purchases in schools; for pregnant women, infants, and preschool children; and for some minor programs. Finally, the 2014 Farm Bill created a new but up-to-now unused Dairy Product Donation Program that would authorize government purchases of dairy products when the milk margins are low.

This chapter does not consider or evaluate environmental and related policies that affect milk supply and cost. Many environmental regulations, such as those dealing with local air quality, water quality, animal care practices, and greenhouse gas emissions are probably the government policies that matter most to many dairy farms and milk processors. Some of these state and federal policies raise milk production and processing costs substantially and must be subject to careful analysis to assure that the environmental benefits match the economic costs.

After reviewing the remarkable productivity improvements and structural changes that have occurred in the US dairy industry and describing the contemporary policy environment, I argue that the current slate of dairy programs does little to benefit the industry and that there is little rationale for continuing the programs. I see marketing regulations that raise the price of beverage milk products as counter to public policy principles and as having negative consequences with little benefit. They raise prices for consumers, especially children, who consume fresh beverage milk, and the programs do little except redistribute revenue among producers. Of course, milk and feed prices will continue to vary from month to month and year to year, but I find that government efforts to mitigate the consequences of such variability are likely to be counterproductive. I note that, as for crops, unless policies to deal with variability are accompanied by substantial subsidy, they do not generate much farm participation. I also note that, as with other farm subsidies, there is no rationale for regular and sustained income transfers from taxpayers to dairy farms. Finally, I argue that moving to a more open market with less government encumbrance would allow the US dairy industry to become stronger.

The US Dairy Industry Is Large, Important, Diverse, and Complex

The farm value of milk was about $40 billion in 2017 and contributes about 10 percent of total US farm cash receipts. Milk is among the most important farm commodities in most states and the top farm commodity in terms of cash receipts in several important agricultural states, such as California and Wisconsin. Milk is also the top farm commodity produced in several of the smaller agricultural states, such as Vermont. The major milk-producing states range from New York and Pennsylvania in the East to Wisconsin and Minnesota in the Midwest to Idaho, New Mexico, and California in the West. Thus, the dairy industry is geographically diverse and important.[5]

Two remarkable transformations in the milk industry have occurred in the past three decades. Table 1 documents these changes. First, from the early 1980s through 2007, milk production and productivity grew rapidly in the West, as represented by California and Idaho in Table 1. From 1984 through 2007, the number of cows doubled in California, and milk

Table 1. Dairy Production and Productivity for Major Dairy States, 1984–2017

		1984	1997	2007	2017
California	Milk Production (Billion Pounds)	15,292	27,582	40,683	39,712
	Milk per Cow (Pounds)	15,636	19,829	22,440	22,698
	Number of Cows (Thousands)	978	1,391	1,813	1,750
Idaho	Milk Production (Billion Pounds)	2,190	5,193	11,549	14,636
	Milk per Cow (Pounds)	13,273	19,092	22,513	24,386
	Number of Cows (Thousands)	165	272	513	600
Wisconsin	Milk Production (Billion Pounds)	23,501	22,368	24,080	30,353
	Milk per Cow (Pounds)	12,856	16,057	19,310	23,737
	Number of Cows (Thousands)	1,828	1,393	1,247	1,278
New York	Milk Production (Billion Pounds)	11,443	11,530	12,103	14,973
	Milk per Cow (Pounds)	12,658	16,495	19,303	24,020
	Number of Cows (Thousands)	904	699	627	623

Source: US Department of Agriculture, National Agricultural Statistics Service, "Quick Stats," https://quickstats.nass.usda. gov/.

production grew by 250 percent as milk production per cow increased by about 50 percent. Growth rates were even faster in Idaho, which emerged as a major dairy state. Over the same period, milk production stagnated in the East and Midwest as represented in Table 1 by Wisconsin and New York, where milk per cow increased rapidly but numbers of cows declined just as rapidly. Between 2007 and 2017, these trends reversed. California has had stagnant milk production with slight declines in cow numbers and slight gains in milk per cow. Idaho experienced much slower growth in cow numbers and milk per cow than in the previous period, and it added less than 30 percent to milk production compared to more than 110 percent in the previous decade. Remarkably, Wisconsin and New York held cow numbers steady as production per cow rose by about 25 percent. The result is that now California, still the largest dairy state by total production, has less milk per cow than the other three dairy production leaders.

Milk production is central to the agricultural economy in the United States. Dairy farms buy and feed grains, especially corn, and oilseeds, especially soybeans. Dairy farms also use huge quantities of forage crops, such as alfalfa hay, other hays, grain silage, and even almond hulls. The US feed industry relies on US dairy farms as a significant source of demand. Dairy demand for forage crops, which tend to be grown near dairy farms, is a major factor in determining the crop landscape in milk-producing regions. Milk tends to be processed near farm production, so milk production also generates considerable downstream economic activity. In many regions, therefore, the dairy industry accounts for much of the activity in the local agricultural economy, directly or indirectly.[6]

Milk marketing cooperatives owned by dairy farmers account for about 84 percent of the milk produced and marketed in the United States. K. Charles Ling reports on 132 cooperatives, many of them small local operations that either process their farmer-owners' milk or, more often, represent the marketing of member milk to other processors, without actually doing any processing themselves.[7] While most cooperatives are small, some are large, well-known national or regional companies such as Dairy Farmers of America, Land O'Lakes, United Dairy Farmers, and Darigold Inc. The top four cooperatives market about 40 percent of all milk in the United States, and the 20 largest cooperatives market about two-thirds of all milk.[8] However, markets for raw milk from the farm are local because milk is heavy and perishable. So local market shares are also relevant, and in some major dairy states such as California and Washington, a few cooperatives market 80 or 90 percent of milk in the state.[9]

As with every agricultural commodity, features of the dairy industry are similar in some respects but different in others when compared to other farm commodity industries. As with eggs and some fruits and vegetables such as strawberries, milk is perishable and harvested every day. Harvest timing for milk is even more crucial given animal welfare considerations. Milk is more homogeneous than many commodities.[10] Like several other commodities, much of the milk in the United States is sold through farmer cooperatives. Also like many commodities, including grains and oilseeds, several end-use products are made from raw milk. The dairy industry also shares some of the features of the cattle feeding, hog, and poultry industries with respect to the change of farm size and migration of the industry across regions. It differs from those industries and is more similar to program crops in the heavy role of government programs in the dairy industry beginning in the 1930s.

Figure 1. Trends in the Dairy Industry: Milk Production, Cow Herd, and Milk per Cow

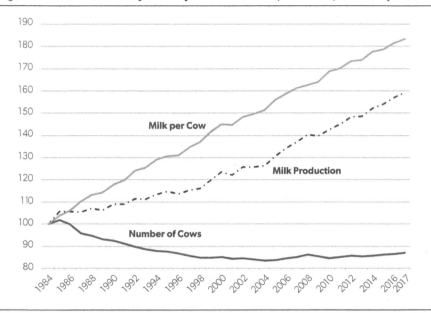

Note: Index numbers with 1984 = 100.
Source: US Department of Agriculture, National Agricultural Statistics Service, "Quick Stats," various years, https://quick-stats.nass.usda.gov/.

Dairy Productivity Growth and Structural Change

The remarkable change in the US dairy industry in recent decades has stimulated much analysis and commentary for many years.[11] Some of the increase in average dairy herd size parallels changes in other parts of US agriculture, but other features are specific to the dairy industry.[12] James McDonald, Jerry Cessna, and Roberto Mosheim show that "midpoint herd size," defined as the herd size for which half of all milk cows are in herds that size or larger, grew from 80 cows in 1987 to 140 cows in 1997, 570 cows in 2007, and 900 cows in 2012, according to Census of Agriculture data.[13] Western states continue to have larger dairy farms, but even in midwestern states such as Michigan and Indiana, more than half the cows were in herds of more than 499 cows.[14] In 2012, according to the US Department of Agriculture (USDA) Census of Agriculture, about half the national milk cow herd was on farms with 1,000 cows or more, and about three-quarters was on farms

Figure 2. Real Milk Prices and Class I Utilization, 1988–2017

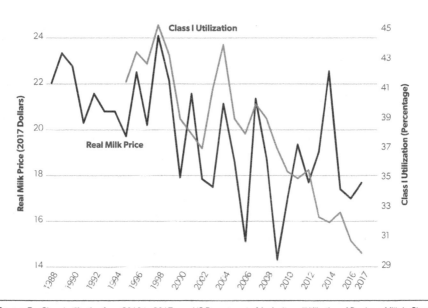

Source: For Class I utilization from 2010 to 2017, see US Department of Agriculture, "Utilization of Producer Milk in Class I," https://www.amc.uoda.gov/resources/marketing-order-statistics/class-I-utilization. For Class I utilization from 1995 to 2009, see Brian W. Gould, "Understanding Dairy Markets," Agricultural and Applied Economics, http://future.aae.wisc.edu/ams_statistics.html.

with 200 cows or more. Ten years earlier, the 1992 Census reported that less than one-third of the milk cows were on farms with 200 cows or more.[15]

Since 1984, milk production in the United States has risen by almost 60 percent, reaching about 216 billion pounds in 2017 (Figure 1). This growth has been made possible by an 83 percent increase in milk production per cow to about 23,000 pounds per cow. The increase in milk per cow has overwhelmed a 13 percent reduction in the number of milk cows to about 9.39 million. The 13 percent decline in milk cows occurred during the decade from 1986 to 1997, and the national herd has been roughly stable since (Figure 1). The increase in milk per cow of about 300 pounds per year has meant that US milk production has increased rapidly over the past 20 years. Among major dairy states, milk per cow has risen most rapidly in the Midwest, while growth has slowed in the West, especially in California, which used to be a leader in milk per cow.[16]

The price of milk has declined in real terms in line with industry-wide productivity growth. Figure 2 shows that since 1988 the national average "all-milk" price has fallen by more than a third from just under $27 per hundredweight (in 2017 dollars) to about $17 per hundredweight. Although the all-milk price has varied by up to $6 per hundredweight from year to year, there has been a stark downward trend in price over the past three decades. Farm milk is processed into many end uses, and, based on the regulations discussed below, beverage products (known in the regulations as Class I milk) command the highest price per unit and contribute to higher all-milk prices. Figure 2 also documents that the Class I utilization percentage has fallen by more than a quarter in just over two decades from about 42 percent in 1995 to about 30 percent in 2017. The decline of beverage milk demand has helped drive down all-milk prices and has caused other issues for milk policy and price regulations.

The increase in milk production, increased production per cow, and reduced cows per farm have accompanied substantial increases in labor productivity and lower milk production costs. Data from the USDA show that costs are substantially lower when the number of cows in a herd rises from a few hundred cows or fewer to 1,000 cows or more.

McDonald, Cessna, and Mosheim[17] provide details on the national patterns by herd size of dairy resource use and costs per hundredweight. They use the USDA Agricultural Resource Management Survey (ARMS) data to document evidence of substantial economies of size. While these tables tell a revealing story, the causation from herd size to lower costs is not as clear because herd size tends to be correlated with regional attributes that may also affect milk production costs. Moreover, for the smallest herds, farms with fewer than 500 cows, a substantial part of the production costs they incur are from cost imputed to unpaid family labor. The USDA cost data are consistent with observations that small dairy farms are either leaving the industry or getting larger, and already-large herds have been getting even larger. These patterns are also consistent with data the California Department of Food and Agriculture compiled using different methods. For example, in the Southern San Joaquin Valley, herds of more than 1,500 cows have consistently lower costs per hundredweight than herds of 1,500 cows or fewer, even when farms use similar technology and are located in the same region of California.[18]

Hired labor costs are higher for farms with larger herds, and the share of hired labor of all labor used on the farm is also higher. Farms with more cows rely on lower-cost hired labor for milking and routine chores.[19] However, total labor hours per unit of milk and labor costs per unit of milk are lower on the larger herds despite farms with more workers paying higher hourly wage rates. Milk per cow is higher for herds with more than 500 cows but shows no pattern above that herd size in the national ARMS data. In the California data from the Southern San Joaquin Valley, milk production per cow is highest for herds with between 1,500 and 2,400 cows and second highest for even larger herds.

The evolution toward larger herds with lower costs has transformed the US dairy industry over the past 30 or 40 years. Most US milk production occurs on farms with more than 1,000 cows operated by owner managers who employ others to feed and milk cows while they concentrate on supervision and improving the operation. The policies of the past are not suited to the farms that produce most of the milk. The USDA and Congress have struggled to maintain a relevant role—and nowhere more so than in trade and trade policy—as the United States has become competitive in global markets.

Brief History of Recent Dairy Policy

Just three decades ago, during the time of the 1985 Farm Bill, US dairy policy included:

1. Price supports for milk and government purchase and storage of processed dairy products;

2. Stock disposal policies that shifted government-owned products into domestic and international food aid;

3. High tariffs and strict quotas to keep out imports;

4. Export subsidies to allow exports to match foreign prices;

5. A "whole herd buyout" that paid farmers to sell their cows for slaughter, shutter their farms, and leave the dairy business;

6. Dozens of regional marketing orders that regulated milk prices by end use and pooled prices paid to farmers; and

7. Food and nutrition programs that subsidized domestic consumption of fluid milk products by children.

All but the last two of these policy features have been removed or are no longer significant. The first five policies were linked by the idea that farm prices for milk needed to be higher than the market would generate, thus the government should set those higher prices. When high government-set prices became incompatible with rapidly improving dairy productivity, support prices were allowed to decline (in real terms) so that eventually they did not interfere with market prices except in rare cases. With price supports no longer relevant, storage programs, surplus disposal, export subsidies, and supply controls also became redundant.

In place of binding support prices, a decade or so later, programs were introduced that used payments to dairy farms to make up the revenue difference between a government-determined price and the market price. The 1996 Farm Bill authorized the Northeast dairy states to begin a program of payments for farms in that region that was followed by Milk Income Loss Contract payments that started with the 2002 Farm Bill. This direct payment program has also now faded away. Finally, after three decades in which the economics of US milk production and marketing were transformed, the 2014 Farm Bill formalized the recognition that US dairy policy was in a new era.

Dairy Trade and Trade Policy

Decades ago, government price supports and federal purchase programs diverted milk supplies into government-held stockpiles of cheese, butter, and nonfat dry milk and into subsidized disposal programs. Eventually, as dairy farms and processors became more efficient, government commodity programs became less intrusive, and global demand increased, the United

States emerged as a major net exporter of several important processed dairy products. Currently, the United States is among the leading commercial dairy exporters while also importing selected products.

On average, US processors export about 14 percent of domestic milk production—a share that has fluctuated from about 12 percent to about 17 percent each month over the past five years. Meanwhile, imports have accounted for the equivalent of between 3 and 4 percent of US production. As a share of production, exporters ship more dry milk powder out of the United States than either cheese or butter. Cheese imports are still significant, and for some specialty cheeses, imports have sizable shares of the market.[20]

Top export products by volume are powders of nonfat milk, whey products (by-products from cheese manufacturing), cheese, butterfat, and lactose. Top dairy export destinations by value are Mexico, Southeast Asia, Canada, China, South America, and South Korea.[21] As with other farm commodities, most of the top dairy markets for US dairy exports have free trade agreements with the United States, and three of the top six markets (Mexico, Canada, and South Korea) are currently subject to "renegotiation" of those agreements. A significant exception, China, is a major buyer of US whey products and skim milk powder and is also the subject of some controversy with the United States, mostly over nonagricultural trade issues.

With recent changes in EU policy that eliminated production quotas and removed explicit export subsidies, several EU member countries are now also commercial exporters that rival the United States, New Zealand, and Australia in global markets. Australia and New Zealand have low domestic subsidies and no substantial trade barriers for dairy products. The EU, like the United States, has residual dairy subsidy programs and maintains import barriers. Nonetheless, global markets for relatively standard traded dairy products such as skim milk powder, standard cheese, whey products, and butter reflect vigorous competition. For major traded products, the four major traders have domestic prices that track each other closely over time.[22]

As noted above, US price support policy precluded commercial exports so long as the US government was ready to buy dairy products at prices higher than those available in export markets. As support prices came down in real terms, however, US food processors had the potential to export dairy products for which they could be competitive. Two further conditions have contributed to expanded exports.

First, the global market for US dairy products has grown because of reduced border barriers, income growth among potential importers, and limits to production expansion in New Zealand and Australia. Global imports have expanded because of income growth, especially in Asia and Mexico; free trade agreements with Korea and other countries; and reduced barriers in other importing countries. Moreover, with heavily pasture-based dairy systems, both Australia and New Zealand have found it difficult to expand enough to supply growing markets.

Second, the United States would have remained a tiny force in global exports if the rapid productivity growth in milk production and dairy processing had not allowed domestic costs to fall substantially. Farm-owned dairy cooperatives have been major participants in the export of milk powder and butter. Commercial cheese companies, some also owned by dairy farmers, have been significant exporters of cheese and whey products. Exports have been more important to western farms and processors because of their access to Mexico and Pacific ports and their distance from large US population centers in the US East and South.

While US firms have expanded commercial exports of dairy products and as US domestic prices are on par with those of other exporters, the United States has maintained hundreds of tariff-rate quotas (TRQs) that are designed to limit imports. A TRQ is a combination of a relatively low, often zero, tariff for a specified quantity of imports and a high, often prohibitively high, tariff for any additional "over-quota" imports. TRQs are often designated for specific tariff lines (for example, blue mold cheese), and they are often assigned to exports from specific countries. TRQs are allowed under World Trade Organization agreements and several free trade agreements. Many of the exporter-specific TRQs have "fill rates," the share of the limit actually imported, of zero or near zero in recent years.

US barriers for dairy products do seem to limit imports in instances in which a country-specific TRQ fills and the general TRQ available to all countries also fills. This may occur even when some of the country-specific TRQs for that item, say a specialty cheese, have not filled. Overall, TRQs do limit US imports but do not keep US dairy prices above world prices because the US exports many of the same product categories that it imports. For butter, commercial exports are about 3 percent of production, and imports are slightly less. For dry milk powder, exports are far larger, and imports are tiny. For cheese, the US imports many specialized and high-priced cheeses and exports more generic cheeses. In all these cases, the limits on imports seem to have small aggregate impacts, and, although import limits may lift the fortunes of particular companies, relaxing the mind-boggling array of TRQ regulations would have negligible aggregate impact on the US dairy industry.

The benefit of a US dairy industry as a champion of free trade could be large. The US could then join other major exporters in pushing for more open markets in every international forum and no longer be vulnerable to claims of hypocrisy and lack of consistent measure on dairy trade. The remarkable gains the US dairy industry has made allow it to leave behind its legacy of protection. The next farm bill could begin the process of clearing away the regulatory clutter that impedes dairy industry competitiveness.

Federal Milk Marketing Orders

The FMMO system in the United States dates from early in the New Deal era of the Great Depression in the 1930s. After the Supreme Court ruled a first version of the program unconstitutional, the Agricultural Marketing Agreement Act of 1937 authorized the USDA to intervene in the dairy markets only if requested by dairy farms in a given region. After the USDA develops a proposed marketing order for a region, it is applied only if favored by farms selling two-thirds of the Grade A milk in that region in a referendum in which cooperatives are allowed to block vote for their members.

The most recent major change to law controlling the FMMO system occurred in the 1996 Farm Bill when the USDA was instructed to reduce the number of orders from more than 30 to between 10 and 14. The resulting changes in the regulations specified 10 marketing orders, altered how minimum prices were calculated, and made other technical adjustments. The rule went into effect on January 1, 2000. Subsequent farm bills, including the 2014 Farm Bill, have retained the revised FMMO system and authorized conditions under which California is scheduled to join the FMMO system. Creating a California FMMO remains an active consideration.

Figure 3. Map of Federal Milk Marketing Orders

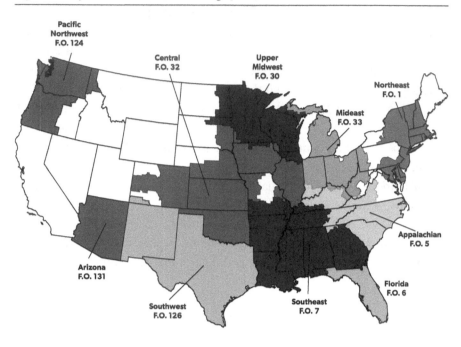

Note: F.O. = Federal Order. Blank areas of the map are regulated by state orders or unregulated. Alaska and Hawaii are not in federal orders.
Source: US Department of Agriculture, Agricultural Marketing Service, "Federal Milk Marketing Order Areas," https://www.ams.usda.gov/sites/default/files/media/Federal%20Milk%20Marketing%20Orders%20Map.pdf.

Figure 3 shows the regions covered by the 10 active FMMOs and regions not covered. Some of the area the FMMOs do not cover produce and process little milk, but others are significant milk regions. California is scheduled to eliminate the state milk marketing order it had operated since the 1930s and adopt a federal order starting in November 2018. That will leave only Idaho among the major dairy states that will not be regulated by a federal marketing order. Some small milk-producing states and parts of other states are covered by state marketing orders rules. In all, about two-thirds of US milk is regulated by the FMMO system and another 20 percent by state milk marketing orders that are similar to the federal orders. When California joins the federal system, that share will be about 85 percent.

The long-standing stated "objectives of the FMMOs are as follows:

- To promote orderly marketing conditions in fluid milk markets,

- To improve the income situation of dairy farmers,

- To supervise the terms of trade in milk markets in such a manner as to achieve more equality of bargaining between producers and milk processors, and

- To assure consumers of adequate supplies of good quality milk at reasonable prices."[23]

Several of these objectives suffer from vagueness of terms such as "orderly marketing," "more equality of bargaining," and "reasonable prices." For most of the American economy, market forces establish prices and create incentives for producers and consumers. For example, the USDA does not operate elaborate price and marketing regulations for strawberries, celery, eggs, corn silage, or alfalfa hay. The one objective that links the FMMO system to other farm programs is "to improve the income." I show in what follows that the price regulations under the FMMO system tend to not only shift revenue from consumers to farmers by raising farm prices of milk used for fluid products but also have many other consequences.

More fundamentally, a natural question is: Why are elaborate arrays of government regulations needed to meet such objectives for milk markets and milk producers? To consider this basic question, I draw on the insights of a standard analytic framework used by economists to examine pool pricing presented (see Appendix A) and provide a description of how the FMMOs actually operate. Even with this level of detail, we must abstract from much of the complexity of the regulations. Indeed, much of the intricacy of the milk marketing orders has developed in attempts to avoid unintended consequences of incentives created by the regulations themselves.

Basic Economics of Milk Marketing Orders. Dozens of studies have addressed the economic effects of milk marketing regulation in the United States.[24] These studies and many more helped establish some economic implications of the FMMOs: Milk marketing orders transfer income from milk consumers to dairy farmers, resulting in a net loss to society. They stimulate milk production and divert production from fluid products into hard products. This research has explored many conceptual and empirical issues and has become more technical and elaborate over the years.

A milk marketing order sets minimum prices that processors must pay for raw milk depending on the product for which the processor uses that milk. FMMOs distinguish between four end-use classes: beverage products (the highest price), soft and frozen products, cheese and whey, and butter and powder. Revenue from each milk class is pooled, and participating producers receive a market-wide average, or blend, price. The details of milk pricing rules have evolved over time, but the key elements of price discrimination and revenue pooling remain.

The quantity and share of milk used for manufactured products is larger under the FMMO pricing system for two important reasons. First, under the FMMO the government sets a high price for fluid milk products that tend to stay in the local regional market. The higher price discourages consumption of those fluid products, and the milk that would otherwise be used for locally consumed products must shift to processed products, which increases supply of those products.

The second reason the FMMO system implies more milk for manufactured products is that the policy stimulates more raw milk production on farms. As a matter of policy, all farms in the system explicitly receive a weighted average "pool" or "blend" price that includes the benefit of the high (government-set) price of milk used for fluid products. That means that even milk that is produced to be used for cheese and whey, or butter and dry milk powders, receives a price above that paid by the manufacturers of those products. That is, the farm receives more than the buyer pays for milk used for manufactured products, with the difference contributed by the fluid milk processors and milk drinkers.

Several simplifications are made in the graphical exposition in Appendix A but not in more complex simulation models that are used for analysis of quantitative impacts of marketing orders. First, in the actual complicated regulations, prices and quantities are specified separately for milk components—fat, protein, and nonfat, nonprotein components. These separate components are combined to generate the price of milk per liquid hundredweight to determine the price paid to the farms. Second, farm milk prices often include some over-order milk price premiums paid directly by the buyer to the farm supplier (or cooperative of farmers) to encourage delivery to a particular buyer. That is, regulations specify price minimums and do not restrict payments above the minimums. Milk hauling costs, milk sanitation, and other farm-specific considerations affect the price farmers receive and processors pay. Despite the simplifications used in the exposition in Appendix A, the structure introduced captures the essential features, subsidy elements, and supply implications of the milk marketing order system.

In practice, FMMOs adjust minimum prices on a monthly basis for components of fat and nonfat solids for Class III milk (used for cheese and whey products) and Class IV milk (used for butter and dry milk powder) based on specific market prices of butter, nonfat dry milk, cheese, and whey products. The market prices of products and the resultant implied component prices used in the minimum milk price calculations do not differ across orders and reflect a national (and international) market for these products and components. The minimum prices of Class III and Class IV milk components are tied directly to market prices of highly traded processed products. The minimum prices of milk fat and skim solid components are market determined, which ties the minimum farm price of milk to these product markets.

Class I (fluid products) and Class II (soft and frozen products) component prices are set by simply adding region-specific differentials to the Class III and Class IV component prices. Thus Class I and Class II minimum prices are higher than those that would exist without the policy.

The Class I price per hundredweight is calculated using the component prices for the *higher of* the Class III and Class IV skim milk component (and the common butterfat component). Importantly, the minimum prices for the subsequent month are based on the recent past market prices of the Class III and Class IV products. The high prices reduce quantities of fluid products demanded by consumers, and therefore less milk is used for these locally consumed products. Moreover, binding future minimum prices to past product price builds in sticky adjustments and additional flux to the markets.

Class II prices are tied only to the market price of nonfat dry milk, which is a Class IV product. In recent years, the Class II price was often below the Class III price because of the low price of nonfat dry milk compared to the price of cheese. Such price differences would not persist under market-driven pricing, given competitive pressures and arbitrage.

As noted above, markets for soft and fluid products are more local, and the quantity demanded for milk used in beverage products consumed locally is relatively insensitive to price changes. That means the higher price caused by the marketing order has relatively small effects on quantities demanded. The markets for the Class III and Class IV products in each marketing order, on the other hand, are national and international, and demands for those products are much more sensitive to price changes, meaning that pushing their prices lower results in relatively large increases in quantities sold.

The marketing orders also maintain a separation between the price paid for milk used for cheese and whey and the price paid for milk used for butter and dry milk powder. In recent years the price of cheese and whey has been relatively high compared to the price of dry milk powder and butter. The result has been a higher price of Class III milk than for Class IV milk. For example, in December 2016, the national average price of Class III milk was $17.40 per hundredweight, while the price of Class IV milk was $14.97. A few months later, in April 2017, the price of Class III milk was $15.22 per hundredweight, while the price of Class IV milk was $14.01 per hundredweight. No such differentials would persist under a market-based price system, given competitive pressures and arbitrage. They reflect inefficiency losses of regulated prices.

The FMMO regions differ in how their milk is used and the Class I price differential. In the Florida order, more than 80 percent of the milk is used for Class I products, and the Class I price differential is $5.40 per hundredweight. At the other extreme, in the Upper Midwest order, about 10 percent of the milk is used for Class I products, and the Class I price differential is $1.80 per hundredweight.[25] Milk is more expensive to produce in Florida, and without the marketing orders, little milk would be produced there. Incentives for geographic arbitrage are standard market forces that would move milk to higher-priced markets. The FMMO system attempts to duplicate such a standard market result with an array of minimum prices and differentials. Of course, government-set differentials can never precisely mimic market forces. The result is that additional high-cost milk is produced in places such as Florida, higher prices are charged to consumers, and less milk is produced in lower-cost regions that are better suited to milk production.

Example of Impacts of a Marketing Order on Prices and Quantities. By setting the price of milk used for Class I products above that of identical milk used for Class III and IV products, the FMMO system causes beverage milk to be more expensive and cheese, whey, butter, and milk powders to be less expensive for buyers. As discussed above, the diversion of milk across uses and the incentive to produce more milk cause economic losses to both consumers and the economy as a whole. The magnitude of the diversions and the losses depends on the shares used for each product, the size of the price differential, and the relevant impacts of price changes on quantities supplied and demanded.

In the Northeast FMMO, for example, the Class I price has been about 40 percent above the Class IV price. Given the usage shares across classes, the blend price has been about 20 percent above the Class IV price. Using a low-price elasticity of demand (the percentage change in quantity demanded for each 1 percent change in price to buyers) for milk used in Class I products (which is about –0.2) and a moderate intermediate term supply elasticity (the percentage change in quantity supplied for a 1 percent change in the price to producers) for raw milk (say, 2.0), these price differences translate into about 8 percent less fluid milk use and about 40 percent more milk produced in the region. Putting these impacts together, the marketing order has a substantial impact on the use of milk for manufactured products in the Northeast.

In states such as Idaho (or California and Wisconsin), marketing orders have much smaller potential impacts on the diversion of milk across uses and incentives for additional milk production. The impacts are small because in these states only a small share of milk is used for Class I products, and there is a small potential Class I differential because so much of the milk is shipped out of the area as processed products. With, say, 15 percent of milk used for Class I and a 15 percent Class I differential, the extra revenue from diversion is just over 2 percent (0.15 x 0.15 = 2.25 percent). Thus, in the regions that are most milk intensive and where most of the milk in the United States is produced, marketing orders do the least to generate additional milk income. These regions also face complications in moving milk out of the region for higher price uses, and the array of complicated marketing order rules may cause more disruption to milk market innovation.

A caveat to these quantitative implications is that, in many regions where marketing orders set minimum prices, buyers pay significant over-order premiums (OOPs) for milk used for fluid products and cheese. Marketing order minimums do not set actual market prices, and buyers often pay more than the minimums. And since the OOPs are not pooled, they provide incentives directly to individual farms to deliver their milk to a specific processor. A second caveat is that in federal orders, some milk processors may choose not to participate in the marketing order.[26] These buyers may operate "non-pool" plants and buy milk directly from producers. Of course, non-pool plants must pay enough to attract farms that would otherwise receive the blend price if they deliver to a pool plant, and the blend price is usually above the minimum price for Class III and Class IV processors. Sometimes, however, when the blend price is low and the minimum Class III or IV price is above what would otherwise be a market price, plants remain outside the order.

Current Issues Facing the FMMO System. No changes to FMMOs are required in the next farm bill. Like crop insurance and some other farm policies, they are not subject to periodic reauthorization.[27] Nonetheless, even if the system remains largely in place, changes are likely on the horizon. These include a California FMMO, complications associated with organic milk, and adjustments to FMMOs to facilitate forward pricing and other risk-management tools used by milk producers.

After years of discussion and prior legislation facilitating transition to a federal order for California, the USDA held public hearings on a California order throughout much of the fall of 2015. Based on this record, the USDA published its "recommended decision," essentially a proposed marketing order in the *Federal Register,* on February 14, 2017. With cooperatives "block voting" for their memberships, the proposed federal order passed with an overwhelming majority.

One stipulation was that the federal order would allow continuation of the California-specific policy that allocates some of the milk revenue to producer owners of California milk "quota" only if the system was operated and regulated by California rather than federal rules. The California Department of Food and Agriculture held a referendum of producers to gauge their approval of a California-operated quota program to accompany the federal order.

Most projections indicated higher minimum milk prices for farms under a federal order, at least initially. A longer-term issue is whether higher farm milk prices imposed by a marketing order would be sustainable, given relatively high processing costs in California and California's reliance on the sale of standard processed products in national and international markets. Among the features of particular interest in a California FMMO is whether California cheese plants are likely to operate outside the marketing order (depooling) and, if they do, how that would affect the pool prices. Cheese plants now offer OOPs to farms that deliver to them, and they may prefer this practice to higher pool prices and diluted price incentives for farms to deliver to them. The issue of allowing processors to leave and remain outside the pool may be contentious in California.[28]

In recent years, organic milk has grown to about 6 percent of fluid use, while overall beverage milk consumption has declined. The challenge for the FMMO system is that the Class I differential and minimum prices are irrelevant for organic milk, which, nonetheless, must remain in the system. Options might be to let organic milk producers opt out of the FMMO system or set up separate orders for organic milk, but both these options might encourage other producers who claim their milk is special also to want to opt out. The broader systemic question is: As conventional milk beverage products become an ever smaller share of milk usage, does the FMMO system cause more complications and added costs than it is worth in terms of milk revenue generated by price discrimination?

Two broader issues for milk marketing orders are that they likely make milk prices more variable and that they reduce the ability of producers and processors to manage price variability. First, minimum prices the FMMOs set use recent prices of manufactured products to set future minimum prices by proposed end use for milk on the farm. One of the most powerful features of markets is that they aggregate participant views of likely supplies and demand and implications for prices. Markets are inherently future oriented. History may be a guide, but there is nothing rigid about the relationships, and market participants have substantial incentives to find and use all relevant information. Formulas simply cannot replicate performance of participants with incentives. That means the FMMO prices send the wrong signals to farms and buyers and cause undue fluctuation as the markets must compensate those signals. The FMMO system regulators are remarkably effective with the tools they have, but they cannot replicate markets.

All agricultural markets have variable supplies and demands and hence variable quantities and prices. Market tools have evolved to allow sellers and buyers to mitigate or offset quantity and price variability that is costly to them. A problem is that marketing order rules make using some of those tools—such as features of long-term contracts, forward pricing, futures and options, and even on-farm production adjustments—more complicated.[29] Regulators have recognized some of these issues and designed special programs (such as the Dairy Forward Pricing Program) to facilitate certain types of contracts. However, Class I milk cannot participate in forward pricing, and risk management for buyers of Class I milk is made more difficult by the FMMO rules. Month-to-month and year-to-year price variability is endemic and natural in agriculture. By restricting options for both buyers and sellers and inserting government regulations into every transaction, the FMMO rules seem to exacerbate costs of dealing with such variability.

The FMMO system is an elaborate and sophisticated set of complicated rules and regulations. It is hard to see how they make milk markets more "orderly" except in the sense that they are now controlled by active government agents rather than forces of supply and demand. It is also hard to picture that milk producers and processors would fail to assure an adequate supply of beverage milk products for consumers. That problem has not plagued the supply of lettuce and strawberries or beverages such as orange juice, soy milk, and almond milk. As to bargaining, some of the largest food companies in the United States are dairy farm cooperatives that bargain for their farmer members. And in local markets the farm cooperatives are often larger than the local cheese companies that buy the milk. No evidence indicates that dairy farms are especially vulnerable and that the FMMO system is effective protection in any case.

The bottom-line question is why, 30 years after the fall of the Berlin Wall and decades after China abandoned rigid Mao-style central planning, the United States maintains Soviet-style milk pricing. The most likely answer is that some farms and some processors gain from the system at the expense of other producers, processors, and consumers.[30] These winners take advantage of political inertia and fatigue among those who would benefit from change.

The Margin Protection Program: An Unpopular Policy in Search of Repair

As noted above, the 2014 Farm Bill removed both the long-standing dairy price support program and the direct payment programs for dairy farms that had tried to provide subsidies after the price supports proved untenable. The problem with price supports was that, if the support price was high enough to satisfy the producer lobby, the program stimulated production of efficient farms, distorted markets, precluded commercial exports, and was prohibitively expensive. Payment schemes (such as Milk Income Loss Contract) substituted deficiency payments to farms for market price interventions but faced the problem that they provided only relatively small per-farm subsidies, even with low dairy-net incomes. So these programs also were not popular with producers. The basic problem for subsidy programs is that the dairy industry is large and diverse and has had remarkable productivity gains concentrated among larger farms. This means any program that provides substantial support to the high-cost farms and is therefore popular among those farms and their advocates is also likely to become expensive for US taxpayers.

The genesis of the MPP that replaced price supports and payment schemes derives from the experience of the previous decade. Dairy farms experienced periods of low and moderate milk prices but disastrous economic conditions in 2009 and negative net revenues again in 2012. In both cases the problem was as much because of high feed prices as low milk prices. The year 2009 was particularly severe. As McDonald, Cessna, and Mosheim document in detail, even the largest low-cost dairy farms experienced negative net revenue in 2009. The dairy industry, as a whole, shed equity and acquired debt, and many farms did not have enough cash flow to service the debt.[31]

The MPP is vulnerable to the same basic problem that has doomed other recent dairy subsidy programs. It seems unpopular with dairy advocates because it does not generate substantial income subsidies.[32] But the budget costs of providing substantial subsidies each year to such a large industry that has not recently had a large share of the farm subsidy budget does not seem feasible. To see the income impacts of the program clearly, we must review a few program specifics and outcomes.

As revised in 2018, the MPP authorizes payments to enrolled farms when the USDA-calculated margin per hundredweight falls below the target margin selected by the farmer.[33] For the first five million pounds of covered production, margins from $4.00 per hundredweight through $5.00 per hundredweight are available with only a nominal enrollment fee and no premium payment. For higher-insured margins, farmers pay a premium scaled to alternative margins that increase in $0.50 intervals from $5 up to $8 per hundredweight. After five million pounds of covered production, premiums are zero for the $4.00 margin and rise rapidly for higher margins. Under the 2018 adjustments, the margins are calculated monthly rather than using a two-month average as in the previous law. The other interesting change is that farms were allowed to enroll for 2018 coverage until mid-June 2018 so that many were eligible to buy the policy after they had already qualified for payments.

The definition of the legislation-defined margin used in calculating possible payments is an approximation of the actual farm-based margins that use readily available national data from the USDA. The milk price used in the calculations is the national all-milk farm price that is not adjusted for any regional differences or any farm-by-farm differences due to quality. The feed-cost index is based on a linear formula of coefficients reflecting share of costs of each of three feeds in an average dairy operation. These coefficients are multiplied by the national average price of corn, soybeans, and alfalfa hay. The coefficients were calibrated to set the feed cost in the base period equal to the average feed cost and movements in calculated feed cost from month to month and to reflect changes in the feed prices. This calculated margin reflects, in rough terms, the movements in the milk price minus cost of feed and does not reflect the true margin for any particular farm or group of farms in recent years. The idea was simply that the movements in the USDA-calculated margin would have a relatively high correlation with the economic fortunes of dairy farms in the United States.

Farms may enroll between 25 percent and 90 percent of their covered production history. The premium per hundredweight is lower for the first 40,000 hundredweight of covered production history.[34] Table 2 shows the premium schedule that is currently operative as written into the legislation.[35] An important feature of the schedule is that premiums were not calibrated by actuaries to general fair premiums with specific subsidy rates, as is the practice with USDA Risk Management Agency crop insurance programs. The premiums for each coverage of production history and protection level are written into law, with some consideration of projections of government budget costs over the five-year life of the farm bill.

Table 2 shows how much premiums increase as protection level increases. This reflects estimates associated with the history of milk-price-minus-feed-cost margins that had occurred in the years before the 2014 legislation. Premiums are much higher for the higher hundredweight of coverage, which would be demanded by larger dairy farms. These higher premiums for larger farms are especially pronounced at higher protection levels. At a protection level of $6.50 per hundredweight, a farm would pay $0.29 per hundredweight more (more than triple) for insured milk in excess of five million pounds. At the highest protection of $8.00 per hundredweight, a farm would pay $1.36 per hundredweight more for the covered milk over five million pounds. The premium rate differences are unlike the laws and regulations governing crop insurance and reflect purely political forces (associated with regional differences) that are unfavorable to larger dairy farms.

We now have three years of experience with the operation of the MPP and can assess how the program has performed so far. First, consider enrollment. In 2015, 24,748 of 45,344 eligible dairy operations signed up for the program, with 44 percent of those enrolling at the free minimum margin of $4.00 per hundredweight and 56 percent of those enrolled paying a premium. Thus, overall, 55 percent of operations enrolled, and 31 percent paid a premium. In 2015, about 81 percent of production enrolled, and about 33 percent enrolled at higher than the minimum. The figures for 2016 and 2017 show gradually fewer farms enrolled at premium paying levels. In 2017, most eligible farms enrolled, but essentially all those producers and their milk coverage enrolled at the minimum $4.00 per hundredweight coverage and paid no premiums.[36]

Farms that have chosen not to enroll or to enroll at the no-premium level have made appropriate financial decisions in the sense that in none of the years was the program payoff enough to be profitable. Of course, if the goal of the program is risk management, it does not seem to have attracted farms to regularly pay premiums, as they do for their unsubsidized insurance policies that cover farm machinery and buildings on the farm. The MPP seems to have the same pattern of participation as subsidized federal crop insurance, where unless reliably profitable, farms do not participate or participate at the minimum coverage that does not require a premium.[37]

Table 2. MPP Premium Rates per Hundredweight of Covered Production History

Margin Protection Level	First 5 Million Pounds of Covered Production History Premium	Covered Production History > 5 Million Pounds Premium
$4.00	$0.000	$0.000
$4.50	$0.000	$0.020
$5.00	$0.000	$0.040
$5.50	$0.000	$0.100
$6.00	$0.009	$0.155
$6.50	$0.040	$0.290
$7.00	$0.063	$0.830
$7.50	$0.087	$1.060
$8.00	$0.142	$1.360

Note: All values are in dollars per hundredweight.
Source: Randy Schnepf, "Dairy Provisions in the 2014 Farm Bill (P.L. 113-79)," Congressional Research Service, September 15, 2014, http://nationalaglawcenter.org/wp-content/uploads/assets/crs/R43465.pdf; and Dave Natzke, "MPP-Dairy 2018 Enrollment Open, April 9 Through June 1," *Progressive Dairyman*, April 3, 2018, https://www.progressivedairy.com/news/industry-news/mpp-dairy-2018-enrollment-open-april-9-june-1.

Several analysts have examined how the MPP would have performed for dairy farms if the program would have been in operation and if farms would have participated in prior years.[38] Much of the data and analysis were provided as the MPP was being finalized to help producers with their enrollment decisions. Using the USDA-provided data and estimates of projected milk and feed prices, an analyst may ask what the payoff to the program would have been under assumptions about coverage and what the farm expected about prices.[39] The USDA provides useful enrollment information for dairy farms that also includes historical information that allows them to assess participation strategies that would have maximized net returns in prior years. The results depend on the amount of milk coverage and whether a farm uses ex ante forecasts of milk and feed prices or assumes the farm has perfect foresight in selecting what turned out to be the optimal coverage to maximize returns, rather than accounting for any risk-management considerations.[40]

Based on ex ante estimated returns, the optimal MPP choice would have been for minimal coverage in half the years over the past decade, even for small farms with fewer than four million pounds enrolled (equivalent to fewer than 200 cows). The enrollment years were 2009 through 2013 when $8.00 coverage would have been the net-income-maximizing choice. For actual returns, there are only three years in which paying premiums to buy coverage would have been optimal: 2009, 2012, and 2013. The same pattern applied to a large farm covering 20 million pounds of annual production.

It is useful to ask how much MPP benefits would have contributed to the farm total revenue and farm margin of milk revenue over feed cost. In most years the payoff would have been zero, but in a few years, especially 2009 and 2012, the net payments from the MPP would have been large. In summary, for small farms, the MPP would have contributed about 2.0 percent to total revenue if the farm followed the projected returns in deciding how to enroll. If the farm could have selected the net-revenue-maximizing enrollment strategy each year, the program would have added 4.0 percent to revenue. Of course, the estimated shares are much higher for the margin over feed costs. The average is 5.7 percent of revenue and 12.0 percent of margin if the optional coverage were chosen each year. For a farm covering 20 million pounds, the impact is about 0.8 percent of revenue following projected returns for enrollment and 2.8 percent of revenue if the best coverage choice were made each year. The large farm would have gained about 2.3 percent of revenue following the projected returns and about 8.3 percent of revenue if the farm could have made the best coverage choice each year.

These calculations show that even a program that would pay off in only a few years in each decade can be profitable to farms. In the case of the MPP, given considerable information available before the farms must make an election decision, it is likely that they may pick years in which margins are likely to be low during the year and years when margins are likely to be high. In that case, the estimates that the program can account for between 1 and 4 percent of long-run dairy farm revenue seem plausible. These calculations suggest that the MPP has provided significant additions to expected revenue and that additional revenue would be available in periods during which farms would otherwise experience low or negative net revenue.

The MPP contributes to a long-run increase in expected net revenue for participating farms and smoothing of revenue variability. These impacts of the program suggest the potential for significant supply response.[41] The impacts on expected revenue and an applicable supply elasticity of about 2.0 indicate that added milk production in the long run may be 4 percent or more. This is in the same order of magnitude as estimates of the impact of crop insurance programs for field crops administered and subsidized by the USDA Risk Management Agency.[42] With the revisions in 2018, the subsidy elements are larger, and the program is even more favorable for small farms.

The bottom-line considerations about MPP also apply to the Livestock Gross Margin for Dairy Cattle insurance program offered by the USDA through the Risk Management Agency. Indeed, the same considerations apply to USDA-subsidized agricultural insurance programs in general. What broad public purpose is served by offering heavily subsidized insurance to farm businesses that choose not to buy such insurance if offered without substantial subsidy? As with other farms, milk producers undertake myriad activities to mitigate production and financial risk. They operate well-managed herds to reduce disease and other supply-side risks, buy feed with forward contracts or use markets to hedge against future feed price increases, diversify into other farm enterprises, vertically integrate into feed production and cooperative marketing, and have off-farm investment, and family members work at nonfarm occupations.

Of course, even with all these tools, farming, including dairy farming, is a risky business. But that fact in itself is not a rationale for subsidy. Without the MPP subsidies, the United States may produce somewhat less milk, which would mean somewhat lower exports. But reduced dairy subsidies would mean that those resources (income taken from taxpayers) could be put to use elsewhere in the economy where they would be more productive.

Concluding Remarks

The recent history of milk productivity and dairy competition tells a remarkable and compelling story. The industry has been transformed by progressive farmers, processors, and marketers. Policy change has also been remarkable. Outmoded policy ideas were simply no match for industry realities. The 2014 Farm Bill cleared away some of the policy thicket, but more remains.

The first policy change is not necessarily part of the farm bill process, but it could be. It is time to eliminate US dairy product trade barriers. An uninitiated observer just counting tariff lines and the number of relatively high tariffs might conclude that there was a massive wall of protection behind which the US dairy industry cowered in fear of imports. But that image is an illusion. In fact, despite dozens of individual tariff lines and TRQs with high second-tier tariffs, the US exports a large range of milk products with no export subsidy, and the domestic price of milk and milk components in the United States is commensurate with prices in other competitive exporters. For the most part, the tariffs are not binding, or they apply to narrowly specified sets of products and therefore have little or no aggregate impact. These residual effective high tariffs protect a few favored companies to the detriment of the industry as a whole. It is time for the United States to help fully open the two-way street to global dairy markets. The FMMO system also does not have to be an issue for a farm bill, but it has been in the farm bill in the past and could be again.

The FMMO system in the United States is among the most byzantine policies in world agriculture, and that is no modest achievement. Perhaps the main reason the system has lasted for 80 years is that advocates for the status quo have successfully challenged critics on the basis that they do not understand how the system operates. Proponents do not acknowledge that a convoluted regulatory system that defies understanding is a government failure, not a success. In fact, the FMMO system is complicated mainly because it has tried to mimic market forces. But the program's history has documented time and again that regulators simply cannot capture the full force of market incentives with regulatory rules.

Marketing orders do not simply gum up the gears of progress for the dairy industry, which is bad enough; they cause higher prices for consumers of beverage milk products (notably children). Marketing orders also transfer revenues among milk producers to favor those least suited to satisfy buyers with lower-cost and innovative products.

Finally, the new dairy subsidy program, the MPP, provides periodic subsidies when the national average margin of milk price is above a USDA-calculated feed price index. Over a decadelong horizon, this program would probably increase milk revenues received by dairy farm businesses by a few percentages. But that is purely a subsidy from taxpayers for no clear public good and with no clear rationale. The program also continues regional and other biases such that US dairy policy is once again transferring income from successful progressive and competitive dairy farms to those likely to be exiting the business.

So the bottom line: It is time to set the cows free. Let the US dairy industry embrace its global competitiveness and innovate unencumbered by outmoded policy ideas.

Appendix A. Basic Economic Framework
of Federal Milk Marketing Orders

Figure A1 is the standard diagram that economists use to illustrate the key elements of milk marketing orders. An important feature of the market depicted in Figure A1 is that demand for raw milk used for fluid products, Q_F, is a function of (P_F) in that marketing order region. Moreover, that demand relationship is inelastic because beverage milk is heavy and expensive to transport and is therefore limited to only relatively local markets. Milk from outside is less available to compete for beverage uses within the marketing order. The opposite is true for the demand for milk that is used for manufactured products such as butter, milk powder, and cheese. Milk within a marketing order faces relatively elastic demand because the products produced from milk in a particular region compete in national and global markets. For simplicity, in Figure A1, demand for manufacturing milk is shown as perfectly elastic, so that the price of manufacturing milk facing the marketing order, P_M, is independent of allocation of this region's milk to this use. The marginal cost of producing raw milk is denoted in the figure as MC_A.

With no price regulation and no milk quality differences, a single price, P_M, prevails for milk in all uses in the single regional market. The total quantity of Grade A milk produced is Q_{A0}, the quantity sold to the fluid market is Q_{F0}, and the difference is sold to the manufacturing market.

Marketing order regulations raise the price of milk used for fluid milk products by a fixed markup D to P_{F1}, and the higher price reduces the quantity sold on the fluid product market to Q_{F1}. The marketing order allows the price for milk used in manufacturing to equal the market-determined price P_M. The blend price paid to producers, found along the curved line labeled P_{blend}, falls as the total quantity of milk sold rises. The blend price is the incentive price for milk producers, resulting in total quantity of milk, Q_{A1}, and blend price, P_{A1}. By reducing fluid consumption and increasing total milk production, the marketing order increases the quantity of milk sold to the manufacturing market, some of which is exported.

Under this depiction, the economic loss to consumers in the market for fluid milk products is equal to area $a + b + c + d$, and the gain to producers is

Figure A1. A Standard Diagram Depicting the Stylized Economics of Milk Marketing Orders

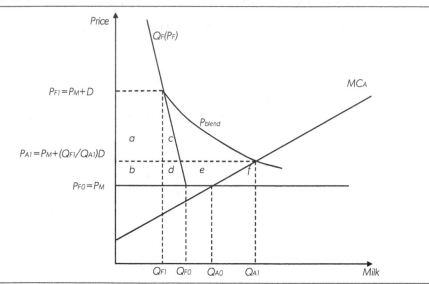

Note: See text for explanations of notation.
Source: Author.

equal to area $b + d + e$. Area c is loss to consumers not transferred to producers. Revenue pooling also induces excess milk production, the cost of which is measured by area f.

This complicated, but conceptually simple, model shows how the FMMO causes the quantity of milk used for manufactured products to be higher. The high government-set price for beverage milk products discourages consumption of those products, so milk that would otherwise be used for locally consumed products shifts to processed products. Second, the higher average price of raw milk stimulates milk production. Milk that is used for the manufactured products receives a price above the price paid by manufacturers of those products. For milk used in manufactured products, the supplying farm receives a higher price than the buyer pays, with the difference contributed by beverage milk processors and milk drinkers.

Without a government marketing order, the price for milk to dairy farms would be the same, independent of the final use of the milk (abstracting from milk component characteristics, transport costs, and so forth).

As noted, the price of milk to the farms in the government system, however, is neither the Class I price of milk used for fluid beverage products nor P_M but is a weighted average of the two, with the weights based on the quantity shares in each use. That is, the price and quantity of milk in the fluid beverage-use market is directly derived from the total quantity and the price and quantity in the market for milk used for manufactured products.

Notes

1. Paul W. MacAvoy, *Federal Milk Marketing Orders and Price Supports*, American Enterprise Institute, 1977; Joseph V. Balagtas, "Milking Consumers and Taxpayers: The Folly of U.S. Dairy Policy," in *American Boondoggle: Fixing the 2012 Farm Bill*, eds. Barry K. Goodwin, Vincent H. Smith, and Daniel A. Sumner (Washington, DC: AEI Press, 2011), http://www.aei.org/feature/american-boondoggle-series/. AEI analyses that include discussion of dairy policy in the context of farm policy more broadly are in Daniel A. Sumner, *Agricultural Policy Reform in the United States* (Washington, DC: AEI Press, 1995). Specifically, see Daniel A. Sumner, Joseph V. Balagtas, and Jisang Yu, "US Dairy Subsidies Remain Convoluted and Costly," in *The Economic Welfare and Trade Relations Implications of the 2014 Farm Bill*, ed. Vincent H. Smith (Bingley, UK: Emerald Group Publishing, 2015).
2. For a recent update in the FMMO system and current issues that may arise in the new farm bill, see Joel L. Greene, "Federal Milk Marketing Orders: An Overview," Congressional Research Service, December 13, 2017.
3. Agricultural Act of 2014, Pub. L. No. 113-79.
4. See Randy Schnepf, "Dairy Provisions in the 2014 Farm Bill (P.L. 113-79)," Congressional Research Service, September 15, 2014, http://nationalaglawcenter.org/wp-content/uploads/assets/crs/R43465.pdf. It includes a side by side of the 2014 Farm Bill dairy title compared to prior law.
5. For the detailed data for recent years, see US Department of Agriculture, Economic Research Service, "Farm Income and Wealth Statistics," 2017, https://www.ers.usda.gov/data-products/farm-income-and-wealth-statistics/cash-receipts-by-commodity/.
6. Dairy-producer groups regularly document the importance of the dairy industry to state and regional economic aggregates. For a California example, see Daniel A. Sumner, Josué Medellín-Azuara, and Eric Coughlin, "Contributions of the California Dairy Industry to the California Economy," University of California Agriculture Issues Center, May 14, 2015, http://aic.ucdavis.edu/publications/CMABReport2015.pdf.
7. K. Charles Ling, "Operations of Dairy Cooperatives, 2012," US Department of Agriculture, Rural Development, Rural Business-Cooperative Programs Research, 2014.
8. See Ling, "Operations of Dairy Cooperatives, 2012," Table 10.
9. Joseph V. Balagtas and M. Cakir, "Estimating Market Power of U.S. Dairy Cooperatives in the Fluid Milk Market," *American Journal of Agricultural Economics* 94, no. 3 (2012): 647–58.
10. The extreme case is wine grapes, for which prices routinely range from $300 per

ton to $6,000 per ton and sometimes much more.

11. For a recent summary in a policy context, see James M. MacDonald, Jerry Cessna, and Roberto Mosheim, "Changing Structure, Financial Risks, and Government Policy for the U.S. Dairy Industry," US Department of Agriculture, Economic Research Service, March 2016, https://www.ers.usda.gov/publications/pub-details/?pubid=45522.

12. For a comparison across commodity industries that draws on USDA data and USDA Economic Research Service discussions, see Daniel A. Sumner, "American Farms Keep Growing: Size, Productivity, and Policy," *Journal of Economic Perspectives* 28, no. 1 (2014): 147–66.

13. MacDonald, Cessna, and Mosheim, "Changing Structure, Financial Risks, and Government Policy for the U.S. Dairy Industry."

14. See MacDonald, Cessna, and Mosheim, "Changing Structure, Financial Risks, and Government Policy for the U.S. Dairy Industry," Table 1.

15. US Department of Agriculture, "2012 Census Publications," https://www.agcensus.usda.gov/2012/.

16. US Department of Agriculture, "2012 Census Publications."

17. MacDonald, Cessna, and Mosheim, "Changing Structure, Financial Risks, and Government Policy for the U.S. Dairy Industry."

18. For California cost data by herd size, see California Department of Food and Agriculture, "Cost of Production Feedback," https://www.cdfa.ca.gov/dairy/cost_of_production_feedback.html.

19. US Department of Agriculture, Economic Research Service, "Milk Cost of Production Estimates," 2017, https://www.ers.usda.gov/data-products/milk-cost-of-production-estimates/milk-cost-of-production-estimates/#Annual.

20. See the data compilation at US Dairy Export Council, "Research & Data," https://www.usdec.org/research-and-data.

21. The US Dairy Export Council provides a convenient display of official export data. US Dairy Export Council, "Top Charts," http://www.usdec.org/research-and-data/top-charts.

22. See MacDonald, Cessna, and Mosheim, "Changing Structure, Financial Risks, and Government Policy for the U.S. Dairy Industry," Figure 6. That figure shows how US commercial exports of skim milk powder were about zero until 2004 when US prices fell below those of Oceania (Australia and New Zealand). Exports have become substantial in the past decade as US prices have remained competitive.

23. Greene, "Federal Milk Marketing Orders."

24. Dozens of studies have developed models, simulations, and econometrics of the economic impacts of milk marketing orders. Among the early studies, see R. A. Ippolito and R. T. Mason, "The Social Cost of Government Regulation of Milk," *Journal of Law and Economics* 21 (1978): 33–65. Among the later studies, see Joseph V. Balagtas, Aaron Smith, and Daniel A. Sumner, "Econometric Analysis of the Effects of Marketing Orders on the U.S. Milk Grade Mix," *American Journal of Agricultural Economics* 89, no. 4 (2007): 839–51. Consider the effect of marketing orders and the shift toward producing Grade A milk. These papers have references to many other articles and chapters.

25. Leonard Sahling, "Federal Milk Marketing Orders and Their Role in Dairy Pricing," CoBank, December 2014, http://www.cobank.com/Knowledge-exchange/~/media/

Files/Unsearchable%20Files/Knowledge%20Exchange/2014/KEReport_FMMO-Dairy-Dec2014.pdf.

26. In the California Milk Marketing Orders, all plants must be in the pool and pay the government-set minimum prices.

27. Greene, "Federal Milk Marketing Orders."

28. An interesting feature of FMMO voting is that milk cooperatives are allowed to "block vote" for their members. In the California case, about 80 percent of the farms with about that share of the milk in the state are members of three large cooperatives. If these three cooperatives vote yes, then the California FMMO would be approved. This could occur even if the measure was favored by a bare majority of each cooperative and favored by few farms that were not members of cooperatives. In this case a majority of all farms may disapprove of the FMMO. But a potential case is more extreme. Two of the cooperatives are national with most of their members and milk purchases outside California. To benefit their national membership, those cooperative could block vote in favor of the California FMMO, even if a majority of their California members opposed the California FMMO.

29. See Greene, "Federal Milk Marketing Orders," 12.

30. For an analysis of milk marketing order pricing as a reflection of political power, see Byeong-il Ahn and Daniel A. Sumner, "Political Market Power Reflected in Milk Pricing Regulations," *American Journal of Agricultural Economics* 91, no. 3 (2009): 723–37.

31. MacDonald, Cessna, and Mosheim, "Changing Structure, Financial Risks, and Government Policy for the U.S. Dairy Industry." Pages 29–43 show the recent history of milk and feed prices and then how the 2009 collapse caused reversals in the economic situation of dairy farms of all economic situations.

32. The MPP is often compared to the Livestock Gross Margin for Dairy (LGM-Dairy), an insurance program offered through the USDA Risk Management Agency The LGM-Dairy program has been available since 2008, well before the MPP was created. It offers insurance for the milk price minus feed costs margins using futures market prices for milk, corn, and soybean meal to compute the margins. Despite significant premium subsidies of up to 50 percent, and flexibility in choosing specific insurance product timing and other features, enrollment in LGM-Dairy has been low.

33. When MPP was first suggested, it was to me accompanied by a supply management program that would hold down milk output when margins were unusually low. For discussion of the issues when supply management was expected to be combined with an MPP-style program, see Joseph V. Balagtas and Daniel A. Sumner, "Evaluation of U.S. Policies and the Supply Management Proposals for Managing Milk Margin Variability," *American Journal of Agricultural Economics* 94, no. 2 (2012): 522–27. In the 2014 Farm Bill, a demand stimulus, the Dairy Product Donation Program, is scheduled to kick in when margins are below $4.00 per hundredweight. So far the program has not been triggered, and such low margins have been quite rare. The program itself is unlikely to make much impact and is not discussed further here.

34. Schnepf, "Dairy Provisions in the 2014 Farm Bill (P.L. 113-79)." The 2018 revisions of the MPP are described in US Department of Agriculture, Farm Service Agency, "Margin Protection Program for Dairy," https://www.fsa.usda.gov/programs-and-services/Dairy-MPP/index; and US Department of Agriculture, Farm Service Agency, "Margin

Protection Program for Dairy Fact Sheet," April 2018, https://www.fsa.usda.gov/Assets/USDA-FSA-Public/usdafiles/FactSheets/2018/mpp_dairy_program_april_2018.pdf.

35. Schnepf, "Dairy Provisions in the 2014 Farm Bill (P.L. 113-79)."

36. Detailed state-by-state enrollment and related data for 2015 and 2017 are available from US Department of Agriculture, Farm Service Agency, "Dairy Margin Protection Program," https://www.fsa.usda.gov/programs-and-services/Dairy-MPP/index.

37. See recent AEI reports, including Vincent H. Smith, Joseph W. Glauber, and Barry K. Goodwin, *Time to Reform the US Federal Agricultural Insurance Program*, American Enterprise Institute, October 13, 2017, http://www.aei.org/publication/time-to-reform-the-us-federal-agricultural-insurance-program/; and Bruce A. Babcock, *Covering Losses with Price Loss Coverage, Agricultural Risk Coverage, and the Stacked Income Protection Plan*, American Enterprise Institute, October 13, 2017, http://www.aei.org/publication/covering-losses-with-price-loss-coverage-agricultural-risk-coverage-and-the-stacked-income-protection-plan/.

38. MacDonald, Cessna, and Mosheim do some of these calculations and cite several others. See MacDonald, Cessna, and Mosheim, "Changing Structure, Financial Risks, and Government Policy for the U.S. Dairy Industry." See also Tyler B. Mark et al., "The Effects of the Margin Protection Program for Dairy Producers," US Department of Agriculture, Economic Research Service, September 2016, https://www.ers.usda.gov/publications/pub-details/?pubid=79414.

39. For the USDA data and calculation, see US Department of Agriculture, "Margin Protection Program for Dairy Producers (MPP-Dairy)," https://www.fsa.usda.gov/programs-and-services/farm-bill/farm-safety-net/dairy-programs/mpp-decision-tool/index.

40. See, for example, US Department of Agriculture, "Margin Protection Program for Dairy Producers (MPP-Dairy)."

41. Analysis of potential supply response has emphasized the risk reduction asked of the program. See Mark et al., "The Effects of the Margin Protection Program for Dairy Producers." They usefully simulate impacts of the MPP by state from 2002 to 2013 by production base for alternative share of production covered and for alternative margins covered.

42. This statement follows from the econometric estimates of Jisang Yu, Aaron Smith, and Daniel A. Sumner, "Effects of Crop Insurance Premium Subsidies on Crop Acreage," *American Journal of Agricultural Economics* 100, no. 1 (2018): 91–114, https://academic.oup.com/ajae/article/100/1/91/4443107.

8

Unraveling Reforms?
Cotton in the 2018 Farm Bill and Beyond

JOSEPH W. GLAUBER

The 2014 Farm Bill introduced many significant changes to US farm programs. Direct payments, in place since the 1996 Farm Bill, were eliminated. Countercyclical payments were replaced, and in 2014, for the duration of a new farm bill, producers had to choose between Price Loss Coverage (PLC), a price-based countercyclical program, and Agricultural Risk Coverage (ARC), a revenue-based countercyclical program. Dairy price supports, a primary fixture of dairy policy dating to the 1930s, were eliminated and replaced with an insurance-like program that guaranteed producers a minimum net margin between the price of raw milk and feed costs. In addition, new area-based crop insurance programs were introduced for many crops that provided supplemental coverage to enable farm businesses to recover a portion of the deductible on their underlying insurance coverage for crop losses on their own farms.

Among the reforms enacted in the 2014 Farm Bill, however, few were more significant than the changes made to the suite of federal subsidy programs for cotton. Direct and countercyclical payments for cotton were eliminated, but, in contrast to programs for other crops such as wheat, feed grains, and rice, cotton producers were not eligible for coverage under the new PLC and ARC programs. Instead, cotton producers were given access to a new cotton-specific supplemental crop insurance program, the Stacked Income Protection Plan (STAX). The STAX program, the blueprint for which originated from the cotton industry itself, is generously subsidized by the federal government. The government pays 80 percent of a farm business' STAX premium costs, which are intended to cover only expected indemnities, and all the administration and other costs associated with the program.

Figure 1. Farms Planting Cotton and Average Cotton Acreage per Farm

Farms (Left Axis) ▬▬ Planted Acres per Farm (Right Axis)

Source: US Department of Agriculture, Census of Agriculture, https://www.agcensus.usda.gov/; and US Department of Agriculture, National Agricultural Statistics Service, "Quick Stats," https://quickstats.nass.usda.gov/.

Further changes were also introduced to the long-standing cotton marketing assistance loans that tied support prices more closely to world prices.

The changes to the cotton program were due, in part, to the settlement of a long-standing trade dispute brought by Brazil to the World Trade Organization (WTO), in which Brazil had successfully brought charges against the US cotton program, arguing that those programs had distorted US production and exports and had depressed world cotton prices. As part of that settlement, Brazil agreed not to challenge US cotton support programs while the 2014 Farm Bill remained in force (that is, until September 30, 2018).[1] As a result, total federal levels of support for cotton have fallen to their lowest levels since the United States began reporting domestic levels of support for agricultural commodities to the WTO in 1995.

Yet, after successfully convincing Congress to adopt changes in the 2014 Farm Bill to implement the heavily subsidized STAX program, the cotton industry has decided that the STAX program must go. Participation in STAX has been low since the program was first offered in 2015. Less than 25 percent of eligible area was enrolled in STAX in 2017 (despite generous payouts to enrollees in 2016). In early 2018, as part of the Bipartisan Budget Act and after successful lobbying by the US cotton industry, Congress agreed to reinstate a new Countercyclical Payment Program, which would potentially boost cotton support levels substantially and thus risk igniting another trade dispute at the WTO.

The US Cotton Industry

Cotton was introduced to the American colonies as early as 1556 in Florida and 1607 in Virginia,[2] and by 1616 colonists were growing cotton along the James River in Virginia. Over the next 300 years, cotton cultivation spread throughout the southern tier of the United States. In 1929, almost two million farms reported growing cotton, and the area planted to cotton topped 44 million acres.[3] Farm and cotton production consolidation began in the 1930s but accelerated dramatically in the 1950s and early 1960s as productivity gains encouraged scale economies and farm numbers shrank (Figure 1). In 1949, 1.1 million farms reported growing cotton, with average cotton plantings of 25 acres. By 2012, only 18,155 farms reported growing cotton, with average plantings of 675 acres.[4]

Cotton is now grown in 17 states in the southern tier of the United States, with principal growing regions in the High Plains of Texas, the Mississippi Delta, and the Piedmont region of the southeast (Figure 2). Over the past 25 years, there has been a relative decline in planted area in the delta and western regions (primarily in California) as cotton returns have been less favorable than returns from competing commodities such as tree crops in California and corn and soybeans in the delta states (Figure 3). In the southeastern states, after a long period of decline due to the boll weevil, in the 1990s cotton plantings increased by some two million acres (due to the success of the Boll Weevil Eradication Program, which had been initiated in the late 1970s). The southern plains states of Texas, Oklahoma, and Kansas remain the largest growing region, accounting for 60 percent of the total area planted to cotton in 2017.

The United States is the world's third-largest cotton producer and the largest exporter, shipping an estimated 14.9 million bales (3.2 million

Figure 2. Upland Cotton Harvested Acres, 2012

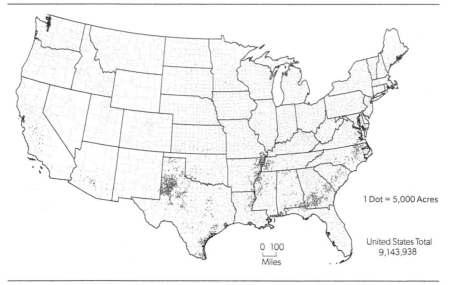

1 Dot = 5,000 Acres

United States Total
9,143,938

0 100
Miles

Source: US Department of Agriculture, National Agricultural Statistics Service, "2012 Census AG Atlas Maps," https://www.agcensus.usda.gov/Publications/2012/Online_Resources/Ag_Atlas_Maps/.

metric tons) of cotton to other countries in the 2016–17 marketing year.[5] Cotton has been a major export crop in the United States since the colonial period. As the US textile industry grew in the 19th and early 20th centuries, domestic milling use increased relative to exports. Nonetheless, cotton exports continued to account for 30–50 percent of total use. Consumption of cotton by US textile mills peaked in 1997 (Figure 4). Since then, US mill use of cotton has plummeted, dropping about 50 percent by 2005 and nearly 70 percent by 2009.

Much of the decline was due to the phaseout of the Multifibre Arrangement (MFA), a system of country and product-specific quotas that had governed world textile production and marketing since the 1950s and that generally disfavored textile production in developing countries.[6] In 1995, the MFA was replaced by the WTO Agreement on Textiles and Clothing, which gradually phased out quotas and brought trade in textiles under the WTO's trade rules. By the mid-2000s most of the decline in US textile production had occurred, as textile production moved offshore, mainly to China, India, and other developing Asian countries.

Figure 3. Cotton Planted Area by Region (Million Acres)

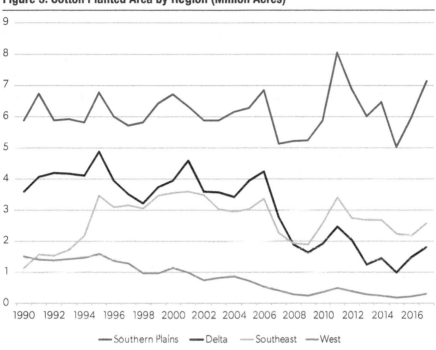

Source: US Department of Agriculture, National Agricultural Statistics Service, "Quick Stats," https://quickstats.nass.usda gov/.

As textile production shifted out of the United States, US cotton exports to textile-producing countries soared. Exports topped 17.6 million bales in 2005 and accounted for 75 percent of total use. The US share of global trade rose from an average of 25 percent in the 1990s to almost 40 percent by the mid-2000s (Figure 5). The increase in US exports and share of global cotton exports came at the expense of other major cotton exporters, including India, Australia, Brazil, several cotton-producing countries in West Africa (Benin, Burkina Faso, Côte d'Ivoire, Mali, and Chad), and several countries in Central Asia (Uzbekistan, Tajikistan, and Turkmenistan). That increase also led to increased scrutiny of US cotton policies that to a large extent had insulated US cotton producers from the drop in market prices following the Asian financial crisis of the late 1990s and the release of cotton stocks on global stocks by China in the early 2000s.

US Cotton Policy

Cotton has enjoyed government support for well over 200 years, and tariff protections for cotton products date back to the early days of the republic. However, as for other row crops such as wheat, corn, and rice, most federal farm programs for cotton date back to the New Deal legislation of the 1930s.

By the late 1990s, cotton producers benefited from a suite of programs including marketing assistance loans, which enabled them to receive a payment equal to the difference between the support price and the world price times their actual production; market loss assistance payments, which would compensate for low market prices; and, beginning in 1996, a direct fixed payment that was payable on historical production regardless of the price level. In 2002, market loss assistance payments were replaced by countercyclical payments, payable on historical production, based on the difference between a target price and the season average price. In addition,

Figure 4. US Cotton Mill Use and Exports (Million Bales)

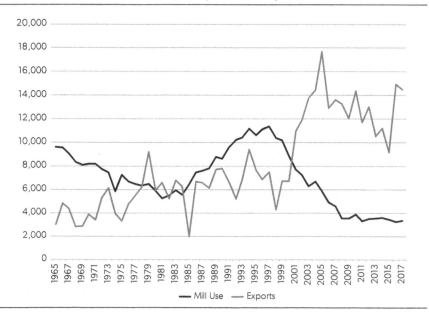

Source: Cotton and Wool Yearbook, "U.S. Cotton Supply and Demand: Table 2," US Department of Agriculture, Economic Research Service, 2018, https://www.ers.usda.gov/data-products/cotton-wool-and-textile-data/cotton-and-wool-yearbook/.

Figure 5. US Share of Global Cotton Exports

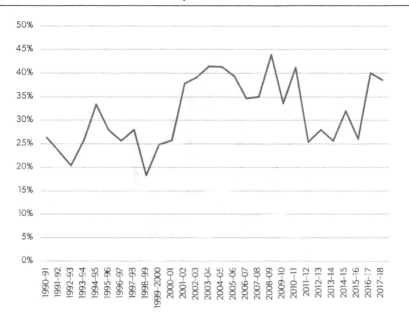

Source: Shares calculated by the author based on data from US Department of Agriculture, Foreign Agricultural Service, "PSD Online," 2018, https://apps.fas.usda.gov/psdonline.

producers were eligible for subsidized crop yield and revenue insurance on their production. To make cotton more competitive in world markets, the government also provided domestic mills and exporters with payments under the Upland Cotton User Marketing Certificate Program (described as Step 2 payments) when global prices fell below US prices and provided importing countries with subsidized credit.

Cotton producers have benefited from substantial levels of government support. Since 1995, total federal subsidies to cotton have averaged almost $2.1 billion annually, about 50 percent of the value of cotton production (Figure 6). Because programs such as countercyclical payments and marketing assistance loans are price based, federal subsidy payments have fluctuated considerably since the early 1990s. Payments averaged less than $1 billion in the mid-1990s when market prices reached then-record highs but more than tripled to over $3.7 billion during the late 1990s as market prices fell. The countercyclical nature of those programs therefore effectively

Figure 6. US Support to Cotton Producers (Million Dollars)

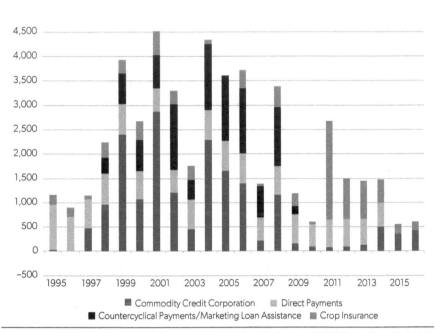

Legend: ■ Commodity Credit Corporation   ■ Direct Payments   ■ Countercyclical Payments/Marketing Loan Assistance   ■ Crop Insurance

Source: For farm program data, see US Department of Agriculture, Farm Service Agency, "CCC Budget Essentials," 2018, https://www.fsa.usda.gov/about-fsa/budget-and-performance-management/budget/ccc-budget-essentials/index. For crop insurance net indemnities, see US Department of Agriculture, Risk Management Agency, "Summary of Business," 2018, https://prodwebnlb.rma.usda.gov/apps/SummaryofBusiness/ReportGenerator.

insulated cotton producers from price declines, obscured market signals, and distorted production decisions. Cotton has also enjoyed large subsidies through the federal crop insurance program and was one of the first crops to be eligible for crop insurance in the late 1930s.[7] Among cotton producers, participation in the federal crop insurance programs has expanded substantially over the past 25 years as crop insurance legislation passed in 1994 and 2000 increased subsidy levels for farmers.[8] Average per-acre premium subsidies for cotton have doubled since 2009 as cotton producers have increased coverage levels and shifted from yield to revenue products (Figure 7).

Net cotton indemnities (indemnities minus producer-paid premiums) averaged $365 million annually between 1995 and 2016. Cotton crop insurance subsidies have been larger than for most competing row crops, both

Table 1. Cotton Crop Insurance Subsidies Relative to Other Row Crops, 2016

Crop	Subsidy per Acre (Dollar per Acre)	Subsidy as a Percentage of Value of Production
Corn	$26.76	4.3%
Soybeans	$15.89	2.8%
Wheat	$16.35	7.7%
Upland Cotton	$48.33	8.6%
Grain Sorghum	$22.94	9.1%
Rice	$20.38	2.4%
Peanuts	$28.81	3.8%

Source: Author's calculations based on data from US Department of Agriculture, Risk Management Agency, "Summary of Business," 2018, https://prodwebnlb.rma.usda.gov/apps/SummaryofBusiness/ReportGenerator; and US Department of Agriculture, National Agricultural Statistics Service, "Quick Stats," https://quickstats.nass.usda.gov/.

in terms of subsidy per acre and as a percentage of the value of production, reflecting the relative riskiness of the crop (Table 1).

Brazil's Case Against US Cotton Subsidies

The large increase in federal spending on cotton subsidies in the late 1990s (Figure 6) derived from a collapse in world cotton prices. That collapse, which persisted into the early 2000s, was precipitated and sustained by many factors, including the Asian financial crisis, which reduced textile demand; global record crops, which lowered agricultural prices generally; a strong US dollar; and policy decisions by China to release large cotton stocks onto world markets. In 2002, Brazil charged that US cotton programs were also contributing to the decline in world market prices by insulating US cotton producers from market prices, thus distorting production decisions. Brazil argued that, by artificially depressing world prices, the US programs reduced the value and quantity of Brazil's cotton market exports, causing economic harm to Brazil's domestic cotton sector.[9] As evidence of the impact of those subsidies, Brazil pointed to the fact that the US export market share nearly doubled over the period 1995–2002. While other factors (such as the phaseout of the MFA) contributed to that increase, the issue was still whether the US share of global exports would have been so large without US cotton subsidy programs.

Figure 7. Cotton Crop Insurance Subsidy per Acre

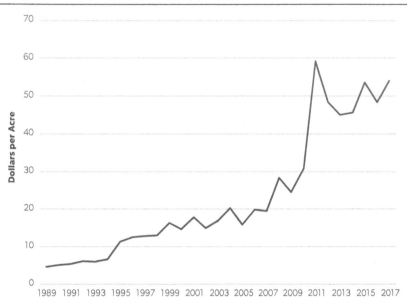

Source: Author's calculations based on data from US Department of Agriculture, Risk Management Agency, "Summary of Business," 2018, https://prodwebnlb.rma.usda.gov/apps/SummaryofBusiness/ReportGenerator.

Brazil's assertions were validated by a wide range of studies conducted by both academics and international organizations, which concluded that the US cotton program caused a decline in world cotton prices.[10] Those price declines were also found to have a detrimental impact on foreign producers, particularly in the least-developed cotton-producing countries, such as those in West Africa.[11]

Brazil initiated a formal dispute settlement case against the US at the WTO in 2002. In September 2004, a WTO dispute settlement panel found that certain price-contingent agricultural support programs were inconsistent with WTO commitments and resulted in serious prejudice in world markets by causing distortions that depressed world cotton prices. Those programs included the cotton marketing assistance loan provisions, the Countercyclical Payment Program, Step 2 payments, and market loss assistance payments (ad hoc payments made in 1998–2001 because of low market prices). The WTO panel recommended that the US take appropriate steps by September 21,

2005, to withdraw price-contingent subsidies or remove the adverse effects. In addition, the panel determined that both Step 2 payments and export credits under the Export Credit Guarantee Program were prohibited export subsidies and recommended that those programs be removed by July 1, 2015.[12]

However, the WTO panel failed to determine that direct payments and crop insurance payments contribute to serious prejudice: "We consider that the nature of the United States subsidies at issue—in terms of their structure, design, and operation—is relevant in assessing whether or not they have price suppressing effects. We see before us two general types of United States subsidies: those that are directly price-contingent, and those that are not."[13] The panel also concluded that crop insurance—along with direct payments and their predecessor, production flexibility contract payments—were not price contingent.

The panel noted that subsidized crop insurance reduced costs, affected risk considerations, and heightened economic security, all of which could have positive ramifications for producer wealth and investment and economic stability.[14] However, the panel concluded that crop insurance subsidies were more in the nature of income support and therefore were not included in the final analysis of price suppression.

In a 2017 analysis, I argue that the panel's serious prejudice ruling for crop insurance seems to ignore that revenue insurance was available to US cotton producers and thus, arguably, was price contingent.[15] Christian Lau, Simon Schropp, and Daniel Sumner pointed out that recent case law from the WTO appellate body ruling in US–Large Civil Aircraft clarified that panels are to include in serious prejudice findings any subsidies with an identifiable impact on production or pricing decisions.[16] Under the new jurisprudence, panels would likely have to take subsidies into account, even if those subsidies are not price contingent but could be shown to affect production or pricing decisions.

In 2005, the US agreed to eliminate Step 2 payments and made changes to its Export Credit Guarantee Program to have it comply with the WTO panel. Brazil argued that the actions were inadequate, and in 2006 a WTO compliance panel ruled in Brazil's favor. Brazil requested authority to impose $3 billion in retaliatory measures against prohibited subsidies. In August 2009, a WTO arbitration panel ruled that Brazil's countermeasures could include both a fixed annual amount of $147.3 million in response to the market-distorting cotton program payments and a variable formula-derived payment based on annual spending under the US Export Credit Guarantee Program. In addition, the panel ruled that Brazil would be entitled to cross-retaliation in sectors outside the agriculture sector (e.g., in the area of copyrights, patents, or other intellectual property).[17]

To avoid sanctions, the US and Brazil negotiated a temporary agreement whereby Brazil would suspend retaliation measures if the US agreed to (1) make annual payments of $147.3 million to Brazil for a fund to be used for technical assistance and capacity building for Brazil's cotton sector and (2) work jointly with Brazil on reaching a mutually agreed-upon solution for the cotton dispute.

On October 14, 2014, Brazil and the US signed a memorandum of understanding (MOU) to end the WTO cotton dispute. Among the provisions was Brazil's agreement to relinquish its right to take countermeasures against US trade and to take no future WTO actions against the US cotton support program while the 2014 Farm Bill cotton program provisions remain in force. Nor would Brazil take action against US credit programs, contingent on the imposition of risk-based fees and a cap on repayment periods of 18 months.[18] The MOU was terminated on September 20, 2018, except for the export credit operations provisions, which remain in effect as long as the credit program complies with the MOU requirements.

The 2014 Farm Bill

A key provision of the 2014 Farm Bill was eliminating direct and counter-cyclical payments for program crops, including upland cotton. However, unlike other program crops, cotton was excluded from ARC and PLC coverage. Instead, cotton producers became eligible for the STAX crop insurance product. In addition, the 2014 Farm Bill made changes to the cotton marketing loans by basing the loan rate on an average of the adjusted world cotton price over the two previous years, capped at a maximum rate of 52 cents a pound (the former loan rate) and cupped at a minimum rate of 45 cents a pound.[19]

The STAX insurance plan provides protection against loss of revenue due to an area-level production loss, a price decline, or both. STAX may be bought

Table 2. Participation in the STAX Program, Percentage of Planted Acres

State	2015	2016	2017
Alabama	54.1%	52.1%	28.1%
Arizona	62.7%	59.6%	64.2%
Arkansas	23.8%	20.5%	25.7%
California	4.8%	2.9%	3.0%
Florida	58.4%	61.3%	16.9%
Georgia	41.8%	38.1%	33.5%
Kansas	2.4%	0.0%	2.0%
Louisiana	41.1%	36.3%	38.0%
Mississippi	46.4%	43.7%	36.4%
Missouri	15.2%	6.3%	32.7%
New Mexico	10.0%	8.9%	5.1%
North Carolina	46.6%	51.8%	54.4%
Oklahoma	48.7%	12.8%	9.6%
South Carolina	37.8%	50.4%	61.9%
Tennessee	20.2%	19.5%	22.6%
Texas	21.5%	19.5%	17.3%
Virginia	60.7%	32.5%	71.0%
United States	30.0%	26.0%	23.9%

Source: Author's calculations based on data from the US Department of Agriculture, Risk Management Agency, "Summary of Business," 2018, https://prodwebnlb.rma.usda.gov/apps/SummaryofBusiness/ReportGenerator; and US Department of Agriculture, National Agricultural Statistics Service, "Quick Stats," 2018, https://quickstats.nass.usda.gov/.

as a stand-alone policy or a supplemental policy to an individual-based yield or revenue policy. The government subsidizes 80 percent of the premium costs (as well as fully subsidizing delivery costs). In its initial forecast of the costs of STAX after passage of the 2014 Farm Bill, the Congressional Budget Office (CBO) estimated annual federal expenditures to be about $330 million.[20]

Initial assessments of the STAX program were mixed. For example, Terry Townsend indicated that because of replacing the Direct Payment and Countercyclical Payment Programs with STAX, cotton outlays under the 2014 Farm Bill would be substantially lower than under the 2002 and 2008 Farm Bills.[21] In contrast, Lau, Schropp, and Sumner argued that the 2014 cotton program, including STAX and federal crop insurance, would continue to cause serious prejudice in world cotton markets, estimating that price suppression could cause damages to global cotton producers worth $6.4 billion annually.[22]

The experience with STAX, however, has suggested that the program has been less popular than many had anticipated (Table 2). In 2015, the first year STAX was offered, cotton producers enrolled only 30 percent of the area eligible for the program. Participation then declined in each subsequent year and has been particularly low in the southern plains (Texas, Oklahoma, and Kansas). Several factors have been cited as reasons why participation is so low. Losses are paid on regional yield and revenue outcomes. Thus, some producers may feel that STAX adds little in the way of additional risk protection, particularly if their yields are not well correlated with county yields.[23] Nick McMichen has argued that participation was low because cotton prices were low.[24] Keith Coble has postulated that good preseason weather in the southern plains in 2015 and 2016 may explain why participation was so low there in those years.[25] Regardless of the reasons, the trend in participation is not encouraging—notwithstanding an 80 percent subsidy on out-of-pocket premium costs.

Through 2017, federal spending on cotton subsidy programs under the 2014 Farm Bill was lower than payments under the 2002 and 2008 Farm Bills and is expected to decline further. Government payments for programs other than for crop insurance averaged $415 million over the 2014–16 crop years. Most of these outlays were made under the cotton marketing assistance loans, which under the new loan provisions must adjust the loan rate for cotton downward if the average world market price over the two preceding years has declined. Those provisions were triggered for the 2017 cotton loan rate, which was lowered to 49.49 cents per pound, reflecting lower world cotton prices in 2015 and 2016.

Given higher expected cotton prices, the CBO currently projects that annual outlays for cotton programs other than crop insurance and STAX will average about $75 million over fiscal years 2018–27.[26] Based on lower participation assumptions, the CBO projects that annual STAX outlays, including delivery costs, will average about $91 million over the same period. Net crop insurance subsidies will involve the largest single program expenditures. Based on recent premium levels, net cotton insurance indemnities (that is, indemnities minus producer-paid premiums) are estimated to average about $500 million annually.

While outlays for cotton production have declined, producers who historically grew cotton (including many who currently produce cotton)

Table 3. Acres Planted and Payments Made on Generic Base Acres

Crop Year	Generic Base Acres on Which PLC or ARC Payments Were Made (Million Acres)	Total Payments Made on Generic Base Acres (Million Dollars)
2014		
Total	2.2	$148.9
Peanuts	0.7	$87.2
2015		
Total	9.7	$443.8
Peanuts	0.9	$169.5
2016		
Total	8.6	$501.1
Peanuts	1.0	$185.7

Source: US Department of Agriculture, Farm Service Agency, "ARC/PLC Program," 2018, https://www.fsa.usda.gov/programs-and-services/arcplc_program/index.

continue to remain eligible for payment on former cotton base acres, the acres eligible for the Direct Payment and Countercyclical Payment Programs before 2015. Under the so-called generic base provisions of the 2014 Farm Bill, producers who grow other crops on former cotton base areas are eligible for ARC or PLC payments for those other crops. Former upland cotton base acres total about 17.6 million acres. In 2016, the US Department of Agriculture (USDA) Farm Service Agency reported that about 8.6 million acres of former cotton base were planted to ARC- and PLC-eligible crops for which payments under those programs totaled more than $500 million (Table 3).

Subsidy payments made on generic base under the ARC and PLC programs are tied to current rather than historical planting decisions. Thus, they are directly coupled and arguably more production distorting than payments made on other crop bases. (On corn base, for example, a producer is eligible for corn ARC or PLC payments regardless of whether those acres are planted to corn or, indeed, planted at all.) In Chapter 9, Vincent Smith and Barry Goodwin argue that generic base provisions have distorted peanut production.[27] Over one million acres of peanuts were planted on generic base in 2017, almost all of which were enrolled in the PLC program. As a result, in 2017, peanut producers received PLC subsidy payments totaling $185 million on those acres. Further, since 2013, total US peanut plantings have increased by over 800,000 acres, suggesting that peanut PLC payments on generic base have played a large part in the increase.

Recent Changes to the Cotton Program: Back to the Future?

Low participation rates in the STAX program led many in the cotton industry to seek changes in current legislation. In late 2015, the National Cotton Council sought to convince the secretary of agriculture to designate cottonseed a "minor oilseed" and hence become eligible for PLC and ARC payments.[28] Secretary of Agriculture Tom Vilsack refused, saying that the USDA lacked the authority to make the changes. In early 2018, as part of the Bipartisan Budget Act, Congress passed an industry-backed proposal to create a new program for "seed cotton"—unginned cottonseed with the attached lint. Under the new seed cotton program, costs for the new PLC program would be offset, at least partially, by savings due to a reduction in generic base acres and the requirement for participating producers to opt out of STAX.

A more detailed analysis of the proposals is presented in Appendix A. While there would be benefits from eliminating generic base acres (and the potential distortions created by tying payments to planting decisions), the analysis suggests that reintroducing a price-based program for cotton producers could lead to a large exposure for the federal budget, particularly for a seed cotton program. For example, based on historical price data for cotton lint and cottonseed for 1980–2016, payment rates under a cottonseed program would have been at the maximum rate in almost two-thirds of those years. The analysis of the seed cotton program also suggests that payments would have exceeded $1 billion in almost half the years between 1980 and 2016.

Tying payments to cotton prices would unequivocally refocus world attention on the US cotton program and especially the program's impacts on developing countries. Large payments would mute market signals, as under the programs in place when Brazil initiated a WTO cotton case in the early 2000s, and could very well result in another WTO case.

Concluding Comments

Cotton producers have lobbied extensively for a new Countercyclical Payment Program, arguing that costs of production for cotton are high relative to other crops.[29] However, providing support to producers to maintain high production levels in the face of lower market prices leads to market distortions that prolong downturns in US and world market prices, with adverse impacts on cotton producers in other countries. Such policies could, therefore, hurt US trade relations and lead to new WTO disputes and dispute settlements that have spillover impacts on other sectors of the US economy, as evidenced by the Brazil cotton case.

Now is not the time to unravel reforms. Rather, reforms should be extended to include elimination of generic base acres either through gradual phaseout or perhaps a one-time buyout based on expected outlays. Market orientation should be the driving focus of federal farm subsidy and other programs for all crops, cotton included.

Appendix A. Estimating the Cost of a Price Loss Coverage Program for Cottonseed and Seed Cotton

The two major proposals for a new Countercyclical Payment Program (CCP) for cotton are as follows. The first proposal would add cottonseed as a commodity eligible for coverage under the Price Loss Coverage (PLC) and Agricultural Risk Coverage programs. The second would create a PLC program for seed cotton. Seed cotton is defined as unginned cottonseed with the attached lint, as it is picked from the cotton boll. Both proposals would allow participating producers to reallocate their generic (old cotton) base acres to the new program. Producers enrolled in the new program would not be eligible for the Stacked Income Protection Plan (STAX).

Current Baseline

In its "June 2017 Baseline for Farm Programs," the Congressional Budget Office estimated that STAX outlays would average $91 million annually over fiscal years (FY) 2018–27 and that payments made on generic base acres would average $335 million per year over the same period.[30] Thus, potential offsets to the new program totaled about $426 million annually over FY2018–27.

Proposed Cottonseed Program

Under the proposed PLC program for cottonseed, a reference price of $0.15 per pound would be established for cottonseed. Producers would receive a payment equal to the difference, if positive, between the reference price and the higher of the season average cottonseed price or the cottonseed loan rate, times eligible production. The proposed cottonseed loan rate is $0.08 per pound. Eligible production is defined as cottonseed base acres times the payment yield. The payment yield is equal to 1.4 times the payment yield established under the CCP defined in the 2008 Farm Bill. Producers would have an opportunity to update their program yields.

Proposed Seed Cotton Program

Under the proposed PLC program for seed cotton, a reference price for seed cotton is established at $0.367 per pound. The PLC payment rate would be equal to the difference, if positive, between the reference price and the higher of the season average price of seed cotton or the seed cotton loan rate. The National Agricultural Statistics Service does not collect data on seed cotton, so a season average price would be imputed based on a weighted average of the lint cotton price and the cottonseed price. The seed cotton loan rate, established for payment calculations only, would be equal to $0.25 per pound. Eligible production would equal 85 percent of the seed cotton base acres times the new payment yield. The seed cotton payment yield equals 2.4 times the payment yield under the 2008 CCP program. Producers would have an opportunity to update their program yields.

Analysis

To calculate potential costs under the two proposals, historical prices for lint cotton and cottonseed for 1980–2016 were used. About 17.6 million acres of cotton base were converted to generic base in the 2014 Farm Bill. The CBO assumes that almost 11 million acres of generic base will be planted annually to covered crops over the 2018–27 marketing years. How much of that area would be enrolled under a new program is uncertain, but based on recent cotton plantings, here I assume that 10 million acres of generic base would be enrolled in a new cottonseed or seed cotton program.[31] The assumption of an average CPP yield of 632 pounds per acre was based on the "CBO's March 2013 Baseline for Farm Programs."[32] No updating of payment yields is taken into account. To calculate a season average price for seed cotton, it is assumed that for every pound of lint, 1.4 pounds of cottonseed are obtained. The seed cotton price is thus equal to the sum of the price of lint cotton plus 1.4 times the price of cottonseed, divided by 2.4. Assumptions for the analysis are summarized in Table A1.

Note that no attempt is made to estimate the potential impact of the program on production decisions, though, as others have shown, producer

Table A1. Proposed Cotton Program Parameters

	Cottonseed Program	Seed Cotton Program
Eligible Base Acres	10 Million Acres	10 Million Acres
Payment Factor	100%	85%
CCP Yield	632 Pounds per Acre	632 Pounds per Acre
Yield Factor	1.4	2.4
Payment Yield	884.8 Pounds per Acre	1,516.8 Pounds per Acre
Eligible Production	8,848 Million Pounds	12,892.8 Million Pounds
Reference Price	$0.15 per Pound	$0.367 per Pound
Loan Rate	$0.08 per Pound	$0.25 per Pound
Maximum Payment Rate	$0.07 per Pound	$0.117 per Pound
Maximum Payment	$619 Million	$1,508 Million

Source: Author's calculations based on data from Congressional Budget Office, "CBO's June 2017 Baseline for Farm Programs," 2017, https://www.cbo.gov/sites/default/files/recurringdata/51317-2017-06-usda.pdf.

responses to subsidy programs can have significant effects on crop prices and program payment levels.[33]

Tables A2 and A3 show the potential costs of the proposed programs for cotton based on historical prices for cotton and cottonseed over the past 37 years. The average annual costs of the cottonseed PLC program would have been $467 million. Note that there were positive outlays in every year, and in over two-thirds of the years, the payment rate would have been at the maximum level of $0.07 per pound. In recent years, due to the increase in oilseed prices, cottonseed prices have been higher. The average annual costs over 2007–16 would have been $407 million. Payments of the seed cotton program would generally have been significantly higher and more variable than under a cottonseed program. Over 1980–2016, payments would have averaged $946 million, with outlays exceeding $1.5 billion in almost one out of every four years. Over the past 10 years, cotton lint and cottonseed prices have been higher. As a result, outlays over 2007–16 would have averaged $561 million.

Table A2. Estimated Costs of a Cottonseed PLC Program

	Cottonseed Price	Payment Rate	PLC Payment
	————Dollars per Hundredweight————		Million Dollars
1980	$6.45	$7.00	$619.4
1981	$4.30	$7.00	$619.4
1982	$3.85	$7.00	$619.4
1983	$8.30	$6.70	$592.8
1984	$4.98	$7.00	$619.4
1985	$3.30	$7.00	$619.4
1986	$4.00	$7.00	$619.4
1987	$4.13	$7.00	$619.4
1988	$5.95	$7.00	$619.4
1989	$5.25	$7.00	$619.4
1990	$6.05	$7.00	$619.4
1991	$3.55	$7.00	$619.4
1992	$4.88	$7.00	$619.4
1993	$5.65	$7.00	$619.4
1994	$5.05	$7.00	$619.4
1995	$5.30	$7.00	$619.4
1996	$6.30	$7.00	$619.4
1997	$6.05	$7.00	$619.4
1998	$6.45	$7.00	$619.4
1999	$4.45	$7.00	$619.4
2000	$5.25	$7.00	$619.4
2001	$4.53	$7.00	$619.4
2002	$5.05	$7.00	$619.4
2003	$5.85	$7.00	$619.4
2004	$5.35	$7.00	$619.4
2005	$4.80	$7.00	$619.4
2006	$5.55	$7.00	$619.4
2007	$8.10	$6.90	$610.5
2008	$11.15	$3.85	$340.6
2009	$7.90	$7.00	$619.4
2010	$8.05	$6.95	$614.9
2011	$13.00	$2.00	$177.0
2012	$12.60	$2.40	$212.4
2013	$12.30	$2.70	$238.9
2014	$9.70	$5.30	$468.9
2015	$11.35	$3.65	$323.0
2016	$9.70	$5.30	$468.9

Source: Author's calculations based on assumptions given in Table A1.

Table A3. Estimated Costs of a Seed Cotton PLC Program

Year	Upland Cotton Lint Price	Price	Weighted Seed Cotton Price	Payment Rate	PLC Payment
	———————Cents per Pound———————			Million Dollars	Dollars per Acre
1980	74.40	6.45	34.76	1.94	$250
1981	54.00	4.30	25.01	11.69	.$1,507
1982	59.50	3.85	27.04	9.66	$1,246
1983	65.30	8.30	32.05	4.65	$600
1984	58.70	4.98	27.36	9.34	$1,204
1985	56.80	3.30	25.59	11.11	$1,432
1986	51.50	4.00	23.79	11.70	$1,508
1987	63.70	4.13	28.95	7.75	$999
1988	55.60	5.95	26.64	10.06	$1,297
1989	63.60	5.25	29.56	7.14	$920
1990	67.10	6.05	31.49	5.21	$672
1991	56.80	3.55	25.74	10.96	$1,413
1992	53.70	4.88	25.22	11.48	$1,480
1993	58.10	5.65	27.50	9.20	$1,186
1994	72.00	5.05	32.95	3.75	$484
1995	75.40	5.30	34.51	2.19	$283
1996	69.30	6.30	32.55	4.15	$535
1997	65.20	6.05	30.70	6.00	$774
1998	60.20	6.45	28.85	7.85	$1,013
1999	45.00	4.45	21.35	11.70	$1,508
2000	49.80	5.25	23.81	11.70	$1,508
2001	29.80	4.53	15.06	11.70	$1,508
2002	44.50	5.05	21.49	11.70	$1,508
2003	61.80	5.85	29.16	7.54	$972
2004	41.60	5.35	20.45	11.70	$1,508
2005	47.70	4.80	22.68	11.70	$1,508
2006	46.50	5.55	22.61	11.70	$1,508
2007	59.30	8.10	29.43	7.27	$937
2008	47.80	11.15	26.42	10.28	$1,325
2009	62.90	7.90	30.82	5.88	$759
2010	81.50	8.05	38.65	0.00	—
2011	88.30	13.00	44.38	0.00	—
2012	72.50	12.60	37.56	0.00	—
2013	77.90	12.30	39.63	0.00	—
2014	61.30	9.70	31.20	5.50	$709
2015	61.20	11.35	32.12	4.58	$590
2016	68.00	9.70	33.99	2.71	$349

Note: Seed cotton price based on weighted average of 1.4 pounds of cottonseed per one pound of cotton lint.
Source: Author's calculations based on assumptions given in Table A1.

Notes

1. Randy Schnepf, "Status of the WTO Brazil-U.S. Cotton Case," Congressional Research Service, October 1, 2014, http://nationalaglawcenter.org/wp-content/uploads/assets/crs/R43336.pdf.

2. National Cotton Council of America, "The Story of Cotton," 2018, https://www.cotton.org/pubs/cottoncounts/story/.

3. US Department of Agriculture, National Agricultural Statistics Service, "Quick Stats," https://quickstats.nass.usda.gov/.

4. US Department of Agriculture, National Agricultural Statistics Service, "Quick Stats."

5. US Department of Agriculture, Foreign Agricultural Service, "PSD Online," 2018, https://apps.fas.usda.gov/psdonline.

6. Stephen MacDonald and Thomas Vollrath, "The Forces Shaping World Cotton Consumption After the Multifiber Arrangement," US Department of Agriculture, Economic Research Service, April 2005, https://www.ers.usda.gov/webdocs/publications/35835/29795_cws05c01_002.pdf.

7. Joseph W. Glauber and Keith J. Collins, "Crop Insurance, Disaster Assistance, and the Role of the Federal Government in Providing Catastrophic Risk Protection," *Agricultural Finance Review* 62, no. 2 (2002): 81–102.

8. Vincent H. Smith, Joseph W. Glauber, and Barry K. Goodwin, *Time to Reform the US Federal Agricultural Insurance Program*, American Enterprise Institute, October 13, 2017, http://www.aei.org/publication/time-to-reform-the-us-federal-agricultural-insuranceprogram/.

9. Schnepf, "Status of the WTO Brazil-U.S. Cotton Case."

10. Stephen Tokarick, "Measuring the Impact of Distortions in Agricultural Trade in Partial and General Equilibrium" (working paper, International Monetary Fund, Washington, DC, 2003); Louis Goreux, "Prejudice Caused by Industrialized Countries' Subsidies to Cotton Sectors in Western and Central Africa," World Bank, January 2004, http://web.worldbank.org/archive/AFRtrade/WEB/PDF/2004_01_.PDF; Daneswar Poonyth et al., "The Impact of Domestic and Trade Policies on the World Cotton Market" (working paper, Food and Agricultural Organization Commodity and Trade Policy Research, Food and Agricultural Organization of the United Nations, April 2004); Ben Shepherd, "The Impact of US Subsidies on the World Cotton Market: A Reassessment," Groupe d'Economie Mondiale, March 2004, www.oecd.org/dataoecd/0/9/31592808.pdf; Food and Agriculture Organization of the United Nations, "Cotton: Impact of Support Policies on Developing Countries—Why Do the Numbers Vary?," 2005, http://www.fao.org/economic/est/publications/trade-policy-briefs/en/; Daniel A. Sumner, "Boxed In: Conflicts Between US Farm Policies and WTO Obligations," Cato Institute, December 5, 2005, https://www.cato.org/publications/trade-policy-analysis/boxed-conflicts-between-us-farm-policies-wtoobligations; Suwen Pan et al., "The Impacts of U.S. Cotton Programs on the World Market: An Analysis of Brazilian WTO Petition," *Journal of Cotton Science* 10 (2006): 180–92, https://ttu-ir.tdl.org/ttu-ir/handle/2346/1648; and Andrew Schmitz, Frederick J. Rossi, and Troy G. Schmitz, "U.S. Cotton Subsidies: Drawing a Fine Line on the Degree of Decoupling," *Journal of Agricultural and Applied Economics* 39, no. 1 (2007):

135–49, https://econpapers.repec.org/article/agsjoaaec/6621.htm.

11. Nicholas Minot and Lisa Daniels, "Impact of Global Cotton Markets on Rural Poverty in Benin," *Agricultural Economics* 33, no. 3 (2005): 453–66, http://onlinelibrary.wiley.com/doi/10.1111/j.1574-0864.2005.00415.x/abstract; Julian M. Alston, Daniel A. Sumner, and Henrich Brunke, "Impacts of Reductions in U.S. Cotton Subsidies on West African Cotton Producers," Oxfam America, 2007, https://www.oxfamamerica.org/static/media/files/paying-the-price.pdf; Fousseini Traoré, "Do Global Cotton Subsidies Affect the Malian Economy? New Evidence from a Multimarket-General Equilibrium Model," *Economics Bulletin* 32, no. 2 (2012): 1640–52; and Fousseini Traoré, "Domestic and Trade Policies Affecting the World Cotton Market," in *Agriculture, Development, and the Global Trading System: 2000–2015*, eds. Antoine Bouët and David Laborde Debucquet (Washington, DC: International Food Policy Research Institute, 2017): 193–230, https://doi.org/10.2499/9780896292499_07.

12. Schnepf, "Status of the WTO Brazil-U.S. Cotton Case."

13. World Trade Organization, "United States—Subsidies on Upland Cotton, Report of the Panel," 2004, https://www.wto.org/english/tratop_e/dispu_e/cases_e/ds267_e.htm.

14. World Trade Organization, "United States—Subsidies on Upland Cotton, Report of the Panel."

15. During the period of investigation of US–Upland Cotton (1999–2002), revenue products accounted for less than 15 percent of insured cotton area in the US. In 2017, they accounted for 81 percent of insured area. Joseph Glauber, "Agricultural Insurance and the WTO," in *Agriculture, Development and the Global Trading System: 2000–2015*, eds. Antoine Bouët and David Laborde (Washington, DC: International Food Policy Research Institute, 2017).

16. Christian Lau, Simon Schropp, and Daniel A. Sumner, "The Economic Effects on the World Market for Cotton of US Cotton Subsidies Under the 2014 US Farm Bill," International Centre for Trade and Sustainable Development, 2015.

17. Typically, compensation is sought through raising tariffs on an equivalent volume of trade. Brazil argued that because agricultural imports from the US were small relative to the level of damages, total compensation could be obtained only if Brazil were allowed to retaliate in sectors outside agriculture.

18. The US also agreed to make a one-time final payment of $300 million to the Brazil Cotton Institute.

19. US Department of Agriculture, Farm Service Agency, "2014 Farm Bill Fact Sheet: Nonrecourse Marketing Assistance Loans and Loan Deficiency Payments," February 2016, https://www.fsa.usda.gov/Assets/USDA-FSA-Public/usdafiles/FactSheets/2016/mal_ldp_2016.pdf.

20. Congressional Budget Office, "CBO's April 2014 Baseline for Farm Programs," 2014, https://www.cbo.gov/sites/default/files/recurringdata/51317-2014-04-usda.pdf.

21. Terry Townsend, "The 2014 U.S. Farm Bill and Cotton: Proof That the WTO Matters," *Choices* 30, no. 2 (2005): 1–5.

22. Lau, Schropp, and Sumner, "The Economic Effects on the World Market for Cotton of US Cotton Subsidies Under the 2014 US Farm Bill."

23. As an area-based plan, STAX is less prone to moral hazard and adverse selection programs. If revenue guarantees are unbiased, STAX should operate much like a fair game

lottery, in which case it is difficult to understand why producers have not signed up given the 80 percent subsidy. See Mario J. Miranda, "Area-Yield Crop Insurance Reconsidered," *American Journal of Agricultural Economics* 73 (1991): 233–42.

24. Nick McMichen, testimony before the Committee on Agriculture, Nutrition and Forestry, US Senate, July 25, 2017, https://www.agriculture.senate.gov/imo/media/doc/TESTIMONY_McMICHEN.pdf.

25. Keith Coble, "STAX and Cotton Crop Insurance: First Year Results" (presentation at the USDA Agricultural Outlook Forum, February 2016), https://ageconsearch.umn.edu/record/236592/files/Cobel%202.pdf.

26. Congressional Budget Office, "CBO's June 2017 Baseline for Farm Programs," 2017, https://www.cbo.gov/sites/default/files/recurringdata/51317-2017-06-usda.pdf.

27. Vincent H. Smith and Barry K. Goodwin, *Reflections on the US Peanut Program: It's Nuts*, American Enterprise Institute, January 29, 2018, http://www.aei.org/publication/reflections-on-the-us-peanut-program-its-nuts/.

28. Jonathan Coppess et al., "The Cottonseed Conundrum," *farmdoc daily* 7 (2017): 77, http://farmdocdaily.illinois.edu/2017/04/thecottonseed-conundrum.html.

29. McMichen, testimony.

30. Congressional Budget Office, "CBO's June 2017 Baseline for Farm Programs."

31. In a recent analysis, Jonathan Coppess et al. assume that as many as 14 million acres of generic base could be enrolled in the seed cotton program. That would increase cost estimates by 40 percent over those estimated here. Jonathan Coppess et al., "Reviewing the Latest Cotton Proposal," *farmdoc daily* 8 (2018): 5, http://farmdocdaily.illinois.edu/pdf/fdd110118.pdf.

32. Congressional Budget Office, "CBO's March 2013 Baseline for Farm Programs," 2013.

33. Sumner, "Boxed In"; and Food and Agriculture Organization of the United Nations, "Cotton."

9

The US Peanut Program: An Exercise in Excess

BARRY K. GOODWIN AND VINCENT H. SMITH

Relatively small, well-funded interest groups are often successful in obtaining funds from federal legislators, either directly through straightforward subsidies or indirectly through regulatory constraints and mandates. Often, the benefits are concentrated among a relatively small number of wealthy individuals or institutions in the group, although such programs are typically rationalized through claims that they target a few financially vulnerable entities. The accompanying rhetoric often uses litanies such as "we need to save the family farm" or "farmers who put food on your table are essential to survival!" Interest groups accomplish their objectives by providing legislators with support through votes and campaign funds.[1] Their policy objectives are typically to obtain new programs and regulations that benefit their members and ensure the continuation and, if feasible, expansion of existing programs. Moreover, when an interest group's current federal program disadvantages other influential lobbies, the groups frequently work together to design new or modified policies that serve both groups, typically at everybody else's expense.[2]

Once upon a time, the programs serving an interest group may have been put in place to address broad public policy objectives such as poverty alleviation in rural communities and low farm incomes, but they have long since ceased to serve those purposes. However, ending such programs is extremely difficult,[3] not least because the revenues the programs generate are used to fund further lobbying by the interest groups that benefit from them.[4] Today's farm-based peanut industry provides an unambiguous example of an interest group that falls into this category and that has been remarkably successful in obtaining and maintaining benefits that have little or no public policy justification.

Beginning with the Agricultural Adjustment Act of 1933, farm businesses growing peanuts have benefited from federal policies that increase their incomes by raising the prices US consumers pay for peanuts. Initially, federal support for peanut production was provided through paid land retirement programs, then price supports, and then, until 2002, via a quota system that raised the price of peanuts used in consumer-oriented products such as peanut butter. Since 2002, farm businesses producing peanuts have sustained highly successful direct raids on the public purse in which legislators with agricultural constituencies have been complicit. Times and industries change, however, as do industry needs that turn into wants for federal programs that generate direct or indirect subsidies. This fact is as true for peanuts as it is for most other major subsectors of the US agricultural production industry.[5]

Today, peanuts are produced in different ways by different commercial entities than they were between 1933 and 1949. Insight into the dramatic nature of that change can be illustrated by comparing United States Department of Agriculture (USDA) Agricultural Census data for 1949 and 2012, shown in Table 1. In 1949, the nation's peanut crop was raised by over 183,000 farms that planted, on average, 12.1 acres of peanuts per farm, with average yields of 808 pounds per acre and average per-farm peanut production of 4.9 tons. These farms also raised other crops but were mostly small-scale enterprises, many of which used the work of every adult family member on a full-time or near to full-time basis, at a time when farm household incomes were generally below the average US household income.

In 2012, 6,561 farm businesses produced the nation's peanut crop, planting an average of 247 acres per farm with average yields of 4,211 pounds per acre[6] and average per-farm peanut production of 525 tons. Most of these farms also produced other agricultural commodities and were sophisticated commercial businesses that used advanced technologies embedded in complex plant varieties, extensive machinery and equipment, and much less labor. Thus, in 2012, on average each peanut farm business' production was over *100 times* larger than the output of the average peanut farm in 1949. Clearly, the businesses producing peanuts in 2012 were nothing like their 1949 counterparts. The business people who own the assets and manage these farm businesses also tend to enjoy household incomes well above those of the average US household in 2012.

Table 1. The Numbers of Farms and Average Acres Planted to Peanuts in 1949 and 2012

Year	Number of Farms	Average Acres Planted to Peanuts	Average Yield per Acre	Average Production per Farm
1949	183,117	12.1	808 Pounds	4.89 Short Tons
2012	6,561	247.1	4,211 Pounds	520.3 Short Tons

Source: US Department of Agriculture, National Agricultural Statistics Service, "1950 Census," http://agcensus.mannlib. cornell.edu/AgCensus/censusParts.do?year=1950; and US Department of Agriculture, National Agricultural Statistics Service, "2012 Census," https://www.agcensus.usda.gov/Publications/2012/#full_report.

The federal programs—which were introduced in 1933, adjusted in 1937, modified in 1941, and expanded in 1948 and again in 1949 with the goal of raising peanut farmers' incomes[7]—could perhaps have been justified as poverty alleviation initiatives at those times. Sixty-five years later, in the context of the 2014 Farm Bill, the peanut lobby's best justification for federal subsidy programs was perhaps their purely normative "entitlement" claim that because peanut operations had benefited from substantial federal subsidies for so long, it would be unfair to take those subsidies from them. In 2002, the peanut lobby made similar "fairness" arguments to validate a $1.3 billion congressional gift of a five-year-long series of substantial program buyout payments to holders of peanut production quotas that had provided high prices for peanuts marketed to US consumers since 1978.

In addition, and on much the same basis, in 2002 farms continuing to produce peanuts were given access to a highly lucrative set of direct subsidy programs, which were already available to growers of "program" commodities such as corn and wheat. Those programs included the now-discontinued Direct Payment Program, through which producers simply received a check in the mail because peanuts had once been grown on the land they owned or farmed. In 2002, peanut growers, far fewer in number than quota holders (many of whom had long since divorced themselves from production agriculture), were also given a quasi–price support Countercyclical Payment Program and the long-standing loan rate program (another farm support program dating back to the early 1940s).

In effect, through a standard lobbying process, in the context of the 2002 Farm Bill, peanut producers used their political influence to obtain funds directly from taxpayers instead of consumers using standard arguments

Figure 1. National Average Peanut Prices and the PLC Reference Price: 2005–16 (Dollars per Ton)

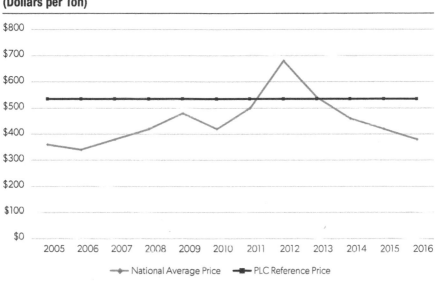

Source: US Department of Agriculture, Farm Service Agency; and US Department of Agriculture, National Agricultural Statistics Service, "Quick Stats," https://quickstats.nass.usda.gov/.

about the dire financial straits of the agriculture sector to cover what really amounted to naked rent-seeking. When their main sources of federal largesse, the Direct Payment and Countercyclical Payment programs, were scheduled for cancellation in the 2014 Farm Bill, peanut growers lobbied successfully for favorable treatment with respect to the new Price Loss Coverage (PLC) program. They ended up with a PLC reference price of $535 per ton, effectively a guaranteed minimum price that applied not to actual production but rather to their historical production reflected in program "base."[8] As shown in Figure 1, the PLC peanut target price substantially exceeded the market prices growers had received in all but two of the previous nine years,[9] or any market price they were likely to receive in the foreseeable future. The PLC program, as structured in 2014, was therefore set up to ensure peanut growers (or individuals with peanut base, whether actually producing peanuts or not) would receive over $300 per acre in taxpayer funds for the duration of the 2014 Farm Bill. To put these subsidies in perspective, $300 per acre on an average of about 250 acres is $75,000 in taxpayer payments to the average-sized peanut operation, over three times the US poverty line wage for a family of three or four, and almost 50 percent higher than the median household income. These subsidies are being paid to business owners with an average net worth that exceeds $1.5 million.

Such is the current state of play in the US federal peanut policy world—a lucrative PLC program, accompanied by a new heavily subsidized crop revenue insurance program also mandated by the 2014 Farm Bill. To hear some lobbyists talk, one might end up thinking that crop insurance initiatives for most commodities are needed because, unlike Main Street business owners who are typically poorer and much more highly leveraged, farm businesses owners are too bereft of financial resources and management skills to handle their own risks. An alternative hypothesis is that, like President Jimmy Carter, most peanut growers are well educated and well financed, and they simply wanted their "fair share" of the highly lucrative $8.5 billion a year of taxpayer-funded federal crop insurance subsidy pie, including a revenue insurance program expected to be more lucrative than a yield insurance program already available to them.

A Short History of Federal Peanut Subsidy and Price Support Programs: 1933–2002

Peanut growers, as well as producers of other more extensively planted crops such as corn and wheat, were the intended beneficiaries of the 1933 Agricultural Adjustment Act. Under the program, farmers made voluntary reductions in acreage in exchange for a payment. The program was modified in 1937, when regional growers associations were formed to purchase peanuts for crushing into oil and meal at a predetermined government minimum price.[10] In 1949, when an expanded loan rate program was introduced, peanuts were produced by over 180,000 farms, most of which were tiny by today's standards and operated by individuals and households with modest or below-average household incomes. As remains the case today, in 1949 peanut production was relatively local and heavily concentrated in a few states (Georgia, North and South Carolina, Virginia, Florida, Texas, and Alabama). Seeking a means for increasing their revenues, peanut producers, through the provisions of the 1949 Agricultural Act and previous farm bills, were given access to a more lucrative loan rate program, effectively a price support program with the support price set above the long-run average price for peanuts, in return for accepting an acreage-based production quota.

In 1978, the peanut program was modified substantially. Growers were subject to a poundage quota; that is, only a fixed amount of production would be eligible for the loan rate program, in which the support price was set well above expected international prices. However, farm businesses would be able to sell "over quota" production on the open market for exports or to a domestic processor for crushing to produce peanut oil and meal. In addition, the secretary of agriculture had the authority to adjust the aggregate peanut production quota on an annual basis to meet estimated domestic demand for edible peanuts (peanuts for human consumption, in peanut butter, and other consumer products such as confectionaries and processed foods). Finally, to ensure the domestic market was insulated from foreign competition, imports from other countries were heavily restricted, although the 1994 World Trade Organization (WTO) agreement market access provisions meant that some imports had to be permitted, which to some extent undermined the domestic production quota system.

In effect, the peanut program became a government-mandated price discrimination program in which peanuts for human consumption would be sold at a much higher price in the United States than peanuts that were exported or used for crush. The quota program was appealing to some congressional members because they and the peanut lobby could claim that, as long as no (or few) peanuts were permanently handed over to the government through the price support program, there was "no cost to the taxpayer."[11] The claim was unequivocally specious, as are current similar claims by sugar producer interest groups, because, of course, consumers (many of whom are taxpayers) were required to pay much higher prices for their peanuts than would otherwise have been the case. Between 1996 and 2002, for example, growers received $610 per ton for quota peanuts but only between $320 and $410 per ton for peanuts sold for export or crush.

The peanut quota program had its critics.[12] Processed food manufacturers objected to the costs the federal government's price discrimination program imposed on them. In addition, in the context of the 1994 North

American Free Trade Agreement and the 1994 WTO Agreement, the US peanut program was increasingly a cause of concern with respect to US trade relations and the potential for trade disputes.[13] In response, in 2002 Congress terminated the quota program and authorized a $1.3 billion buyout of quota holder rights from just under 70,000 quota holders. Congress also established access for farm businesses producing peanuts to the Direct Payment Program (at $36 per ton for eligible peanut production) and the Countercyclical Payment Program (triggered when peanut prices dropped below $459 per ton) for what, in 2002, were about 9,000 peanut producers. The details of the buyout and accompanying changes to policy that characterize the current peanut program are discussed in detail in the next section.

Almost certainly, the policy goal of the 2002 "reforms" was to ensure that whatever peanut growers lost on the swings of policy misfortune in the 2002 Farm Bill (farewell, price discrimination), they at least made up in the legislation's roundabouts of policy joy (hello, direct payments and a generous Countercyclical Payment Program). An added bonus for legislators was that at least the food-processing sector would no longer complain about the peanut program. While the peanut program's costs would now directly fall on taxpayers, hopefully, they would not notice a $500 or $600 million annual giveaway at, in 2002, an expected average of over $55,000 per peanut farm business, in a federal budget of around $3 trillion.

Contemporary (Post-2002) Policy Issues

The modern era of peanut policy began in 2002, when the farm bill established a quota buyout program that awarded quota owners (not necessarily peanut producers) $220 per short ton of quota. The national quota in 2001–02 was 2.36 billion pounds. The largest owner of quota at the time of the buyout was the John Hancock Mutual Life Insurance Company of Boston, which controlled 3.8 million pounds of quota—an amount worth $2.1 million under the terms of the buyout.[14] Many peanut producers were not quota owners and either paid to grow peanuts under quota rental arrangements or grew peanuts for the crush and export markets. Such growers were not eligible for the generous terms of the quota buyout, but beginning in 2003 they became the beneficiaries of direct payments on newly established peanut base (if they had a history of producing peanuts over 1998–2001) and significant marketing loans that established a floor on producer prices.

Several aspects of the contemporary peanut program are unique, notable, and expensive for taxpayers. The 2002 quota buyout effectively endowed peanut producers with two separate payment limits. They are limited to the same $125,000 payment limit on all crops other than peanuts that applies to other base crops. However, peanut producers also benefit from a separate $125,000 payment limit on program payments made only on peanuts. A spouse who is actively engaged in farming is eligible for a separate limit on both programs, essentially setting a $500,000 limit on payments to a farm operation growing peanuts and other program crops. This higher payment limit has persisted over the past 15 years, as the limit was retained in the two farm bills (in 2008 and 2014) that followed the buyout. As is the case with other crops, marketing loan gains and loan deficiency payments made in the form of generic commodity certificates are not subject to any payment limitations. The marketing loan rate is currently set at $355 per short ton, and the national market price for 2016–17 was $394 per short ton, highlighting the potential for significant payments if prices fall lower.

A second important feature of the current peanut program relates to the generous levels of support the PLC program provides through its target price for peanuts. Randy Schnepf has compared levels of support across different crops.[15] Figure 2 illustrates total government support between 2014 and 2016 as a share of the value of the commodity. Figure 3 presents support outlays per acre. Such acreage-based comparisons depend on yields, which vary across regions and crops. However, the exceptionally generous support provided to peanuts is obvious from the figures. Government support is nearly half the value of production for peanuts. This level far exceeds the next nearest crop—rice. Likewise, support per acre for peanuts significantly surpasses that provided to other crops, with each acre representing government outlays that average $341.19.

This significant level of support is largely due to the substantial target price for peanuts. As is true with other commodities, peanut producers were provided the option of enrolling in the Agricultural Risk Coverage (ARC)

Figure 2. Government Support as a Share of the Value of Production

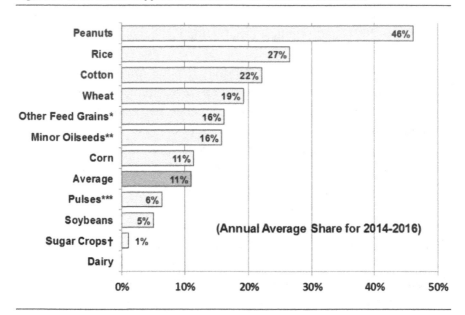

Source: Based on Congressional Research Service calculations for crop years 2014–16 using Commodity Credit Corporation program data from Farm Service Agency; the Congressional Budget Office's June 29, 2017, baseline of farm programs; and crop insurance data from Risk Management Agency as of April 24, 2017. See Randy Schnepf, "Farm Safety-Net Payments Under the 2014 Farm Bill: Comparison by Program Crop," Congressional Research Service, August 11, 2017, https://fas.org/sgp/crs/misc/R44914.pdf.

or PLC programs under the 2014 Farm Bill. Almost all peanut growers (99.7 percent) opted to join the PLC program. Schnepf notes that "peanuts have a statutory reference price that is set disproportionately above historical market prices."[16] The PLC reference price for peanuts is $535 per short ton, a level that, as shown in Figure 1, has continually exceeded market prices since the 2014 legislation was enacted.

The generous support afforded to peanuts reflects the geographically concentrated nature of production. As Bruce Gardner noted, geographically concentrated commodities are likely to face lower lobbying costs and secure higher levels of support than is typically the case for commodities with more dispersed production.[17] Table 2 presents state-level harvested peanut acreage for 2016. Georgia is the largest peanut-producing state, with 45 percent of the US total acreage. Texas and Alabama also have

Figure 3. Government Support Outlays per Acre

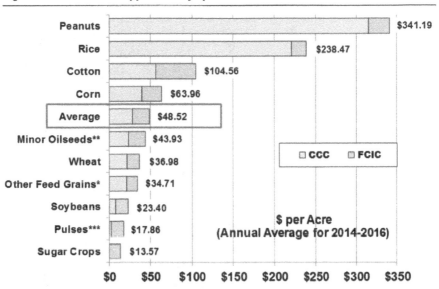

Source: Based on Congressional Research Service calculations for crop years 2014–16 using Commodity Credit Corporation program data from Farm Service Agency; the Congressional Budget Office's June 29, 2017, baseline of farm programs; and crop insurance data from Risk Management Agency as of April 24, 2017. See Randy Schnepf, "Farm Safety-Net Payments Under the 2014 Farm Bill: Comparison by Program Crop," Congressional Research Service, August 11, 2017, https://fas.org/sgp/crs/misc/R44914.pdf.

Table 2. Harvested Acreage for Peanuts in 2016

State	Acres	Percentage of Total
Alabama	172,000	10.98%
Arkansas	23,000	1.47%
Florida	146,000	9.32%
Georgia	706,000	45.05%
Mississippi	38,000	2.43%
New Mexico	8,000	0.51%
North Carolina	99,000	6.32%
Oklahoma	12,000	0.77%
South Carolina	106,000	6.76%
Texas	205,000	13.08%
Virginia	21,000	1.34%
Other States	31,000	1.98%
Total	1,567,000	

Source: US Department of Agriculture, National Agricultural Statistics Service, "Quick Stats," https://quickstats.nass.usda.gov/.

Figure 4. Geography of Peanut Production for 2010–14 (with State Percentages of Total Production)

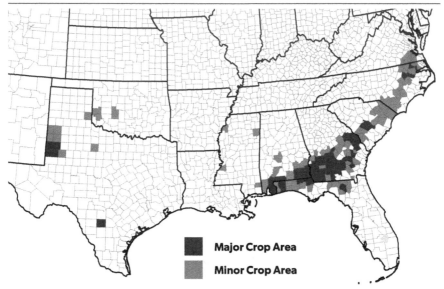

Major Crop Area
Minor Crop Area

Source: Randy Schnepf, "US Peanut Program and Issues," Congressional Research Service, September 27, 2016, https://fas.org/sgp/crs/misc/R44156.pdf.

Table 3. Total Government Outlays on Peanut Subsidies by Program

Peanut Subsidy Program	Total Payments 1995–2016
Peanut Quota Buyout Program	$1,289,001,708
Countercyclical Payment—Peanuts	$1,012,300,870
Direct Payment—Peanuts	$799,931,547
Crop Insurance Premium Subsidy—Peanuts	$572,653,814
Peanut Marketing Assistance	$172,798,128
Market Gains—Peanuts	$120,994,835
Loan Deficiency—Peanuts	$27,656,359
Commodity Certificates—Peanuts	$16,572,530
Average Crop Revenue Election Direct Payments—Peanuts	$1,162,720
Direct Payment Violation—Peanuts	−$816
Loan Deficiency Refund—Peanuts	−$7,419

Source: Environmental Working Group, "Farm Subsidy Database," https://farm.ewg.org/.

Table 4. Top 20 Payment Peanut Payment Recipients, 1995–2016

Rank	Recipient	Location	1995–2016 Peanut Subsidies
1	American Peanut Marketing Association	Leary, GA 39862	$20,333,433
2	Concordia Allied Producers LLC	Ashburn, GA 31714	$18,910,605
3	Cecil Everton	Gorman, TX 76454	$5,098,940
4	Peanut Loan Processing Center	Gorman, TX 76454	$5,075,293
5	Killarney Farm Partnership	Jakin, GA 39861	$3,771,637
6	35 Farms Peanut Venture	Gainesville, FL 32635	$3,732,881
7	T. H. Birdsong III	Gorman, TX 76454	$3,683,024
8	Peanut Marketing Loan Services LLC	Stephenville, TX 76401	$3,650,830
9	V-C Peanut Dma LLC	Franklin, VA 23851	$3,391,521
10	GFA Peanut Association	Camilla, GA 31730	$3,294,720
11	P. G. C. Farms	Brinson, GA 39825	$3,218,759
12	Scott Farms	Brinson, GA 39825	$3,214,384
13	Glenn Heard Farms	Brinson, GA 39825	$3,005,231
14	Luther Griffin Farm	Bainbridge, GA 39817	$2,919,752
15	Sayer Farms Family Partnership	Wray, GA 31798	$2,908,593
16	Lahey Farms Ptn	Brownfield, TX 79316	$2,686,798
17	Driskell Cotton Farms	Grand Bay, AL 36541	$2,460,002
18	John Hancock Mutual Life Insurance	Savoy, IL 61874	$2,209,861
19	Brock Farms	Bainbridge, GA 39817	$2,187,963
20	River Rock Farms	Camilla, GA 31730	$2,158,119

Source: Environmental Working Group, "Farm Subsidy Database," https://farm.ewg.org/.

significant shares of total acreage. These states are well represented on the House and Senate Agriculture Committees. In these states, production is further concentrated (Figure 4). Taxpayer outlays to support this relatively limited number of peanut farmers exceeded $4 billion in nominal terms over 1995–2016.

According to the Environmental Working Group's farm subsidies database, the top 1 percent of growers received 24 percent of payments, while the top 15 percent received 80 percent of all payments. Table 3 presents summary statistics on the distribution of these subsidies across individual subsidy programs, with the 2002 buyout being the largest single budgetary item. The top individual recipients over this same period are presented in Table 4. The (non) peanut operation known as John Hancock Mutual Life

Table 5. Top Peanut Subsidy Recipients 2016

Rank	Recipient	Location	2016 Peanut Subsidies
1	Sanchez Farms*	Old Town, FL 32680	$125,000
2	83 Farms LLC*	Bell, FL 32619	$125,000
3	Tillis Farms LLC*	Chiefland, FL 32644	$120,904
4	TEC Farms Inc.*	Blakely, GA 39823	$120,654
5	Herman H. Sanchez Jr.	Old Town, FL 32680	$92,500
6	Keith L. Philman	Bell, FL 32619	$88,285
7	Morell Jones Farms*	Enfield, NC 27823	$76,461
8	Simpson Acres LLC*	Bell, FL 32619	$71,010
9	Sayer Farms Family Partnership*	Wray, GA 31798	$66,062
10	K & S Farming LLC*	Warsaw, NC 28398	$62,259
11	Tammie W. Holt	Andalusia, AL 36420	$62,163
12	Lillian Farms LLC*	Elberta, AL 36530	$61,395
13	Rachelle Philman	Bell, FL 32619	$55,159
14	Harold Tillis	Chiefland, FL 32644	$49,343
15	Kelby Sanchez	Old Town, FL 32680	$36,469
16	O. J. Smith Farms Inc.*	Whitakers, NC 27891	$30,958
17	Betty Wier	Charlotte, TX 78011	$28,173
18	J & J Peanut Inc.*	Trenton, FL 32693	$21,071
19	I Arlene Bell	Williston, FL 32696	$20,534
20	D & D Farms LLC*	Allendale, SC 29810	$15,242
21	Galen T. Watson	Trenton, FL 32693	$14,856
22	Everswood Farms LLC	Murfreesboro, NC 27855	$14,334
23	Virginia Lorraine Sanchez	Old Town, FL 32680	$12,198
24	J & R Farms*	Williston, FL 32696	$10,010
25	Herman Harvey Sanchez III	Old Town, FL 32680	$9,881
26	Benton Farms Inc.*	Bronson, FL 32621	$9,817
27	L. L. Hiers Jr.	Dunnellon, FL 34431	$9,515
28	Rodney Clayton Watson	Fort White, FL 32038	$9,003
29	Al Darley	Lyons, GA 30436	$8,089
30	Donnie Lee Blankenship	Willow, OK 73673	$7,264
31	Charles P Millican Dba Millican F	Sylvania, GA 30467	$6,475
32	Stephen Edison Dowless Jr.	Bladenboro, NC 28320	$4,963
33	Cleve Lloyd Kilgore	Coolidge, GA 31738	$4,945
34	Hardee Farms*	Chiefland, FL 32626	$4,776
35	Grass Roots Farming LLC*	Dublin, TX 76446	$4,732
36	Stephenson-Mclean Farms Inc.*	Murfreesboro, NC 27855	$4,386
37	Edwards Farms Inc.*	Dublin, NC 28332	$4,181
38	Jerry M. Mills Jr.	Morriston, FL 32668	$3,897
39	Cameron Farms LLC*	Orangeburg, SC 29116	$3,694
40	Dexter Day Gilbert	Campbellton, FL 32426	$2,469

Note: *It is notable that on the list several individuals and entities have common surnames or addresses (or both) that appear multiple times.

Source: Environmental Working Group, "Farm Subsidy Database," https://farm.ewg.org/.

Insurance Company of Savoy, Illinois, was the 18th largest payment recipient. In addition, a president of a Texas oil company received over $5 million in peanut subsidies. Table 5 presents a detailed distribution of peanut subsidy payments to individuals in 2016. It is notable that on the list several individuals and entities have common surnames or addresses (or both) that appear multiple times, as indicated by the starred entries. This evidence indicates that payment limits are not as directly binding as an uninformed observer might believe, though in no way does this imply any violation of payment limit regulations.

The concentration of payments among farm businesses raising peanuts echoes points raised in congressional testimony on June 24, 2017. Virginia Sanchez (see entry 23 in Table 5) presented a "parable" of three peanut farmers in her testimony.

> These three farmers are neighbors. They go to church together, they hunt together, and their kids play ball together. . . . The farmer to the west tells his wife; well I'm going to start planting today even though peanut prices are very low. We have base and qualify for a PLC payment. We will be ok. The government is providing us a safety net. The farmer in the middle tells his wife. I'm starting to plant today and I'm worried sick because of low prices. We don't have any base and don't qualify for the PLC payment. All we can hope for is that somewhere/somehow there is a shortage of peanuts this year and prices will go up. He says I'm really worried. We've got peanut equipment and land payments. Now the farmer to the east is sitting on his front porch and tells his wife. Well I don't think I'll plant peanuts this year. We've got base and qualify for a $250,000 PLC payment regardless if I plant or not. We don't have any land payments. I paid our land off when the government bought out my peanut quota in 2002. I think I just won't hire any employees, buy any equipment, fuel, fertilizer or supplies. We will just pocket the $250,000. Heck, lets you and I just go fishing today. . . . The 2014 farm bill has created the haves, have-nots and the ones that don't have to do anything.[18]

Figure 5. Area Planted to Peanuts: 2000–17 (Acres)

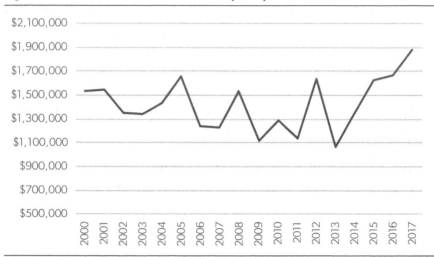

Source: US Department of Agriculture, National Agricultural Statistics Service, "Quick Stats," https://quickstats.nass.usda. gov/.

Following the 2014 Farm Bill, farmers were provided with the generous target price PLC program described above. Payments are made on historical base and not on current production—hence, the "farmer/recreational fisherman to the east" described in the testimony. Farmers are also entitled to marketing loans and loan deficiency payments on current production, whether they have base acreage or not. As noted above, the potential that price declines will trigger these additional payments is nontrivial.

The current peanut policy situation has been significantly complicated by the elimination of the cotton program in the 2014 Farm Bill. Land that was formerly cotton base became "generic base," meaning that the crop actually grown on the base would be the relevant crop for PLC or ARC payments. This essentially recoupled payments to current production, an action that conceivably could raise concerns in WTO negotiations. The provision created 17.5 million acres of generic base, of which a considerable proportion was subsequently planted to peanuts. Cotton shares a similar geography with peanuts, and land suitable for cotton is also typically suitable for peanuts. Peanut acreage jumped significantly from about one million acres in 2013 to over 1.5 million acres in 2015 and about 1.9 million acres in 2017, as shown

Table 6. Peanut Plantings, Peanut Base, and Generic Base

State	Peanut Base	Generic Base	Peanut Planted Acreage (Thousands)				
			2012	2013	2014	2015	2016
Georgia	753,328	1,456,949	735	430	600	785	760
Texas	401,032	7,204,323	150	120	130	170	190
Alabama	260,991	657,231	220	140	175	200	175
North Carolina	157,643	866,638	107	82	94	90	80
Florida	152,206	105,308	210	140	175	190	145
Oklahoma	93,010	589,031	24	17	12	10	13
South Carolina	78,770	347,713	110	81	112	112	115
Virginia	75,516	103,423	20	16	19	19	20
New Mexico	24,267	98,088	10	7	4.5	5	5
Mississippi	14,144	1,623,887	52	34	32	44	40
Other	9,336	4,530,320	—	—	—	—	20
Total	2,020,243	17,582,911	1,638	1,067	1,353	1,625	1,563

Source: Randy Schnepf, "Farm Safety-Net Payments Under the 2014 Farm Bill: Comparison by Program Crop," Congressional Research Service, August 11, 2017, https://fas.org/sgp/crs/misc/R44914.pdf.

in Figure 5. This, coupled with strong growth in peanut yields, led to a significant increase in peanut production and lower peanut prices, which triggered even larger PLC payments. Further exacerbating this situation, the lucrative nature of PLC payments for peanuts has also led many growers to alter their rotation patterns and produce more peanuts. Table 6 presents summary statistics for peanut base, generic base, and actual peanut plantings. These statistics and the data presented in Figure 5, which show the rapid increase in area planted to peanuts since 2013, demonstrate the impacts of generic base following the 2014 Farm Bill and the rise in peanut plantings.[19]

The increase in US peanut production has also led to an expansion of US peanut exports. As shown in Figure 6, peanut exports have been substantially higher since 2013–14. Exports of agricultural commodities are generally relatively volatile because, while from one year to the next domestic consumption is relatively stable, domestic production varies because of weather and other effects on average yields. This makes "one year to the next" comparisons of changes in exports somewhat misleading. However, a comparison of average US exports over the peanut marketing year for the four-year period 2014–15 to 2017–18 (618,000 tons) compared to the

Figure 6. US Peanut Exports: 2001–17 (Thousands of Tons)

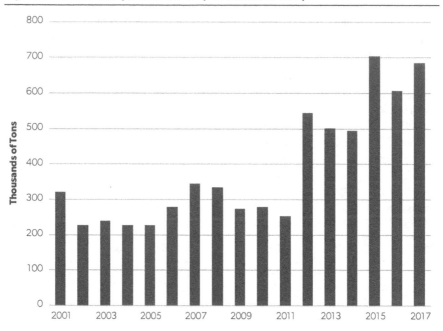

Source: Oil Crops Yearbook, "Table 11," US Department of Agriculture, Economic Research Service, 2017.

previous four-year period 2010–11 to 2013–14 (390,000 tons) indicates that peanut exports have been 55 percent higher since the passage of the 2014 Farm Bill.

The impact of the 2014 Farm Bill provisions on US peanut exports since 2014 has been substantial (Figure 6) and, especially when combined with the price-suppression effects of increased US peanut production on world prices, created the potential for challenges by other countries under the WTO Subsidies and Countervailing Measures Agreement on behalf of their adversely affected domestic peanut industries. Thus, the US peanut program has also created the potential for important adverse effects on US trade relations with other countries. For example, the increase in US peanut production and acquisition of stocks by the USDA under the loan rate program was associated with a controversial USDA proposal to ship 15,000 tons of peanuts to Haiti in the spring of 2016 in the form of US aid. Haiti's largely impoverished peanut producers responded that all those shipments would only lower the prices they received for their own production. Subsequently, numerous nongovernment organizations involved in international humanitarian aid wrote a publicly released letter to the secretary of agriculture strongly criticizing the proposed action.[20]

Finally, domestic and international peanut prices have become considerably more volatile and, because of the 2014 Farm Bill's treatment of orphan acres, almost certainly lower than would otherwise have been the case. At one point in 2010 the national posted price for peanuts was over $1,200 per short ton. In 2014, posted prices briefly fell below the $355 loan rate before settling around $400 per short ton. The 2014 Farm Bill therefore also mandated the establishment of a peanut revenue insurance policy that would address both yield and price volatility. This presented significant challenges for the USDA as peanuts are not traded on any futures market that enables any transparent price discovery process. In 2016, the new peanut revenue insurance plan covered 920,587 acres and had a liability of $481 million. The program paid out $67 million in indemnities while collecting only $20 million in premium from farmers (with an additional $31 million in premium covered by taxpayer subsidies). The program loss ratio (ratio of total indemnities to total premium) was 1.30, but because taxpayers contribute about 60 percent of the premiums, on average farmers received about $3.35 in indemnity payments for every $1 they paid in premium.[21] This program was just introduced in 2015, and it remains to be seen whether this reflects a poor insurance year or yet another expensive transfer of wealth to peanut producers and base owners.

Summary

The peanut lobby is essentially an ideal example of how interest groups can successfully extract funds from the federal government. The peanut industry is relatively small, currently consisting of about 6,000 generally affluent and financially secure farm businesses, and geographically concentrated, operating in a relatively small number of counties in a small number of states. The lobby has been exceptionally well rewarded by farm state legislators. Given the size of the industry, benefits from peanut subsidy programs, which averaged over $900 million a year from 2014 to 2016,[22] have been massive, providing over $350 per acre of peanuts and accounting for over 40 percent of peanut grower revenues. Many of those growers do not even need to plant peanuts to obtain their subsidies because payments are based on histories of production, not current plantings. Nevertheless, in part because of changes in the US cotton program, the US peanut program has in fact led to substantial increases in heavily subsidized peanut production, increased US exports, and created the potential for otherwise unnecessary trade disputes.

Further, subsidies are heavily concentrated among the largest operations that grow peanuts and those businesses that enjoy extremely generous limits on the total subsidy payments they can receive, up to $1.5 million per farm. Moreover, the evidence presented in this chapter indicates that when payment limits could become binding, peanut growers are likely to have reorganized the structures of their businesses to (legally) avoid even that $0.5 million constraint on the amount of PLC payments they can obtain. In addition, as if up to $0.5 million in taxpayer-funded handouts for a producer were not enough, Congress mandated that peanut businesses have access to a heavily subsidized crop insurance program that in its first year paid out $57 million in indemnities on polices that cost growers only $20 million. That program has a long history of encouraging farmers to adopt production practices that lead to resource misallocations, economic inefficiency, and complex and in some important ways adverse environmental outcomes.[23]

The US peanut subsidy program is a great deal if you can get it, especially when there is no real public interest reason for subsidizing peanut production businesses that typically are technically sophisticated operations owned and managed by well-educated and wealthy individuals and corporations.

How should the peanut program be reformed in the next farm bill? If there is no public purpose being served, then the answer seems clear. Terminate all the subsidy programs and let the peanut industry operate like most other small and midsize businesses. At a minimum, the rationale for allowing peanut growers separate payment limits and an extremely generous PLC reference price is elusive; thus, such special entitlements should be eliminated. The current peanut program represents an extreme among extremes as agricultural subsidies go. Therefore, major changes are needed, if not to eliminate such an unmerited waste of scarce taxpayer resources, then at least to bring levels of support into line with what other (generously supported) commodities enjoy. Continuing this out-of-control fiscal train wreck is, to put it mildly, simply nuts.

Notes

1. Gary S. Becker, "Public Policies, Pressure Groups, and Dead Weight Costs," *Journal of Public Economics* 28, no. 3 (1985): 329–47; and Sam Peltzman, "Toward a More General Theory of Regulation," *Journal of Law and Economics* 19, no. 2 (1976): 211–40.

2. Vincent H. Smith, "The US Federal Crop Insurance Program: A Case Study in Rent Seeking" (working paper, Mercatus Center, 2017).

3. Becker, "Public Policies, Pressure Groups, and Dead Weight Costs."

4. Mancur Olsen, *The Logic of Collective Action: Public Goods and the Theory of Groups* (Cambridge, MA: Harvard Economic Studies, 1965).

5. Vincent H. Smith et al., *Agricultural Policy in Disarray: Reforming the Farm Bill—An Overview*, American Enterprise Institute, October 13, 2017, http://www.aei.org/publication/agricultural-policy-in-disarray-reforming-the-farm-bill-an-overview/.

6. A cautionary note: Peanut yields in the US hit their record high in the 2012 census year. However, over the five-year period 2012–16, nationally, peanut yields averaged 3,931 pounds per acre, indicating that on average today's peanut producers each consistently produce well over 100 times the amount produced by their 1949 counterparts.

7. A detailed history of peanut policy up to 1990 is provided by Brad Crowder et al., *Soybeans and Peanuts: Background for 1990 Farm Legislation*, US Department of Agriculture, Economic Research Service, March 1990, https://www.ers.usda.gov/publications/pub-details/?pubid=42022.

8. As we discuss in detail below, the conversion of cotton base into "generic base" effectively coupled current peanut production to the PLC price for those peanut farmers who formerly had cotton base.

9. Vincent H. Smith, "A Midterm Review of the 2014 Farm Bill," American Enterprise Institute, February 10, 2016, http://www.aei.org/publication/a-midterm-review-of-the-2014-farm-bill/.

10. Jan Chvosta et al., "The End of Supply Controls: The Economic Effects of Recent Change in Federal Peanut Policy" (paper presented at the Southern Agricultural Economic Association Annual Meetings, Mobile, AL, 2003).

11. Erik Dohlman and Janet Livezey, "Peanut Backgrounder," US Department of Agriculture, Economic Research Service, 2006.

12. Chvosta et al., "The End of Supply Controls."

13. Dohlman and Livezey, "Peanut Backgrounder."

14. Elizabeth Becker, "Peanut Proposals Put a New Wrinkle on Farm Subsidies," *New York Times*, March 4, 2002, http://www.nytimes.com/2002/03/04/us/peanut-proposals-

put-a-new-wrinkle-on-farm-subsidies.html.

15. Randy Schnepf, "Farm Safety-Net Payments Under the 2014 Farm Bill: Comparison by Program Crop," Congressional Research Service, August 11, 2017, https://fas.org/sgp/crs/misc/R44914.pdf.

16. Randy Schnepf, "US Peanut Program and Issues," Congressional Research Service, September 27, 2016, https://fas.org/sgp/crs/misc/R44156.pdf.

17. Bruce Gardner, "Causes of U.S. Farm Commodity Programs," *Journal of Political Economy* 95, no. 2 (1997): 290–310, https://www.jstor.org/stable/1832073?seq=1#page_scan_tab_contents.

18. Virginia Sanchez, "Startling Truth About a Peanut Farmer's Struggle," testimony before the Agriculture Committee, US House of Representatives, June 24, 2017, https://www.jordanagency.com/blog/startling-truth-about-a-peanut-farmers-struggle.aspx.

19. The growth in peanut yields over the past 15 years in part traces back to the 2002 buyout of quota. The presence of quota, which typically could not be exchanged over county lines, essentially kept production locked into high-cost areas. Once the quota restrictions were eliminated, significant reallocation of acreage toward low-cost regions, such as Georgia, occurred.

20. The issue was also widely discussed and generally criticized by a broad spectrum of the media. See, for example, Associated Press, "Donation of Surplus Peanuts from US Dismays Haitian Farmers," Fox News, April 15, 2016, http://www.foxnews.com/world/2016/04/15/donation-surplus-peanuts-from-us-dismays-haiti-farmers.html.

21. For a detailed discussion and assessment of the current US federal crop insurance program, see Vincent H. Smith, Joseph W. Glauber, and Barry K. Goodwin, *Time to Reform the US Federal Crop Insurance Program*, American Enterprise Institute, October 13, 2017, http://www.aei.org/publication/time-to-reform-the-us-federal-agricultural-insurance-program/.

22. US Department of Agriculture, Farm Service Agency, *Commodity Estimates Book FY 2017 President's Budget Commodity Credit Corporation*, February 9, 2016, https://www.fsa.usda.gov/about-fsa/budget-and-performance-management/budget/commodityestimates-book-and-reports/index.

23. Smith, Glauber, and Goodwin, *Time to Reform the US Federal Crop Insurance Program*.

Conclusion

The 19 studies included in this two volume assessment of agricultural policy in the United States examine a wide spectrum of federal government initiatives that affect, and for the most part substantially benefit, the agricultural sector and related upstream input supply and downstream processing industries. The picture these studies paint consists of a compellingly chaotic, apparently randomly structured collage of individual programs that, nevertheless, almost always serve to benefit carefully selected constituencies at the expense of taxpayers and consumers. In doing so, most of those programs create incentives that result in wasted resources and provide subsidies that overwhelmingly flow to large agribusiness-style farm operations owned by relatively wealthy and very wealthy households (Chapter 1, Volume I; Chapter 2, Volume I).

Despite persistent claims to the contrary by farm interest groups and farm state legislators, farm subsidy initiatives do nothing to alleviate poverty in either rural or urban areas (Chapter 1, Volume II). One exception is the suite of nutrition programs the US Department of Agriculture manages that do help millions of US households in poverty (Chapter 2, Volume II). However, some farm state legislators have regularly sought to shift funds from the Supplementary Nutrition Assistance Program, the largest program that currently helps just under 40 million people, to farm subsidy programs that mainly benefit much wealthier constituents (Chapter 1, Volume I).

Some major subsidy programs (e.g., crop insurance) harm the environment and involve substantial administrative costs (Chapter 3, Volume I). Others address environmental and resource degradation problems in inefficient and inane ways (Chapter 6, Volume II; Chapter 7, Volume II; Chapter 8, Volume II). Many agricultural commodity subsidy and tariff programs also create serious challenges for the United States regarding international trade in agriculture and other commodities and services (Chapter 5, Volume I).

In addition, effective support from agricultural lobbies for public investments in agricultural research and development (R&D) has withered over the past 30 years. Frequently, those lobbies have chosen to trade away from federal spending on agricultural R&D and shift funds to short-term direct subsidy programs. The result has had substantial adverse impacts on productivity growth in the agricultural sector (Chapter 4, Volume II). One R&D policy mistake US legislators have not yet made, but policymakers in other countries have, involves overregulation and even proscription of the development and use of genetically modified organism (GMO) technologies. As Gary Brester and Joseph Atwood discuss (Chapter 5, Volume II), in the United States those technologies appear to have been an important source of productivity growth for corn and soybeans—crops that are mainly used for biofuels and animal feed rather than for human consumption (a purpose for which, in any case, non-GMO varieties of those crops are available).

The various components of US agricultural policy frequently work at cross-purposes, with offsetting impacts that result from delivering benefits to different groups with conflicting objectives. For example, paid land retirement programs encourage soil conservation, while the federal crop insurance program incentivizes farm businesses to plant crops on fragile lands. Nutrition programs, which from a policy perspective are antipoverty programs that help millions of people, somewhat anachronistically continue to be included in farm bill legislation even though they have not measurably affected prices farm businesses receive for their products for at least the past 30 years. In contrast, sugar and dairy product tariffs are explicitly designed to increase domestic food prices and have substantial adverse effects on employment opportunities in the food-processing sector (Chapter 6, Volume I; Chapter 7, Volume I). Further, somewhat ironically, some government funds flow to industry-based organizations for agricultural export promotion (e.g., US Wheat Associates); at the same time, other programs are explicitly designed to impede international trade (Chapter 5, Volume I).

The studies in these volumes reflect several common themes and realities regarding agricultural policy in the United States. First, most policies are largely designed to benefit, and are effectively determined by, relatively small interest groups. Many of these organizations consist of farm businesses (e.g., the National Corn Growers Association, the American Sugar Alliance, the National Cotton Council, the American Soybean Association, the National Milk Producers Federation, the American Farm Bureau Federation, and the National Farmers Union). Others consist of industries that service the agricultural sector, such as crop insurance companies, input supply organizations, and downstream processing companies. These include organizations such as the National Association of Professional Insurance Agents, National Crop Insurance Services, the Fertilizer Institute, the American Bankers Association, and the Food Products Association, as well as large multinational companies with their own lobbyists. When it comes to the inefficiencies and waste associated with US international food aid programs, as Stephanie Mercier, Erin Lentz, and Christopher Barrett discuss (Chapter 3, Volume II), groups such as the National Mariners Association and USA Maritime have pushed to retain mandates that provide rents mainly for shipping companies. Those mandates use up about 30 percent of the federal funds available for such aid and are estimated annually to prevent US international food aid programs from meeting the needs of an additional four million or more people in dire poverty who are experiencing hunger and malnutrition.

Second, other players in the agricultural policy process include environmental and other more broadly focused interest groups such as the World Wildlife Fund and the Sierra Club, as well as other special interest groups such as the Renewable Fuels Association. However, as Erik Lichtenberg points out (Chapter 6, Volume II), often the polices those groups end up supporting involve payoffs to the agricultural sector (e.g., through paid land retirement initiatives such as the Conservation Reserve Program and through subsidies for working-lands programs to encourage the adoption of conservation practices by farm businesses).

These outcomes reflect political compromises between interest groups with otherwise conflicting interests that impose costs on the rest of society. In contrast, pollution in other US economy sectors is typically addressed through government regulations and other approaches (e.g., marketable permits) that require compliance and impose emissions-control costs on polluters rather than taxpayers. The Renewable Fuel Standard, notionally intended to reduce greenhouse gas emissions (Chapter 8, Volume II), also results in similar outcomes. Higher prices for corn and soybeans impose substantial costs on all US consumers in the form of higher food and fuel prices, with substantial adverse environmental effects associated with increased chemical use by farm businesses that produce biofuels crops, especially in the Midwest.

Third, little attention, if any, is given to consumers or the poor in forming and implementing farm subsidy programs or the efficient and effective use of federal resources allocated for humanitarian aid (Chapter 3, Volume II), despite assertions to the contrary from vested farm and other interest groups. Consumers and families in poverty are more likely to be taxed either directly or through higher prices for agricultural commodities.

Fourth, US agricultural policies rarely take account of the international trade relations implications associated with their operations, even though the US is a net exporter of agricultural commodities. Examples include subsidy programs for cotton, dairy products, and major row crops such as corn, cotton, rice, soybeans, and wheat, as well as sugar program initiatives that place arbitrary ad hoc restrictions on imports from trading partners such as Mexico.

Finally, in the vast majority of cases, agricultural subsidies and other policies are deliberately structured to funnel federal funds to a small number of large farm businesses that would be financially successful without any help from the US taxpayer or consumer. Most of these policies have nothing to do with ensuring food security in the United States, the survival of the US agricultural sector, or poverty, and farm interests appear to be increasingly disinterested in policies that do, such as public R&D investments. American farm programs are far more likely to be driven by rent-seeking, through what independent observers have increasingly described as crony capitalism. Thus, it is simply no accident that, as the scholars who have contributed to these volumes document, agricultural policy in the United States remains in disarray.

About the Authors

John C. Beghin is professor and head of the department of agricultural and resource economics at North Carolina State University. His research interests and expertise are in the economics of international agriculture and food markets.

Anton Bekkerman is an associate professor in the Department of Agricultural Economics and Economics at Montana State University.

Eric J. Belasco is an associate professor in the Department of Agricultural Economics and Economics at Montana State University and a visiting scholar at the American Enterprise Institute.

Amani Elobeid is an adjunct assistant professor in the economics department at Iowa State University. Before this appointment, she was the international sugar and ethanol analyst with the Food and Agricultural Policy Research Institute at Iowa State University.

Joseph W. Glauber is a senior research fellow at the International Food Policy Research Institute and a visiting scholar at the American Enterprise Institute.

Barry K. Goodwin is William Neal Reynolds Distinguished Professor of Agricultural Economics at North Carolina State University and a visiting scholar at the American Enterprise Institute.

Vincent H. Smith is professor of economics in the Department of Agricultural Economics and Economics at Montana State University (MSU), codirector of MSU's Agricultural Marketing Policy Center, and a visiting scholar and director of Agricultural Policy Studies at the American Enterprise Institute.

Daniel A. Sumner is the director of the University of California Agricultural Issues Center and the Frank H. Buck Jr. Professor in the Department of Agricultural and Resource Economics at the University of California, Davis.

Acknowledgments

This work would not have been possible without the support and contributions of dozens of gifted individuals. The editors truly appreciate the 17 nationally recognized scholars who as authors have made major contributions to this detailed study of US agricultural policy, and we are especially beholden to them for their focus on making their work accessible to the nonspecialist. Daniel Sumner, in particular, deserves particular recognition for his study of dairy policy and the important insights he shared with the editors drawn from his exceptional understanding of the economics of agricultural policy.

We also owe a major vote of thanks to the many wonderful individuals at the American Enterprise Institute who have helped make this project successful. The AEI in-house editing team has been astonishingly effective in improving the quality of the manuscript, and, as a consequence, we are deeply indebted to Rachel Jelinek, Sarah Crain, and Claude Aubert for their painstaking work, their creative contributions, and, above all, their patience with the foibles of the editors. We also want to thank Michael Pratt, John Cusey, and Emily Rapp for their vision and support in enabling this project to move forward and Ryan Nabil and Isabelle Staff for the extensive logistical support they provided in organizing the workshops and events through which this two-volume study was developed.

Finally, the editors would like to acknowledge their intellectual and personal debts to two giants in the field of agricultural economics, both closely associated with AEI throughout their distinguished careers. The first is D. Gale Johnson, professor of economics at the University of Chicago and past president of the American Economic Association, to whose memory this volume is dedicated. The second is Bruce Gardner, professor of agricultural economics and former undersecretary for economics at the US Department of Agriculture, who succeeded Johnson in leading the AEI agricultural policy program until he passed away in 2009. The intellectual and personal contributions of these two wonderful scholars have influenced every study included in this work, for which we are truly grateful.

Index